DANGER
TO SOCIETY

ELAINE MOORE'S STORY

with *Tony McCullagh*

MERLIN

PUBLISHING

First published in 2003 by
Merlin Publishing
16 Upper Pembroke Street,
Dublin 2, Ireland
Tel: +353 1 676 4373
Fax: +353 1 676 4368
publishing@merlin.ie
www.merlin-publishing.com

A CIP catalogue record for this book is available
from the British Library

ISBN: 1-903582-47-4

5 4 3 2 1

All photographs courtesy of Elaine Moore's family
unless otherwise stated in the photo section.

Cover Images supplied by Maxwell Photo Agency and RTÉ
Cover Design by Graham Thew Design
Typeset by Gough Typesetting Services
Printed and bound by Nørhaven Paperback A/S

Dedicated in loving memory of

Evelyn O'Reilly

Mary (May) Monaghan

and

Chloe Mulvaney O'Neill

ACKNOWLEDGEMENTS

Elaine Moore

One can become self-absorbed during a time of personal crisis. In this regard, those people who offer support are often overlooked, albeit temporarily. In writing this book, I was forced to revisit each chapter of that period in my life. Rather than focusing on its troubled aspects, I prefer to savour the countless acts of selfless kindness made on my behalf, which have served to reinforce my belief in humanity. Accordingly, there are many notable people to whom I'd like to express my deepest appreciation; not only for their dedication to my pursuit for justice, but for also understanding my neglect over the past several months.

My Dad Martin, brother Robert *'forever'* and niece Saoire for their constant love and support; my relatives and friends; the entire Reilly clan; Deirdre Casey, Patrick Fay and Tracy Mulvaney; Tom Beirne and Margaret Martin for the pivotal role they played. A sincere word of gratitude is due to those people who played an integral role in securing my bail, by not hesitating to either lodge bail money or act as sureties, with particular thanks to a dear family friend, John Shaw; also to Tom Callanan, Peter Barry, Mary Banotti, Lynn Solomon, Tyrone Falls, Eric Lynch, Ambrose Gordon, Joe Raff and the many others who came forward. I would also like to record my thanks for the several hundred letters of inspiration and character references I received while incarcerated. I am deeply grateful for the assistance, guidance and courtesy of my legal team in London – Nigel Leskin, Tim Greene and Michael Mansfield QC; also, Tracy, Alistair, Unmesh and Hoppy; to my legal team back home at Michael E Hanahoe Solicitors, in particular, Carthage Conlon.

I am eternally indebted to the kindness bestowed upon me by all the priests and staff at Tollington Park, Fr Gerry O'Flynn of the IPO, Carmel, Sr Mary Carroll and the Columban Brothers on Reddington Road who gave me shelter. To Rory Hearty, whose dedication and constant support carried me through. The then residents of Queen's Crescent, Niall Hearty, Paddy 'Scruffy Murphy' Cohen and my former colleagues at Netlink for standing by me. I also wish to thank An Taoiseach, Bertie Ahern and the staff at his constituency office; the Department of Foreign Affairs and the Irish Embassy in London; David Powderly for his advice; Paul May of the BIHRC and his colleagues, the BIRW and Kevin McNamara MP. The media, in particular Pat Kenny, Bill Malone, Cathy Moore, Sean Whelan, Brian O'Connell, Bernard Purcell, Mark Lloyd, Aidan Hennigan, Rachel Donnelly, Brian Carroll, Owen Corcoran, Frank Connolly, Barry O'Kelly, Karl Brophy, Cathy Kelly, John Mooney and Tim Pat Coogan. To my co-author Tony McCullagh, for his remarkable sensitivity; my colleagues at the Programme Management Association; Paul Donegan, for his love, understanding and constant encouragement to remain focused on completing this book. I will be forever grateful to my solicitor, Gareth Peirce. Never in my life have I been so effected by a person's dynamic professionalism, capacity to care and 'angelic' presence. Finally, to Mum, a truly beautiful, courageous and selfless woman. Your determination, unconditional love and belief in me coaxed me from the shadows.

Tony McCullagh

First and foremost, I would like to thank Kathryn, for her love, patience and calming influence, not to mention her help with transcribing the seemingly endless hours of interviews I conducted for this book; the McCullagh clan – Tony Snr, Phyllis, Sharyn, Jamie and Chloe – all of whom I badly neglected during the long months of writing; my grandfather, Peter Seagrave, a longstanding and dedicated supporter of my work; the Flynn and Lynch clans, for listening and believing; the team at the *Dublin People Group*, particularly Ray O'Neill and Robin Webb, for tolerating my extended periods of absence; photographer Darren Kinsclla, for his invaluable help with the photo section; journalist/author Neil Fetherstonhaugh, for his endless encouragement and advice; Elaine Moore, for agreeing to share her deeply personal story with me; Kathy and Robert Moore, for giving so generously of their time; Rory Hearty, for the courtesy he showed me in London; Gareth Peirce, for cramming me into her impossibly busy schedule; Mary Banotti MEP and Geraldine, for their cooperation; Rosaleen Rogers, at Aideen Secretarial Services, for her professionalism and efficiency; to Bobby, for his continued inspiration and for warning me about the disease of conceit; to Jasper, for the weekly respite at the Harbour Bar; and, finally, to The Privateers, for the musical interludes – God damn them all!

Tony McCullagh and Elaine Moore would both like to thank: Aoife Barrett, Chenile Keogh and Selga Medenieks, at Merlin Publishing, for supporting this project since its inception; editor Síne Quinn, whose contribution to this book is immeasurable; our publicist Linda Kenny, for the anticipated good press; and solicitor

Gerard Fanning, for his expert legal advice. Any omission in this acknowledgement has not been deliberate, so to those of you inadvertently left out, a sincere thank you from us both.

CONTENTS

PROLOGUE

Friday, 10 July 1998

"Are ye up yet, Moore?" Rory joked as Elaine struggled to wake up. "I'll be around at your place in a few minutes."

The morning had started badly for Elaine Moore. She was abruptly awoken by the loud shrill of the telephone beside her bed. Panic set in as she realised she had overslept, having subconsciously ignored her alarm clock. The call was from Rory Hearty, who had become Elaine's closest friend and confidant since she moved to London four months earlier. Occasionally, he'd drive her to work in Central London, usually picking her up at around 8 a.m.

It was already 7.50 a.m. Elaine frantically leapt out of bed and gathered her clothes. There was no time to shower – something that would take on major significance in the days and months that lay ahead. She had a quick wash at the sink and pulled on her clothes before grabbing her bag and coat.

The phone rang once – Rory's signal to Elaine that he was waiting for her outside. Before running out the door, Elaine knocked on the bedroom in which an overnight guest from Dublin was sleeping. There was no answer the first or second time but he responded after the third knock.

"Will ye get up, some of us have to go to work," she said light-heartedly.

"Thanks Elaine, I'm up," he replied, sticking his head out of the room. "I'll see you later."

She hurried down the stairs, grabbing her mail as she went out the door and jumped into Rory's car.

"You're unbelievable, Moore, look at the state of you – you're only out of bed."

"I know, I know . . . I'm sorry," she laughed, reflecting on the fact that she was already paying dearly for yet another late night out, which was becoming something of a pattern of London life for Elaine. She was a firm believer that a bad start to a morning would be reflected in the remainder of the day – little did she realise how bad this day would get.

During the drive to the office things picked up slightly as she opened her mail. Her provisional driving licence had finally arrived. Elaine's latest goal was to obtain her full driver's licence before returning home to Ireland the following March and Rory had been giving her regular driving lessons. Her aim was to purchase a brand new car; after all, she wanted something to show for having left home to work in London. Elaine and Rory joked and laughed, as they always did. Rory's brother, Niall, who was another close friend of Elaine's, was leaving for America the next day for a couple of months so plans were hatched to give him a send-off that night. They'd also be belatedly celebrating Niall's twenty-fourth birthday, which they had missed the week before as he was stuck in university in Oxford.

Arriving at her office, feeling slightly worse for wear from lack of sleep, Elaine consoled herself with thoughts of the weekend festivities that lay ahead. Apart from going out to lunch with some colleagues and taking her standard cigarette break outside at around 4 p.m., it was a busy but otherwise uneventful day. Elaine was slightly concerned to receive a call from her mother, Kathy, in the late afternoon with some bad news about her brother. The previous night, twenty-three-year-old Robert Moore had been out for a few drinks in Dublin's so-called cultural quarter, Temple Bar, and had been the victim of an unprovoked assault. Unable to go to work, he was at home in Coolock recovering from a nasty jaw injury.

Just after 6 p.m., Simon, a sales executive, told Elaine to have a nice weekend and got up from his desk to leave. A short time later, he returned to the office with a bewildered look on his face. A colleague asked him why he had not yet left the office. He said that the street outside had been cordoned off and there were police everywhere. Police had issued instructions that no one was allowed to leave the building. There was a buzz of excitement as Simon related the story and staff speculated about what was possibly going on. Their company, Netlink, had been experiencing problems with computer hacking and this was offered as one possible explanation. Elaine was intrigued, but turned to the more pressing matter of finishing a report she needed to complete for the following Monday. She was due to meet with the Netlink account manager from America On-Line with a view to securing a lucrative contract.

At this stage, Elaine was unaware of the growing police presence in the building's lobby. No more than 10 minutes had passed when Netlink's managing director, Mark Kotetche, entered her office and asked if he could speak to her in private. "Of course, I'll be with you now," she replied before getting up from her desk and proceeding to the lobby. Elaine glanced at the curious faces of her colleagues and simply smiled back at them.

On entering the lobby, Elaine was immediately confronted by between 10 to 12 male and female police officers. She felt instantly intimidated by their intense stares. Her boss motioned her towards a disused office, which she approached with a degree of trepidation. Here, she was met by two more police officers: a tall, overpowering man and – perhaps by comparison – a rather petite woman. They introduced themselves as Detective Sergeant Nolan and Detectice Constable Peters respectively, from the Anti-Terrorist Branch of New Scotland Yard.

"Are you Elaine Moore?" they asked, producing warrant cards by way of identifying themselves.

"Yes," she simply replied.

After requesting and confirming her address as 43 Parkhill Road, DS Nolan stood forward and stated: "I have to inform you that I am arresting you for the suspected involvement in the commission and preparation and instigation of acts of terrorism and I'll caution you now. You don't have to say anything but it may harm your defence if you don't mention when questioned anything you may later rely on in court. Anything you do say may be given in evidence. Do you understand?"

Elaine did understand, insofar that she had heard the words before on television. Now, however, she was struggling to comprehend their relevance in the context of her situation.

"Am I under arrest?" she asked.

The response from DS Nolan was a blunt and un-ambiguous "Yes".

"You've got to be kidding me!" Elaine snapped back.

The four walls seemed to be closing in on her as Elaine suddenly felt cold and agitated. She noticed the stunned expression on her boss's face, which, she was sure, mirrored her own. DS Nolan continued to brief her. He stated that owing to the nature of the suspected offence, everyone would have to wear protective clothing. DC Peters then produced 'forensic suits'. They repeatedly referred to Elaine as 'the prisoner' as they fumbled through their 'arrest kits'. Both police officers donned forensic overalls, hoods, over-shoes and gloves, lending a surreal feel to the unfolding events. Again, they turned their attention to Elaine. DS Nolan's next question deeply troubled the frightened twenty-one-year-old.

"Since we have officers who will be going to your address, is there anything there which may be of harm to them?" he asked.

"No . . . not to my knowledge," she replied slowly in stunned disbelief.

DC Peters then conducted a 'safety search' on Elaine. As she was wearing a tight pair of trousers and a fitted shirt, it would have been obvious to a casual observer that she wasn't concealing anything. She was instructed to remove her sandals. Her hands and feet were individually bound in nylon bags, which were secured to her wrists and ankles. She was requested to step into a full-bodied, white forensic suit. A hood was placed over her head. Elaine's mind was racing in all directions and she felt a rush of emotions ranging from horror to complete embarrassment. Mark Kotetche, who had been present throughout her ordeal, was then asked to sign a witness statement. Elaine was somewhat relieved to learn that her boss had dispersed her curious colleagues to a separate part of the office to lessen the humiliation. Some of them had gone down to the local pub to wait for her, not realising the seriousness of the situation.

When asked if she had any belongings with her, Elaine informed them that her coat and handbag were by her desk in the front office. They wanted to know if her desk was her sole work station. She replied that it was. She also told the arresting officers that she had recently emptied her paper recycling bin, the contents of which were now stored in an adjoining office.

According to police records, Elaine had been arrested some time just after 6.17 p.m. It was 7.03 p.m. before she was escorted from the building and locked in the back of a waiting police van with DC Peters. She was not handcuffed at this stage, but merely led by the elbow.

The back of the police van was completely covered, from top to bottom, in white plastic. Elaine sat in silence, trying desperately to take in the enormity of what had just happened. What was it all about? Rory used Elaine's garage to store equipment for his car. Could that – and the fact that Rory was from the North of Ireland – in some way have led to her arrest? At 7.12 p.m. the van arrived at Charing Cross police station and parked in the yard. Time tormented Elaine; the minutes felt like hours. She was suddenly overwhelmed by tiredness and fell asleep, secure in the knowledge that this was all just a big misunderstanding and would be cleared up in no time.

Chapter One

LONDON LIVING

At the age of nineteen Elaine had her first real taste of freedom when she spent the summer of 1996 living in Wildwood, New Jersey. She had travelled over to the States with 10 friends and worked as a waitress. It was in Wildwood that Elaine first met County Armagh man Niall Hearty, who – along with his brother Rory – would go on to play an important role in her future life in London.

Returning from America in September 1996, Elaine found herself at a crossroads. Although she had her heart set on a career in counselling, potential opportunities were hampered by her young age. She soon landed her first 'real job' with America On-Line, the Internet Service Provider giants, as a customer service representative at their Dublin division in East Point Business Park. It was an exciting time to be involved in the Information Technology industry, as Ireland entered into the era of the 'Celtic Tiger' economy. This was Elaine's first taste of the World Wide Web and email and she quickly developed a keen interest in computers. She worked hard and was soon promoted to join a specialist team involved in problem-solving and accounts saving. There was a strong social aspect to working at AOL, too, with regular social nights organised on pay days and extravagant staff parties. Elaine was a popular employee and made many new friends at the company during her time there.

After a year and a half with AOL, Elaine began to feel restless. Her career seemed to have arrived at a cul-desac and there weren't many new prospects or opportunities in sight. Her decision to leave was also prompted by personal issues. Elaine had recently finished an 18-month long relationship with a boyfriend who also worked at AOL. She felt uncomfortable having to sit just a few desks away from him each day in the office. The situation was awkward – it was time for a change.

Elaine ended up moving to London through sheer fate. Breda Doyle, a colleague at AOL, had just been offered a position with Netlink Internet Services in London. The company specialised in domain name registrations for websites and offered complementary services to AOL. Breda's London career move was stopped in its tracks when she found out she was pregnant. Knowing of Elaine's restlessness at AOL, Breda suggested that she should apply for the now vacant position at Netlink. It was too good an opportunity to miss. In February 1998, Elaine travelled over to London for an interview and was more or less offered the job on the spot. Her brother, Robert, and his then girlfriend, Sharon, accompanied her that weekend. They stayed with their cousin, Mark Reilly, who lived in Slough, a suburb in west London.

On her return to Dublin, Elaine decided to accept the Netlink position and handed in her notice. A colleague, Paul Walsh, had originally planned to move to London with Breda, who was his flatmate in Dublin. As he had an interview lined up for a job in Weybridge, Surrey, he suggested to Elaine that they travel over together with a view to finding a place to live. On 27 February, Elaine and Paul went to London for a weekend. The night after Paul's interview, they stayed with friends of his in Reading. The next day, Elaine met up with Rory Hearty, who would soon become the epicentre of her London existence.

She had kept in contact with Rory's brother, Niall, since the summer she spent in New Jersey. In November 1997, she had visited Niall, who was now studying at the Oxford Institute of Legal Practice, and immediately hit it off with his older brother, Rory, who was twenty-eight. Although Elaine and Paul were supposed to be checking out the accommodation situation in London, they were easily distracted by Rory's gregarious company and spent most of the weekend drinking and socialising.

* * *

Unconsciously, Elaine had always surrounded herself predominantly with male friends. During her primary school years, her best friend had been Eileen Flood. At secondary school, she became extremely close to Tracy Mulvaney, who she would later go on to study with at college. Elaine and Tracy were more like sisters and still remain as close as ever. The rest of Elaine's friends, however, were 'blokes'. "Apart from Tracy and one or two others, my friends throughout my teens consisted of 12 lads who I cared very deeply for," she explains. "As a child I was a tomboy, spending a lot of time with my brother and his friends. I always felt extremely comfortable with the lads I knew. They were less judgmental and certainly more laid back than a lot of the girls I knew growing up. There was rarely a dull moment with them, as there was always something happening."

Returning briefly to Dublin, Elaine was given a major send-off by her AOL colleagues with a going away party in Clontarf Yacht Club. She was mortified when she discovered that a strip-a-gram, dressed as a policeman, had been booked in her honour. However, the evening was somewhat marred when Paul Walsh got into a bust up in the toilets with Elaine's ex-boyfriend. She recalls Walsh coming up to her at the party and yelling: "Keep that boyfriend of yours away from me!" Even though Elaine had split up with her boyfriend, he had apparently accused Walsh of trying to get her away from him. The incident with Walsh unsettled Elaine, particularly as they were due to fly to London together the next day. Before leaving Dublin, she spoke to him on the phone and said she no longer wanted to move in with him. This was as a direct result of the way he had turned on her the night before.

Their first night in London was spent in an old Georgian house, with large bare rooms. Elaine felt very uneasy sleeping in her room as the window backed out onto the street with only a small lock providing protection from uninvited guests. Feeling nervous, she went to bed fully clothed – just in case. Paul Walsh was also unhappy with the accommodation. "Paul knocked loudly on my door and called out to me," Elaine recalls of that night. "I opened the door and he stormed into my bedroom, saying he couldn't sleep in his room any longer." There and then, Elaine decided that she wanted to live alone. She was an extremely private person and felt that she would be happier on her own.

Elaine and Paul commenced their search for somewhere to live the following day. In the meantime, they had to stay in bed and breakfast accommodation. They knew it would take them time to settle, at least two or three weeks, and they were both due to start work that coming Monday. They found a B&B, which was far from ideal but would have to do. The owner was in the process of selling the property and offered Elaine and Paul temporary accommodation in a basement flat. Reluctantly, Elaine agreed to move into the virtually condemned building, which was located in the Camden area of London, as a temporary measure until they found permanent accommodation. "It was a complete dump," she recalls. "It was dirty and mouldy and infested with mice. There was no privacy at all. The kitchen had a window that looked directly into the bathroom. It was a scary place: an absolute slum." The temporary decision to move into the flat put considerable strain on Elaine and Paul's already fragile friendship – a friendship that would end acrimoniously four months later.

Relations between Elaine and Paul began to unravel as soon as they moved in together temporarily. She felt he was distant and unfriendly towards her while they were living in the B&B. As Elaine and Rory Hearty developed an immediate close bond, Paul seemed to become increasingly removed and unsociable, eventually declining invitations to go out drinking with them. Elaine suspected that he was somehow jealous of her friendship with Rory.

For Elaine, meeting up with Rory was a godsend. Although London seemed vaguely familiar to her with its red buses and black mini cabs, it could be a daunting and intimidating city for a newcomer. Elaine found the London Underground rail system, for example, next to impossible to navigate during her early days there. Rory not only showed her how to get around the city, he opened up his entire social circle to her. They quickly became inseparable, although their relationship was platonic. "Being with Rory was like having the perfect relationship without all the emotional baggage that goes with it," she explains. "He is an incredibly lovely, decent person and is always the centre of everything that is happening. When I arrived in London, I couldn't believe the way Rory and his friends just accepted me."

Apart from her far from perfect domestic arrangements

at the B&B, Elaine began to relax and enjoy her new life
in London. She quickly warmed to her colleagues at
Netlink and made many new friends of all nationalities
there. There was always something going on and there
seemed to be far more places to go than Dublin. A typical
week could include going out to dinner, a night at the
cinema or simply hanging out at Scruffy Murphy's, a
once well-known Irish pub in central London that has
since been renamed under new management.

From the outset, Elaine made it clear to Paul that she
was going to try to find a flat on her own, but he continued
to look for a place with two bedrooms. She viewed a
number of dingy studio apartments, most of which were
tiny or had dark, secluded entrances. For Elaine, this was
the fear factor that rendered them unsuitable. The fact
that she had no history of bank accounts or utility bills in
the UK presented her with further obstacles. She was
also unable to provide prospective landlords with references
as she had previously lived mainly with her mother, apart
from that summer in the States. Rory came to the rescue
when he found a spacious two bedroomed, third floor
apartment on Parkhill Road, located in the upmarket
Hampstead area of north-west London. The rent was
expensive – £640 per month each – and it meant having
to move in with Paul. But Elaine was starting to despair
of ever finding a place on her own and she decided against
her better judgement to take the flat. The property came
with a lock-up garage located at the rear of the building.
Elaine and Paul both agreed to let Rory use it for his car.
This would be their way of thanking him for the considerable amount of time and assistance he had given them
since they arrived in London. The garage was soon one
of the first things that Elaine and Paul argued over. He
later claimed that his preference had been to let it out.

Elaine was immensely proud of her new flat. Finally, she had a place where she could invite people to stay, particularly her family, who would be regular visitors to London. "I was very conscious of what mum would think if she had seen me living in that dirty B&B or some poky flat. Even though the rent ate up most of my wages, it was worth every penny. Living in such a lovely place not only gave me peace of mind but also made me feel that I had achieved something by moving to London." In a letter to her mother, dated 19 March 1998, Elaine enthused about her beautiful new apartment and king-size bed. "Of course, it hasn't a patch on home but it's perfect for over here, especially because I'm beside Rory," she wrote. Kathy was thrilled to hear Elaine's news and replied immediately by fax. "You're going to be a yuppie, so!" she teased. Protective as ever, Kathy asked, "Promise me you won't smoke in bed – I worry about that a lot."

Conscious of the hospitality she had been shown by Rory and his friends when she had first arrived in London, Elaine was always happy to put people up in her flat – even complete strangers. This openness and casual – almost carefree – attitude towards hospitality would land her in the deepest trouble of her life.

The apparent open door policy at Flat 6, 43 Parkhill Road, is best exemplified by the following story. Elaine often socialised in her favourite pub. She became friendly with a young barman there. One weekend he was expecting guests, a young Belfast couple, but the landlord of the pub was being awkward about letting them stay. On learning of his dilemma, Elaine immediately offered to put them up, much to his relief. The first time she laid eyes on the couple, Elaine presented them with a set of keys she had had cut specifically for them. She did not want their time spent in London to revolve around her schedule. This way, they could come and go as they pleased. Her hospitality also extended to giving the couple her bedroom for the weekend while she slept on the couch in the lounge, even though she was in work that Friday. "I really hit it off with them; they were a lovely couple," she says. "I brought them out in Central London one night. Their friend, the barman, was supposed to show up but he didn't, so I stayed with them anyway and we had a great time."

Despite moving to London, Elaine saw her family as often as possible. She made a number of weekend trips home to Dublin and her mother and brother were regular guests at her Parkhill Road flat. Her brother, Robert, visited her twice in London, accompanied on both occasions by Sharon. They first stayed with Elaine in May 1998 and spent the weekend shopping, taking in the sights and socialising with Rory and his friends. Robert brought Sharon back to London on Thursday, 2 July, as a birthday treat – she had recently celebrated her twenty-first. This time, they made a long weekend out of it and didn't return to Dublin until the following Monday.

While the flat was comfortable and spacious, the atmosphere there was often tense due to the serious deterioration in Elaine's relationship with her flatmate, Paul Walsh, which had reached breaking point. "It was like being in a bad marriage. Some weeks I was hardly in the flat at all and would go out as often as possible just to avoid him." The feeling was mutual. One day, Paul announced that he would be moving out on 4 July, ostensibly because of the long commute to work each day from Hampstead to Surrey. The reality was that Elaine and Paul could no longer stand the sight of each other. By her own admission, Elaine was somewhat obsessive about the tidiness of the flat. Although Paul was reasonably tidy, she felt she was continuously picking up after him. The smallest things got on her nerves.

* * *

One afternoon, Elaine received an unexpected phone call at work. It was from a twenty-five-year-old Dubliner, Anthony Hyland, who Elaine only vaguely remembered. Hyland had attended University College Dublin with her brother, Robert, and Elaine had met him a few years earlier in the students' bar on campus. Robert Moore and Anthony Hyland both studied economics at UCD and were more casual acquaintances than friends. Hyland was a year ahead of Robert in college and would sometimes give him course notes. Elaine was somewhat taken aback to hear from Hyland out of the blue when she moved to London but simply assumed that somebody – possibly her brother – had given him her number. Hyland casually asked Elaine if she wanted to meet up for a drink while he was in London. She told him it wouldn't suit her as she had a friend staying over with her at the time.

On Monday, 22 June, Anthony Hyland turned up at Elaine's flat. It was mostly small talk between them. Hyland mentioned something about interviews for college or university and explained to Elaine that he wasn't working back in Ireland. He stayed for less than an hour and then left. Elaine remembers him being extremely polite and well mannered. He was tall and studious looking, with dark hair and glasses. Feeling at ease with him, she told him he was welcome any time.

Elaine didn't hear from Hyland again until Friday, 3 July, when he showed up at her flat and asked if he could stay the night. As Robert and Sharon were over again that weekend and Elaine had given them her room,

Hyland's timing wasn't great. Paul Walsh wasn't moving out until the next day so his room couldn't be used either. On top of that, the atmosphere in the flat was uncomfortable as Robert and Sharon had just had 'a domestic' and weren't talking to each other. Elaine offered to share the lounge area with Hyland, with each of them sleeping on separate couches. He gratefully accepted.

Elaine, Rory, Robert and Sharon had planned a night out in Scruffy Murphy's pub, but Hyland politely declined their invitation to join them, saying he had to meet a friend. He then left the flat. Rory soon arrived and he phoned for a cab. As the four of them were leaving, Elaine left a spare key under the mat for Hyland to use for when he came back later that night. Before going to the pub, they went for a Chinese meal. When Elaine, Robert and Sharon returned to the flat, having first dropped Rory home, Anthony Hyland was already there. Paul Walsh was in his bedroom with his girlfriend for what was to be his last night in the flat. Elaine was fairly drunk when she got home and can't clearly recollect what she and Hyland talked about as they settled down to sleep on their respective couches. She mostly rambled on about what a great night they had had, although she vaguely remembers him mentioning that he had an interview the next day.

At 9 a.m. the next morning, Saturday, 4 July, Elaine was woken up by the sound of the door buzzer. As she went to answer it, she noticed that Hyland was dressed in a smart suit, sitting at the table reading a newspaper. She imagined it was because he was going for a job or college interview. She answered the door; it was a courier with Robert's bag, which had been lost by Ryanair en route to Stanstead Airport in London. After signing for the bag she spoke briefly to Hyland, offering him a cup of tea. He said he hadn't time for one as he had to go out. After he left, Elaine knocked excitedly on the door of the bedroom in which Robert and Sharon were sleeping. Robert had brought over photographs of the first weekend they had spent in London together and Elaine was dying to see them. She left the bag outside the room and glanced through the pictures. Robert shortly emerged and grabbed some clothes from the bag before taking a shower.

Later that afternoon, Hyland returned to the flat. He chatted and joked with Elaine, Robert and Sharon and then left after about an hour, saying he had to catch his flight home to Dublin. Taking his bags with him, he thanked Elaine for her hospitality and apologised for not making it out the previous night. As he left, he said he would give her a shout the next time he was over in London.

Prior to her arrest on 10 July, Elaine's most pressing concern was letting out the bedroom vacated by Paul Walsh, who had moved out the previous Saturday. One young couple had committed themselves to taking the room but pulled out at the last minute. Elaine was concerned that Paul would lose his deposit unless someone took his bedroom. Besides, there was no way she could afford to stay at Parkhill Road on her own. Given her earlier experiences of trying to find decent accommodation in London, Elaine didn't savour the prospect of being evicted. A second couple and a man from New Zealand had also viewed the flat but didn't follow up on it.

Fresh hope came when a Welsh woman, Nicky, phoned and asked if she could see the flat. Although she didn't have a distinct Welsh accent, Elaine remembers her saying on the phone: "Us Celts must stick together". She was bemused by the comment. An attractive, professional looking woman in her late twenties with shoulder-length blonde hair, Nicky confided in Elaine that she was in the middle of a messy relationship break-up and needed to make a fresh start. Elaine could empathise with the woman's situation. Nicky appeared to have a warm and kind nature and Elaine felt she was someone she could get on really well with as a housemate. She immediately offered Nicky the room and arrangements were made for her to return later in the week to meet the landlord and sign the lease. Elaine's mini crisis had ended. Her exciting new life in London was back on track.

On Thursday, 9 July, Elaine was surprised to receive a phone call at work again from Anthony Hyland, who was already back in London. She assumed he had been offered a job or college place as a result of his interview the previous weekend. He asked if she wanted to meet for a drink but Elaine told him she couldn't as she was going to Oxford that night to see Rory's brother, Niall, who had just finished at university there. That weekend, Niall was going to America for two months but planned to move back to London when he returned. Elaine had offered to store some of Niall's belongings at her place while he was in the States. The plan was that Rory would pick up Elaine at around 8 p.m. that evening and give her a driving lesson en route to Oxford. Niall had a final exam to sit the next day on Friday but would be coming up to London immediately afterwards. Rory and Elaine planned to give him a major send-off that night as they had missed his birthday the previous weekend.

The phone conversation with Anthony Hyland was brief, which suited Elaine as she was having a busy day at work. He seemed undeterred by the fact that she was going to Oxford that evening and said he would drop by later anyway. She told him she'd be home at around 7 p.m. Elaine dived back into her workload and didn't end up leaving the office until 6.30 p.m. She arrived at the flat at around 7.20 p.m. and jumped into the shower. Time was tight. Rory was due to pick her up in around 40 minutes and the landlord – and Nicky, her new flatmate – were also to call around and sign the lease agreement for the vacant bedroom. Elaine put on some music while she frantically dried her hair.

Hyland, who had called to the flat earlier but got no answer, then arrived. She brought him in and chatted away as she continued to get herself ready, self-consciously realising that she was still in her nightdress. Noticing his large rucksack, Elaine figured that Hyland was expecting to stay the night. She explained that Paul had moved out and his room was still free. As the Welsh woman would not be moving in until at least Monday, Elaine told Hyland he was welcome to the room until Sunday. "That'll be brilliant," he replied, without saying how long he intended to stay.

Hyland was chatting to Elaine in her bedroom when the landlord and his wife called. She apologised to them for rushing around the place, explaining that she was being picked up at 8 p.m. to go to Oxford. Having offered them tea while they waited for Nicky to arrive, Elaine then returned to her room to iron some clothes and continued to chat to Hyland. Much to Elaine's relief, Nicky turned up as planned and was going through the lease arrangements with the landlord while Hyland remained in the bedroom, emerging only once to use the bathroom. Elaine had requested that he remain in her bedroom, as she preferred for him not to be there while the contract and money were being discussed. She believed that the landlord would not have appreciated the presence of an uninvolved third party.

Nicky signed the lease, paid the deposit and was given

her own set of keys to the flat. She then indicated that she might return later that night with a male friend to show him the apartment. Elaine assured her that she could come and go as she pleased. Crucially, Elaine asked Hyland to leave his rucksack in her room because Nicky would possibly be returning to the flat and she didn't want her to know that someone was staying in what was now technically her room. Elaine planned to keep her bedroom door locked because she didn't want Nicky to see her bedroom before she moved in. Elaine's room was much larger and nicer than the one Nicky was taking, yet they would both be paying the same amount of rent. Elaine wanted to ensure that the lease was signed and everything was formalised first so Nicky wouldn't try to haggle over the rent or – worse still – back out of the deal. She certainly didn't want to get off on the wrong foot with her new flatmate. It was an innocent request that would have severe ramifications for her. Elaine left her bedroom key in the bathroom and informed Hyland where it would be in case he came back before her and wanted to get his bag.

Elaine apologised to Hyland for all the rushing around and for being absent during his visit. He assured her he was fine, telling her he had to meet some friends. She gave him a spare set of keys for the flat to let himself back in. Her phone rang once, meaning Rory was waiting for her outside. She told Hyland to have a nice evening and dashed out the door.

Significantly, Elaine neglected to mention Hyland's visit to Rory as they drove to Oxford. She had more important things on her mind. Elaine took advantage of the trip to avail of a driving lesson from Rory, which required her maximum concentration. Things didn't go well and a disaster was only narrowly averted when Elaine swerved to avoid another car, which appeared from nowhere, and Rory violently yanked the handbrake. Elaine stumbled out of the car in shock. The tyre marks left on the road bore testament to their narrow escape. They continued on to Oxford, this time with Rory behind the wheel.

When they arrived in Oxford, Niall Hearty was still packing. Elaine and Rory went for a quick drink to get out of his way. They later returned to Niall's and loaded up the car before heading back to London. It was around 1 a.m. by the time they returned to the flat. Rory came up briefly, carrying a stereo system that Niall had loaned to Elaine while he was away in America. Noticing that the light was on in Paul's old room, Rory went to open the bedroom door. Hyland called out that he'd be out in a minute; he was just getting dressed. Elaine's guest emerged from the room and said a quick hello to Rory, who left shortly afterwards.

Elaine made herself and Hyland a cup of tea and they watched telly, chatting casually. Before going to bed, Elaine reminded Hyland to leave his bag back in her room when she went to work the next day as Nicky would be moving some of her stuff in. By this stage, his rucksack was back in the spare bedroom where he was sleeping. Hyland went to bed first, asking Elaine to give him a shout before she left for work the next morning. She tidied up and went to her room, cursing herself for staying up so late on a work night.

It was to be Elaine's last night sleeping in her bed at 43 Parkhill Road.

Chapter Two

LOSS OF LIBERTY

Elaine awoke to the sound of the rear door of the police van opening. DS Chris Nolan, the arresting officer, was standing there, still wearing his forensic overalls. Elaine had been sitting in the back of the van in the yard of Charing Cross police station, which is located in the heart of London, for almost two hours since her dramatic arrest at work and was intermittently falling into an uneasy sleep. The internal fan in the vehicle was switched on to provide some respite from the warm summer's evening but it had no discernible effect. Elaine was sweating profusely under the hood of the forensic suit, with strands of wet hair stuck awkwardly to her face. Despite her discomfort, she was unable to do anything to remove the hair as her hands were restricted under the plastic covering that had been taped over them just after her arrest at Netlink's offices. She tried to compose herself by taking long, deep breaths, mindful that an asthma attack could be triggered off by the confined conditions. Elaine sat upright and looked DS Nolan defiantly in the face.

Accompanying Elaine in the back of the van was DC Peters, the policewoman who was present when she was arrested earlier. At 9.01 p.m. DS Nolan conducted what is known as an 'urgent safety interview' with Elaine. It was only then that she realised the full extent of the trouble she was in. He read the words aloud:

DS Nolan: "You have been arrested along with others under Section 14 of the Prevention of Terrorism Act

1989 as a person reasonably suspected of being or having been concerned in the commission, preparation or instigation of acts of terrorism. The purpose of this interview is solely to avert any possible risk that may be present to any person as a result of your activities recently. Following today's arrests, a number of improvised explosive devices were recovered by police. Do you know of the whereabouts of any such devices?"

Elaine Moore: "I thought that this was about a friend of mine who keeps diesel for his car in my garage. I have no knowledge of what you ask me."

DS Nolan: "I would like you to think again. As I have told you, we have already recovered a number of explosive devices. We want to find all of them before any innocent people get hurt."

Elaine Moore: "I can't, I have no knowledge . . ."

DS Nolan: "Are there any explosive devices in your home or anything that you think might be an explosive device?"

Elaine Moore: "Diesel in the garage, but that's not flammable."

DS Nolan: "Are you sure that there is nothing inside your flat which could be an explosive device?"

Elaine Moore: "Positive."

According to DS Nolan's arrest notes, this statement was recorded and read out to Elaine, who refused to sign it in the absence of a solicitor. However, Elaine insisted that she did sign the statement because police told her it was urgent. The serious nature of the questions caused Elaine great distress. What she was accused of was the complete antitheses of her kind and caring manner. After completing her Leaving Certificate in 1995, Elaine went on to study social studies graduating two years later with a diploma. Throughout her late teens, Elaine was actively involved in voluntary work. While at secondary school, she would spend two evenings a week helping out at the Arch Youth Reach Club in Coolock. For two summers she volunteered at a refuge centre for abused women and their children in Rathmines, where her mother works.

"Being accused of such dreadful acts stripped me of my life as I knew it," she says. "It was the most unimaginable scenario. There I was, a self-professed pacifist, being asked if there was something in my flat that could cause harm to anyone. I couldn't believe they were insinuating that I was capable of hurting anybody. My sense of shock was compounded by the fact that I had no one to turn to and seek clarity or reassurance that this misunderstanding was simply that – a misunderstanding. Never in my life did I feel so alone. Humiliation had been replaced by horror. These people were serious and I appeared to already have been convicted in their eyes. Perhaps that was just a police technique, but having never been in trouble in my life for so much as littering the streets, that was the perception I got when I looked them in the face. 'Jaysus, what next?' I thought."

Elaine was eventually brought into the police station at 9.13 p.m. She had been in the back of the van for the best part of three hours. She was frog-marched up a dual level ramp, similar to one designed for wheelchair users, which was fitted with a panic alarm system. Inside, there were t-shaped corridors, a large reception area and what looked like a control room in the background. Behind two doors was a hallway that resembled a hospital corridor. DS Nolan briefed the desk sergeant as he handed over Elaine's belongings. She was astounded by the heavy police presence and felt unnerved by their fixed stares.

"I could feel their contempt and disgust," she remembers. "Many of them looked at me in disbelief, as if they were wondering what a young woman like me was doing caught up in something like this."

Police recorded full details of Elaine's stay at Charing Cross in a journal of detainment. This generally includes a breakdown of any incidents involving a detainee while in custody. The full particulars of all officers – including rank and number – have to be included in the journal, except in terrorist cases like Elaine's. Presumably, this is because custody records are eventually handed over to a suspect when the prosecution case is being prepared and they don't want police officers' details ending up in the 'wrong' hands. As Elaine stood in the corridor she was again informed of the grounds for her detention under the Prevention of Terrorism Act. Police records state that 'the detainee' made no comment or reply. Looking back, Elaine isn't sure if she did or not. "Perhaps I didn't comment because I was disorientated and fearful," she reasons.

At 10.35 p.m. Elaine was placed in sterile cell No. 55. She sat down to compose herself. As she did, she glanced around at her strange new surroundings. There was a small, blacked-out window positioned high above a concrete slab with a dark navy, plastic mattress. To the left of the cell door was a small reinforced-glass hatch, which she later learned was used by police to monitor her. A toilet was located to the right of the door, which was partially shielded by a small wall. This meant that Elaine's head and shoulders could be seen at all times while still allowing a modicum of privacy.

Elaine could hear a gathering of voices that appeared to be coming from immediately outside her cell. A short while later, the door opened to reveal a temporary desk station that had been set up to conduct the induction interview. A rather senior looking policeman was sitting at the desk preparing some paperwork while other officers stood around him. Elaine imagined the heavy police presence was there to ensure that she didn't try to escape. Not that the notion had ever crossed her mind – she was too paralysed with fear most of the time.

The arresting officer, DS Nolan, carried out the induction interview outlining the circumstances of her arrest. He informed Elaine that she had been detained under Section 14 of the Prevention of Terrorism Act to "secure and preserve evidence by questioning and forensic examination". An extract from a notice of Elaine's rights was read out and a copy handed over to her. She was also provided with a written notice setting out her entitlements while in police custody.

Elaine's entitlements included access to a duty solicitor and she was told that one would be provided upon her request. DS Nolan also informed her that she had the right to nominate a person whom she wished to be contacted. Elaine signed a form requesting the appointment of a duty solicitor at 10.48 p.m. and asked that her friend, Rory Hearty, be informed of her whereabouts. They had made plans to meet up that evening and she thought he would be worried by her non-appearance. Rory was, in fact, abundantly aware of Elaine's situation. Unbeknownst to her, he had also been arrested as part of the operation and was being questioned down a corridor in the same police station. However, Elaine was told that due to the nature of the offence and after consultation with the officer in charge, her right to have someone informed was being withheld. Asked if she understood this, she replied: "I don't understand any of this." Elaine could not comprehend why police would inform her of her rights, only to suddenly decide that she was not entitled to them.

At 11.00 p.m. a police officer enquired if she suffered

from any illness or injury that required medication. She responded that she took "Ventalin" to prevent asthma attacks. She was asked what type of passport she held: "Irish," she replied. The duty solicitor scheme, which provides free legal aid, was then contacted on her behalf.

Elaine was asked to sign the following statement at 11.50 p.m. "I, Elaine Nan Moore, have been informed that non-intimate samples, namely hand swabs, are required from me as I am suspected of being involved in the Commission, Preparation or Instigation of Acts of Terrorism and that the taking of a sample will tend to prove or disprove my involvement in the offence. I have been informed that Inspector Warrant 183091 has authorised the taking of the samples." Elaine signed the statement and also gave consent for her fingerprints and photograph to be taken.

In the meantime, a call had been received at the station from solicitor Nigel Leskin of Birnberg & Co, who enquired if Elaine Moore was in custody. This was confirmed to him when police phoned him back at 11.55 p.m. He was informed that Elaine had already requested a duty solicitor. However, Mr Leskin told the officer to tell Elaine that he had been arranged to represent her through solicitors in Ireland at the request of her mother, Kathy. This message was not passed on to Elaine until 12.40 a.m. as 'forensications' were being carried out. She was horrified to learn that her mother had become aware of her situation.

"The feeling could be compared to that of a child; you only realise how much trouble you're in when your mother gets involved," says Elaine. "I had hoped against hope that the situation would be cleared up in no time and there would be no need to worry my family, particularly my mother. That's why I requested that Rory be informed of my whereabouts. But it made everything more real when I was told that my mother knew what was happening to me. I couldn't understand how she knew what was going on."

At this stage, Elaine was not aware that a similar drama was unfolding back home in Dublin. Just hours earlier, her brother, Robert, and his then girlfriend, Sharon, had been arrested by gardaí on suspicion of terrorist offences as part of a joint Irish and UK police operation, which saw 10 people detained.

When she found out that legal representation had already been arranged for her through a solicitors' firm in Dublin, Elaine replied: "I'll go with what my mother said." Because she was a foreign national, she was asked if she wanted the Irish Embassy contacted on her behalf. She said yes, although she wasn't sure what good it would do her. "I was grasping at straws, I suppose."

Nothing could have prepared Elaine for what happened next. She was forced to undergo her first strip-search at 1.05 a.m. According to custody records from Charing Cross police station, the ordeal lasted for 20 minutes. In the presence of two female police officers, DC Warrant and PC Gaolev, Elaine was told to stand on a white plastic sheet while all her jewellery and clothing were removed, including a wrist watch, bangle, four rings, a necklace, a pair of trousers, a pair of briefs, one blouse and her bra. Each item taken from her was bagged, further prolonging the experience. Police said they removed Elaine's belongings "to prevent harm, escape and [to use] as evidence of the offences." Standing naked in the cell, Elaine felt utterly degraded. She can't even recall if the cell door was shut or not, although police records state that it was.

"I felt that I had been molested in the most sinister

manner imaginable to me. I couldn't believe that this was 'routine' or they had a right to treat me this way. My world had collapsed. From that point on, my identity was lost, replaced by one that labelled me as dangerous and evil. I became the property of Charing Cross police station. Like a child, I was told when I could eat, sleep, use the bathroom, speak – basic things that were no longer my right."

Elaine was provided with a fresh paper suit, which felt strange against her bare skin. She refused the offer of "ridiculous looking" plimsolls and instead accepted a pair of overshoes. The cell door was reopened and her belongings were passed out in bags to an officer who recorded the contents as he received them. At 1.45 a.m., her detention under the Prevention of Terrorism Act was renewed. As she was having her fingerprints taken, a police officer told Elaine that a period of further detention was necessary "in order to obtain evidence by questioning and to preserve/secure evidence". She was returned to her cell where she declined an offer of food and drink at 2.15 a.m. This was not a form of protest – she was simply too traumatised to eat. She did, however, accept a cigarette and two blankets, as she was feeling the cold under the flimsy paper suit. This time, the cell door was kept open, although Elaine was still heavily guarded. Late as it was, the induction process was in no way over.

Elaine first met her solicitor, Nigel Leskin, at 2.39 a.m. and was allowed out of her cell briefly to talk to him. She remembers him as a tall but gentle, warm man, with an extremely relaxing manner. She felt immediately at ease in his presence. However, Elaine broke down for the first time after the solicitor calmly informed her that her brother, his girlfriend and Rory had also been arrested.

"I felt numb and would have willingly keeled over

and died at that moment," she admits. "It was bad enough that Mum knew what was happening. When I learned about Robert, I was crushed not only because of what he was obviously being put through, but also due to the fact that Mum didn't have him by her side. At that point I became a blubbering mess, unable to form a thought or complete a proper sentence."

Elaine desperately tried to regain her composure. She refused to wallow in self-pity. The lives of people she loved now also had to be considered. Being weak was no longer an option. She continued her consultation with Nigel Leskin, who briefed her on what to expect during the police interviews, which would start the next day.

Following this initial legal consultation, Elaine was photographed by police at 3.17 a.m. While the photographs were being taken, she received a 'welfare visit' from the duty inspector to see if she had any requests or complaints. She simply asked for another cigarette. It was 3.25 a.m. before Elaine was returned to her cell and the lights were dimmed. Only then was she allowed to use the lavatory for the first time since her arrest – police had feared she would have used the opportunity to destroy evidence. She collapsed, exhausted, onto the makeshift bed, which comprised of a concrete slab, rubber mattress, two blankets and a disposable pillow. According to police records, Elaine was checked every half hour and appeared to be sleeping.

When she awoke, Elaine declined two offers of breakfast at 7.30 a.m. and 8.10 a.m. She was visited by a doctor in her cell at 9.51 a.m. who deemed her fit to be detained and interviewed. Elaine was allowed out of her cell for a wash and changed into yet another boiler suit. She remembers a "butch looking" police woman telling her to keep the curtain open the first time she showered on the Saturday morning.

"In my eyes she looked like a man and there was no way I was going to shower naked in front of her – or anyone else for that matter," recalls Elaine. "To protect my dignity I had a shower while still wearing the forensic suit, which seemed to make her angry. The next time I was allowed to shower in complete privacy, which led me to believe that my instincts about this particular police woman were correct."

Conditions at Charing Cross police station throughout her induction period were "appalling", Elaine recollects. After washing or showering, she had to dry herself with paper towels and was given a man's comb to brush her long hair. She was handcuffed for the first time when briefly brought outside to 'exercise' – this involved walking around the police station's courtyard in circles. Elaine noticed that the entire perimeter of the yard was patrolled by police officers with dogs. Feeling decidedly uncomfortable, she asked that the exercise period be cut short and was returned to her cell.

At 11.05 a.m. she was allowed out of her cell to speak with Nigel Leskin. She needed to ask her solicitor's advice on police requests for an intimate sample of blood which would 'allow comparison with other forensic evidence and may help to determine her involvement in the commission, preparation or instigation of acts of terrorism.' She granted authority for the blood sample at 11.55 a.m. According to Elaine, this procedure was carried out "roughly" by a doctor and she believes the needle was pulled out too quickly, resulting in blood squirting everywhere. In fact, Rory Hearty would later notice the bloodstains left by Elaine when police brought him into the same room.

Chapter Three

THE FEAR FACTOR

Four days of gruelling police interrogations followed. Elaine was subjected to intense scrutiny of her private life: family background, ex-boyfriends, sexual history, political views – anything and everything was open to discussion. The interviews were conducted by two Scotland Yard detectives in the presence of her solicitor, Nigel Leskin, who was "incredibly supportive" throughout the sessions and made her feel secure. Elaine didn't underestimate the importance of these interrogations, knowing they could determine her future. But at least she would be able to tell her side of the story – for once.

The mood of the detectives fluctuated wildly. They would go from being kind, caring and almost compassionate before suddenly turning sarcastic and aggressive. Sometimes they'd shout at her; she'd shout back. Elaine felt they were constantly trying to intimidate her, speaking in disbelieving and disapproving tones or not allowing her to complete sentences. It was, she says, a classic "good cop, bad cop" scenario.

"At one stage I sarcastically apologised for not giving them the answers they were looking for," Elaine recalls. "They seemed uninterested in the truth. Initially I cooperated in a sheepish manner. I knew the severity of my situation and in a crude sense understood why they were treating me so harshly. But the boredom and monotony was beginning to overcome any fear I felt. I became frustrated and tired of cooperating – at times I could see no point. It was a harrowing experience. I knew they were looking for keywords; any minor discrepancies in my story; anything that could question the validity of my statements. I would almost begin to panic if I could not remember slight details – dates, names, chance encounters, all of which had suddenly become extremely relevant."

The detectives would occasionally try to placate her with sporadic acts of kindness, offering her a blanket when they thought she was cold and repeatedly asking if she wanted something to eat. Elaine had eaten nothing since her arrest and on several occasions throughout the interview sessions it was stated by detectives that this was simply because she didn't feel like it. In other words, her refusal of food was not a form of protest or hunger strike. All interviews were tape recorded and sealed.

The first interview with Elaine took place on Saturday, 11 July at 2.48 p.m. Present were Detective Constable Gary Powell and Detective Constable James Guest, as well as Nigel Leskin. DC Powell first asked Elaine if her asthma was okay and said the interview would be stopped straight away if she required any medication for the condition. A disclosure notice, which had been served on her solicitor that morning, was read out by DC Powell, outlining the reasons for Elaine's arrest. The notice revealed that she had been the subject of surveillance on various dates and had been seen to meet with other persons 'who are also believed to be concerned in acts of terrorism'. Elaine was bemused to learn that Scotland Yard had allocated her the code name 'Delicious Food' during the surveillance operation. She was described as "an associate" of a man known as 'Wheat Bran', the code name of 'Tony' Hyland.

'Wheat Bran stayed the night of the 9 July at 43 Parkhill

Road, NW3, which is believed to be the address of Elaine Moore,' a section of the disclosure notice read. 'He had previously visited the flat on 04/07/98. He was carrying a bag on his arrest on the 10/7/98. When it was examined it was found to contain six improvised explosive devices. The address of Moore was searched on the 10/7/98 and a bag containing improvised explosive devices and Semtex were [*sic*] discovered.'

Nigel Leskin then read the arrest notes taken by Detective Sergeant Chris Nolan. Elaine felt that there had been some omissions from these notes so her solicitor advised her not to sign it as a complete record. Just over 14 minutes passed before the interview properly commenced, starting with an intensive trawl through her personal details and family background. Elaine was questioned on every facet of her life growing up in Dublin, from schools and employment details to relationships. She also recounted the circumstances that had led to her decision to leave her job at America On-Line in Dublin and make the career move to London.

Despite the fact that she had been under surveillance, British police knew very little about Elaine. Gardaí, who had liased with the UK authorities as part of the anti-terrorist operation, also admitted to Scotland Yard that she was not known to them. As the interrogations began, detectives attempted to build a profile of this easy-going twenty-one-year-old woman who was accused of the most serious offences.

Elaine was born in Holles Street hospital in Dublin on 22 September 1976. Her early years were spent living in the north-city suburb of Kilbarrack. When Elaine was five-years-old, her parents, Martin and Kathy Moore, split up. Elaine went to live with her mother while her brother, Robert – who is 20 months older than her –

stayed with his dad. Despite the break-up of their relationship, both parents continued to play a full and active
role in their children's upbringing. Martin and Kathy
would later go on to develop a strong friendship, even
after their divorce in 1998. Family life for the Moores
may not have been conventional but they were close and
tight knit nevertheless. She was particularly close to her
brother, who was completely protective of his little sister.
They saw each other almost every day after school and
Elaine spent most of her childhood hanging out with
Robert and his friends. "I was a complete tomboy!" she
remembers.

After covering Elaine's background in Dublin,
detectives moved on to the people who had visited or
stayed in Elaine's flat over the previous four months. She
was grilled on the nature of her relationship with people
like Paul Walsh, her former flatmate in London. For
example, they wanted to know if Elaine had ever had sex
with Paul. She responded with an emphatic "No!" She
explained that he had moved out the previous weekend
and told of her efforts to let out his room. Elaine also had
to recall, in detail, the exact circumstances of the two
recent visits to London by her brother Robert and Sharon.

Police also probed Rory Hearty's use of Elaine's garage,
located to the rear of her flat. She said he sometimes left
his car there but mainly used it to store equipment.
Protective clothing and gloves had been found in the
garage, which Elaine attributed to the fact that Rory was
allergic to oil. A few days into the interrogations, she was
relieved to learn that Robert, Sharon and Rory had been
released without charge. It gave her a slight glimmer of
hope.

"I now felt their fate would reflect my own and found
a new source of strength in that," she says. "I was

comforted by the fact that they were now safe. You think a situation is bad until you realise that the people you love are experiencing the same hardship. I could cope now that I was the only one in trouble – deep trouble – but at least I knew they were no longer being subjected to this harsh regime. There was now light at the end of the tunnel."

Of particular interest to the detectives was Elaine's knowledge of Anthony Hyland, the twenty-five-year-old Dubliner who had stayed in her flat on two separate occasions, including the night before their arrest. British police seemed unable to understand why anyone would offer such casual hospitality to a person they were only vaguely acquainted with. Elaine's explanation that it was very much an Irish thing was lost on them and treated with suspicion. She told them about the kindness she had been shown by Rory and his friends when she first arrived in London; about how the Irish look out for each other when they are in a different country; that the phenomenon of 'friends of friends' looking for accommodation was very common among young Irish people in London. However, such behaviour seemed completely beyond the detectives' comprehension.

Elaine tried to outline the circumstances that led to Hyland's rucksack being locked in her bedroom on the evening of Thursday, 9 July. She denied that she had touched the bag at any stage. To the best of her knowledge, it had been removed from her bedroom by the time she returned from Oxford in the early hours of Friday, 10 July. Police were highly suspicious of the fact that Elaine had failed to tell her closest friend, Rory Hearty, that she had a guest from Dublin staying in her flat for the night. By way of explanation, she told of her disastrous driving lesson on the way to Oxford that evening, when she narrowly avoided colliding with another car that had cut across her path. That incident, coupled with the fact that it was 'no big deal', were the only explanation she could offer.

Elaine was at pains to point out that she had never made any attempt to hide the fact that Anthony Hyland was staying with her. On one occasion she had left him waiting outside her flat because she was in no particular hurry to get home from work – hardly the actions of a person wishing to harbour a terrorist. In fact, surveillance footage would later verify Elaine's account of this. That same evening, Anthony Hyland had been seen in her flat by Nicky – the Welsh girl who was supposed to be moving in – as well as Elaine's landlord and his wife.

Then there was Elaine's apparent failure to question Hyland about where he had gone or who he had met on the two occasions he had stayed with her. Elaine replied that she was not a nosy person by nature; it had never crossed her mind to ask him where hc'd been or who he was with. She had last heard from Hyland a few hours before her arrest. He had phoned her in work to inquire if Nicky would be coming over to the flat to move some of her stuff in. Elaine had previously reminded Hyland that his rucksack was not to be left in Nicky's room and told him he could put it in her bedroom. And that's exactly where it was found when police raided her flat.

Elaine was shown a number of photographs of other people who had been arrested as part of 'an operation' and as a result of the items found in her bedroom. The first was of Rory Hearty. She didn't recognise the men in the second or third photographs but later learned they were Liam Grogan and Darren Mulholland. The fourth picture was of a young, attractive woman, who was known to Elaine; she was a girlfriend of one of Rory's housemates.

Elaine had learned that the woman was arrested along with Rory on Euston Road in central London.

Another police theory was that Elaine and Anthony Hyland were having a sexual relationship. DC Guest put this to her when she identified Hyland from a photograph shown to her. A used condom had allegedly been found in a bin in Elaine's bedroom, which she denied all knowledge of. Elaine suggested that the Belfast couple who had stayed in her room some weeks earlier, or even Robert and Sharon, who had visited just the previous weekend, could have left the condom. Elaine insisted she was single; that Rory was the closest thing she had to a boyfriend, even though they were just friends. DC Guest sounded sceptical.

"You see, there is a thought that you have been having sex with Tony Hyland, and you have had a relationship with him, hence he's been using your flat and been storing his belongings, and for want of a better word, his terrorist paraphernalia, at your flat," DC Guest said.

"That's not true," Elaine responded, clearly exasperated. "If there's any tests that you can do on me you'll [find that] I did not have sex with him."

The only explanation was that she had simply forgotten to empty the bin and was unaware of the existence of the condom. Furthermore, she stressed that forensic evidence would uphold her assertion that Hyland had never slept in her bed. "The condom's nothing to do with me," she said. "You can check me."

Finishing this line of questioning, DC Guest continued: "But nonetheless, the most important thing is that your flat was used as a storage facility and possible bomb making factory for a man, a man and a group of men that were going to bomb London. And you're saying you've been duped."

Elaine repeated that she had no reason to be suspicious of Hyland and had absolutely no idea what he had allegedly brought into her flat. "Do you honestly think that if I knew what was in them [Hyland's bags], what he'd put [*sic*] in my room, that I would sleep?" Elaine asked. She recounted for police the occasion that she had let the young couple from Belfast stay in her room for the weekend, despite the fact that she had never met them before. She even got keys cut for them.

This led to another hypothesis being put forward by the detectives. It was suggested to Elaine that Hyland didn't simply call her up out of the blue. Somebody must have told him that her flat was a safe place to prepare explosives before planting them in London. DC Guest said: "I'm saying, if they accept you're innocent, somebody tipped him off that there's a trusting woman that will let people come and go from her flat, and here's an ideal place to use. Somebody did, if you're innocent." Elaine refused to believe that anyone she knew would put her in such a dangerous position.

Growing up in Dublin, Elaine had been a shy, insecure teenager and was particularly uncomfortable meeting people for the first time. As a result, she always maintained a tight circle of friends. Rory had helped to bring Elaine out of her shell and life in London had opened up a wealth of new experiences and opportunities.

Her love of Michael Collins, the pivotal figure associated with Irish independence from Britain, set her apart from her peers. She worshipped Collins in the same way that teenage girls idolise pop stars. Her fascination with Collins began when Elaine was around fifteen-years-old. Walking down O'Connell Street in Dublin's city centre one Saturday, she noticed a poster of Michael Collins being sold on the street. "I was captivated by the image of Collins dressed in his Free State uniform," she remembers. "The picture triggered a fascination with him that I still hold dear to this day."

Elaine then immersed herself in anything to do with Michael Collins, from books and newspaper articles to photographs and films. She was particularly enamoured with the portrayal of Collins by the Dublin actor, Brendan Gleeson, in the television series, *The Treaty*. She was less impressed by the choice of Liam Neeson for the titular role in Neil Jordan's film, *Michael Collins*. Elaine's interest in Collins bordered on the fanatical. She would pay a high price for her devotion of him.

During the interrogation sessions, the detectives made repeated references to what they called the "republican paraphernalia" found in Elaine's room. This mainly related to pictures of Michael Collins, as well as newspaper articles, books and a gold necklace with a pendant in the shape of a map of Ireland. Elaine tried – to the best of her ability – to offer a simple analysis of Michael Collins's important role in Irish history. "The majority of republicans hate him because they feel he sold out the six counties," she declared. "I don't believe that. I believe that he tried to get a united Ireland through peaceful means. He viewed the Treaty as a stepping stone which would eventually lead to the overall objective of an independent, united Ireland."

She told of the Irish Civil War that followed the signing of the Treaty between Ireland and Britain, a war that would ultimately lead to the assassination of Collins in 1922. To Elaine, Michael Collins was a hobby, a historical icon who held her interest from a young age. "My bedroom back home is like a shrine to Michael Collins. Everyone knows I love him."

Elaine made no secret of her nationalistic sentiments

and the fact that she would like to see a united Ireland – but through peaceful means. She said she supported the Sinn Féin President, Gerry Adams, whom she described as a "second kind of Michael Collins". Like Collins, Adams was also being branded a traitor in certain quarters, she believed. Elaine was asked about her attitude towards the splinter groups that had broken away from the IRA. She replied that she didn't know much about them because she had been living in London. She believed, however, that there would probably be a united Ireland achieved through the Northern Ireland Assembly, which had been proposed as part of the Good Friday Agreement in 1998. Asked if she would support the use of violence to achieve that aim, she responded: "No way!"

Elaine had also downloaded pages of An Phoblacht, a republican newspaper, from the Internet. One of the articles was in Irish: Elaine had been trying to improve her grasp of the language. Three books about Michael Collins had been found in her room, as well as one written by Bobby Sands, the republican prisoner who had died on hunger strike in May 1981. She had also been loaned a book about the INLA. Elaine emphasised that it was not unusual for Irish people to have an interest in Irish history.

"It's the way Irish people are," she said.

"But most people don't have Semtex in their bedroom," DC Guest sarcastically retorted.

The atmosphere in the interview room suddenly became tense. Elaine could not believe what she was hearing. She had openly displayed the pictures of Michael Collins and the Irish tricolour on her bedroom walls and left the books there for anyone to find. It wasn't as if she was trying to hide anything.

She was asked what she now thought about Hyland,

assuming he had left the Semtex and improvised explosive devices in her flat. There was a long pause before she finally answered. "Umm . . . I'm not happy at all. You know (sighs), I don't even want to think like that because that is just me being completely betrayed by opening up my home to someone and I'm in trouble for doing so. And plus that's obviously endangering me if I'm sleeping in an apartment where there's explosives."

Elaine was clearly appalled when asked how she would feel about a bomb going off in London. " . . . I'm a normal person, I'd say it's fucking deplorable. I have friends in London, I have a lot of English friends in London. I wouldn't like to see anybody getting hurt. My attitude is like that of any normal person."

Elaine speculated that Anthony Hyland was the only possible person who could have brought explosive devices into her flat – definitely not members of her family or close friends like Rory, who she trusted with her life. "I know they'd never have betrayed me. They most certainly wouldn't have put me in this poxy position." Neither did she believe that Sharon, nor Paul Walsh, were involved.

By Monday, 13 July, the detectives seemed increasingly concerned at Elaine's refusal to eat. Apart from a small bar of chocolate given to her by her solicitor, Elaine had declined all offers of food since being brought to Charing Cross police station the previous Friday night. DC Powell said she was to let them know at any stage during her custody if she wanted food or special food arranged.

Close scrutiny of documents, bills and letters found in Elaine's flat had further aroused the detectives' suspicions. They wanted to know, for example, why herself and Paul Walsh had separate phone numbers for the same flat. The explanation for this was simple: firstly, she didn't want her ex-boyfriend back in Dublin to know that she was living with Paul Wash; secondly, Walsh did a lot of work involving his laptop computer and needed a separate connection for the Internet. But it was a letter from one of her best friends back home that presented Elaine with greater difficulties. Half way down Elaine 'Beag' O'Neill's letter were the words 'FREEDOM' in block capitals, followed by ('up the Ra') in brackets. Elaine guessed the reference to freedom related to her break up from her boyfriend in addition to her newfound freedom in London. 'Up the Ra', while indicating support for the IRA, was just something that is 'abused' in Ireland – at football matches, for instance. It's a slogan, something that is chanted by people who attach little significance to its true meaning.

"It just seems a funny thing to put into a letter to a best friend who must know your views," DC Powell commented.

"It only seems so funny because of what has happened now," Elaine responded. "There's nothing wrong with that; I probably would have giggled when I read that, especially because Elaine 'Beag' wrote it. She would have little notion of who Gerry Adams is, let alone know anything about the IRA."

A map of the London underground had also been found in the flat. Certain sections of the map had been circled, including the Canary Wharf area of London's docklands. According to Elaine, the map had been written on during the time when she and Paul Walsh were trying to find a place to live. Apartments at Canary Wharf had been advertised and either herself or Paul, she couldn't recollect, had marked the Tube lines that would bring them to work from there. Walsh could easily clarify that matter. Police would later speculate in the media that some of the explosive devices recovered in London may have been destined for the London underground system.

Elaine had to explain the significance of even the most mundane items found in her flat. Two empty packs of Duracell batteries had been discovered in a bag of rubbish in her bedroom. Elaine had bought the batteries for a weight toner kit, only to discover that she could simply plug the device in. Not needing the batteries, she left them in an Argos bag. In case she was in any doubt about what the detectives were trying to imply, she was then asked if she had heard of or seen Semtex explosives before.

"I don't think so," she answered sarcastically.

"Well, it's an explosive used widely by the IRA," said DC Powell, showing her a photograph of the contents of the rucksack allegedly found in her bedroom. "It's a very, very dangerous explosive. That's why they use it. Let's be honest, it wasn't brought over here and put together for no other reason [sic] but to hurt, maim and cause serious damage in the City of London. That was found in your bedroom. Have you anything to say about that?"

Elaine paused, before answering: "Well, I've never seen it before. How can I possibly comment?"

The next photographed exhibit Elaine was shown was of a Tupperware type box filled with talcum powder, with two kilograms of Semtex in the middle. The presence of talcum powder in the container would eventually mitigate in Elaine's favour. On the morning of her arrest, 10 July, she had slept late and had no time to shower. If she had showered, there was every chance she would have used talcum powder afterwards. Conceivably, this could have presented police with the only potentially damning piece of forensic evidence against her.

Elaine's attitude towards the British was also explored in detail. She was frankly honest when asked what she thought about the English. She said she didn't hold the

"British establishment" in high regard but got on "fantastically well" with the "ordinary" English people. DC Powell opportunistically seized upon her comments.

"Say somebody came over here and placed a bomb [at] the Houses of Parliament . . . what would your view be of that?" he asked.

"I don't agree with bombs at all," Elaine responded. "There's always a danger . . ."

"Well, you don't like the British establishment," he interrupted. "You've already said that."

Elaine stressed that she would not like to see a British soldier being shot dead. It was all human life to her. She did not agree with violence – full stop. She had never heard anyone back in Ireland talk about "bombing the shit out of the Brits", as DC Guest crudely put it to her. DC Powell was also sceptical: "You disagree with all the violence, all that killing, but then we find two packs, two kilograms of Semtex in your room . . . we cannot bring ourselves to believe that you just did not know anything about all this stuff being in your room."

Elaine was quizzed on her knowledge of the 32 County Sovereignty Committee, which had links with dissident republicans opposed to the peace process in Northern Ireland. She didn't know much about the organisation, she said, because she had been living in London and was somewhat out of touch with events back home. She even had difficulty restating its name when responding to the question. DC Powell wasn't convinced. He described Elaine as something of an Irish "historian". He noted that she had printed off Irish news stories from the AOL website, copies of which had been found in her flat. Elaine insisted that these stories had simply related to the conflict on the Garvaghy Road, an annual flash point between Catholics and Protestants during the so-called marching season in Northern Ireland. The articles had simply caught her attention. Powell offered Elaine his assessment of the 32 County Sovereignty Committee: "They don't agree with all this Peace Treaty. They don't agree with the Assembly. They don't want to get on with the English people, the British people. They want a united Ireland blar, blar, blar . . . whatever. That's right, isn't it?"

Elaine said she wouldn't be living in London if she held those views; if she had such a hatred of English people. Besides, a lot of English people didn't like the Irish, she pointed out. She had been called 'Paddy' loads of times. Powell asked her if she was sure she wasn't "a bit fed up" with the peace process and had decided to assist Hyland with some sort of campaign. Elaine was "absolutely positive" that this was not the case. The interrogations were becoming increasingly difficult for Elaine to bear. The constant bombardment of accusations and insinuations, coupled with the detectives' apparent lack of knowledge or understanding of Irish history and current affairs, began to erode the little fate Elaine had that she could eliminate herself from their suspicions.

DC Guest painted another scenario for Elaine. What, for instance, would she have done if the bombs had gone off and there had been pictures of Anthony Hyland in the press? Would she have contacted the police on recognising him? Elaine suddenly lost her temper. She stated that such an incident would have terrified her and she would have gone to the police before they came to her, especially if people had been hurt. She would not have been concerned that certain people back in Ireland would possibly frown upon her cooperation with police.

Elaine found it curious that the detectives seemed reluctant to check the accuracy of her story with one key witness – the Welsh girl, Nicky, who was supposed to have been moving into her flat. Nicky would verify, she believed, one important aspect of her account: that she had been welcomed into the flat and told that she could come and go as she liked when moving her stuff in. Furthermore, Nicky would have seen Anthony Hyland in the flat on the night she signed the lease with the landlord. This would prove that Elaine was not trying to hide him. But Nicky was not all that she seemed. This would account for the detectives' lack of interest in her during the interrogations. They also derailed any effort Elaine made to weave the young couple from Belfast into the equation in a bid to substantiate her hospitable nature.

The final interview session with Elaine at Charing Cross police station took place on the afternoon of Tuesday, 14 July 1998. Earlier that morning, she had received another welfare visit to ensure she had no complaints about her treatment while in custody. A few hours later, Nigel Leskin entered her cell for a private consultation with his client. They were interrupted by DC Powell, who handed the solicitor a statement, one that he had hoped he would not receive. Leskin quietly read the statement and then spoke with Powell for a couple of minutes. It was now apparent that the period in which they were authorised to detain Elaine was fast coming to an end. The Crown Prosecution Service would soon have to decide whether to press charges or release her.

Turning to Elaine, Nigel Leskin informed her that there would be one final interview session with detectives. Deep in her heart, she knew that this interview could ultimately determine her fate. Elaine had cooperated as fully as possible at all times, even when it came to volunteering for forensic examinations. She had never refused to answer any question she was asked and had always followed police instructions. The ridiculous prospect of absconding had never even entered her mind. Paralysed by fear half the time, she didn't dare make a sudden movement, let alone a bid to escape custody.

Custody records show that at 1.52 p.m., the duty officer was informed that an application had been made to the then Home Secretary, Jack Straw, for a further period of detention for Elaine. Unable to contact Nigel Leskin, the message had been passed on to his colleague, Gareth Peirce, who was visiting a client at Charing Cross police station at the time. Nigel Leskin learned of the news 30 minutes later but chose not to inform Elaine of this latest development. He didn't want to unduly worry her; after all, it was merely an application at that point in time. The interview was delayed due to the unavailability of a suitable room. The solicitor returned to Elaine's cell and noticed that she had become extremely anxious.

Elaine asked Nigel Leskin about the upcoming interview. What further information could the detectives possibly want clarified? She had answered every conceivable question over the previous three days. Leskin enquired if there was anyone who might try to contradict her account of events. To the best of her knowledge there wasn't, certainly not in relation to anything of major significance. Elaine was confident that she had no enemies who would deliberately try to damage her case.

At approximately 3 p.m., the duty officer was informed that the Home Secretary had just signed and authorised a further 24-hour period of detention. It would take effect from 4.00 p.m. that afternoon. Nigel Leskin asked the officer to ensure that his client was kept in the dark about this as he feared it would cause her considerable distress. The solicitor knew that Elaine would construe the news as a major setback. She was understandably terrified about the possibility of being charged and this development seemed to bring that prospect a step closer to reality. Leskin needed Elaine, more than ever, to remain focused. Now was not the time for unwelcome distractions.

Shortly after the interview commenced at 3.25 p.m., Elaine was shown a photograph of a necklace, with a pendant in the shape of a map of Ireland. The intricate lines on the map separated each county. It was a symbol, police suggested, for the 32 County Sovereignty Committee. Elaine was flabbergasted. The necklace had been bought for her as a Christmas present in 1995 by her brother, Robert, long before the formation of this dissident republican organisation. It was simply a map of Ireland, she protested, that could be purchased in any gift shop back home. She was asked if she would like to see a united Ireland. She said she would and could see it happening in 20 or 30 years' time. She expressed her admiration for the "fantastic things" being done for the peace process by the British Prime Minister, Tony Blair, and the SDLP's John Hume. Elaine was certainly in favour of a united Ireland – but through peaceful means only. She could not emphasise this point enough but felt that it was falling on deaf ears.

As the interview approached its conclusion, Elaine heard something that shocked her deeply. The police alleged that somebody had told them that not only was Elaine a Sinn Féin supporter but also claimed she had "a connection" with the IRA. Pressed on the Sinn Féin reference, Elaine spoke again of her personal admiration for the role being played in the peace process by the party's president, Gerry Adams. She knew very little about the other "Shinners". She had never gone on a Sinn Féin march but had attended two or three rallies outside the GPO in Dublin to commemorate the 1916 Easter Rising, purely for their historical value. As for the IRA connection,

Elaine had absolutely no idea why anyone would say such a thing to the police and doubted the validity of the detectives' claim. Although deeply disturbed by the alleged statement, Elaine honestly didn't believe that it was said.

Sitting in on the final interview was Detective Constable John Boitel-Gill, who was attached to the Anti-Terrorist Branch at New Scotland Yard. A large, intimidating looking man, he remarked that Elaine had been "quite open" about her "republican, nationalist, whatever" sympathies. He wanted to know if anyone from a republican organisation had asked her to put somebody up in her flat. "The answer is no," she said. "I'm telling you the truth. Do you think anyone – friends or family – would endanger me like this? My whole life is ruined."

The tape was stopped at 3.51 p.m. and Elaine was returned to her cell for what would be the longest night of her life.

Chapter Four

CAUGHT IN THE NET

On the morning of 10 July 1998, Kathy Moore went upstairs and entered her son's bedroom. She'd usually bring Robert up a cup of tea before heading off to work. Kathy was concerned to notice his bloodstained shirt lying on the floor. She recoiled in horror when she saw his battered, swollen face.

Robert explained that he had been involved in a fracas in Dublin's Temple Bar the previous night. After leaving work in the Central Bank, he had bumped into a friend's brother and gone for a quick pint with him. One drink led to another and the two lads found themselves in Eamon Doran's bar some hours later. While Robert was up at the bar, he noticed some sort of commotion involving his friend and two burly looking men. When the door staff became involved in the mêlée, Robert decided it was time to go and ushered his drinking companion out the door. As they were walking away, the two men involved in the scuffle came out of the pub after them. Before words were even exchanged, Robert was floored by a powerful punch that cut the inside of his mouth and left his face visibly swollen. He stumbled to his feet; dazed, he realised the well-dressed thugs had now turned their aggression on his friend. As he staggered over to help, somebody mentioned that the gardaí were around. With that, the two men simply walked away. Robert remembers them as respectable looking and well spoken – certainly not your typical Dublin hooligans out looking for trouble. Whatever their motive or background, they had inflicted serious damage on Robert's jaw. There was no way he could go to work in that state. He asked his mother to phone in sick for him.

Kathy travelled across the city to the Rathmines Women's Refuge Centre, where she worked as the manager. She had been involved with the centre since it first opened in the mid-1980s, initially as a social worker and counsellor. The centre offers crisis accommodation for women and their children who are victims of domestic abuse. It could be a challenging and stressful environment at times, but Kathy loved her job. Later in the day she phoned home to see how Robert was feeling. He had spent the afternoon relaxing and generally feeling sorry for himself. He passed the day watching a video, *In the Name of the Father*, the harrowing true story of the Guildford Four. His girlfriend had bought the video for him but he never had a chance to watch it, until then. Robert's choice of T-shirt that day was also unfortunate; bought at a Shane McGowan concert, it prominently featured the Irish tricolour.

Kathy phoned Elaine in London before she left work. They usually spoke to each other every day. Elaine was concerned to hear about Robert being attacked but her mother assured her that he was feeling much better and his injuries were not serious. Elaine told her mum about her weekend plans. There was a going away party for Niall Hearty in central London that evening so she was heading there straight from work.

* * *

Elaine's father, Martin, was the first to realise that his children were in some sort of trouble. At approximately

5.30 p.m., the door of his Ballyfermot home was violently burst open by gardaí using a steel battering ram. He was confronted by six armed members of the Garda's Emergency Response Unit who repeatedly ordered him to lie on the floor – but he defiantly refused to. His two dogs were clearly distressed and protectively ran to their master's side, barking incessantly at the intruders. Martin asked the police to refrain from pointing their weapons at him. He initially believed that this was a botched drug bust; the guards must have had the wrong address. But then he was asked where Robert was. "He lives with his mother," Martin replied, knowing now that they had intentionally raided his house. Having heard of the previous night's incident in Temple Bar, Martin's next assumption was that Robert had perhaps seriously injured – or even inadvertently killed – one of his attackers. Judging by the extreme measures taken by the gardaí, Robert must have been in deep trouble. Martin held his dogs in his arms as the police searched the house. One of the officers took a call on his mobile phone and then announced to the others that they "had him". Martin stood frozen on the spot. A guard pointed to a picture of Elaine on his wall and sarcastically asked who she was. "That's my daughter," he said quietly, puzzled by the tone of the question. The raid on his home lasted about 30 minutes, during which items were removed without explanation. One Garda sergeant struck him as being more sympathetic and compassionate than the others. He told Martin, sincerely, that he hoped everything would be all right.

Over in Rathmines, Kathy's long-term partner, Tom Beirne, a retired Garda who now ran a bed and breakfast business in the north-city area, picked her up from work. Arriving home to Coolock, they were met at the front door by Robert, who was in a clearly distraught state.

"The guards are here," he told them. "They've arrested Sharon." Kathy couldn't believe what she was hearing. Sharon, a petite twenty-one-year-old woman, was Robert's girlfriend at the time. She had been arrested in her family's home in Ballyfermot. Kathy couldn't believe what she was hearing. Detective Sergeant Tony Fennessey, who knew Tom personally from their early days as gardaí, was standing in the kitchen. He asked Kathy and Tom their names and if they owned the house.

"Is it true that Sharon has been arrested?" Kathy asked him.

"Yeah," Fennessey replied.

"Is Robert in any trouble?" she continued.

"He most certainly is," said Fennessey, who then walked over to Robert and put his hand on his shoulder, stating: "I'm arresting you under Section 30 of the Offences Against the State Act."

When he had answered the door to gardaí just minutes earlier, Robert could only imagine that they were looking for a local drug dealer but had mistakenly come to the wrong address. He was then told that they had a search warrant which had been issued as a result of the "bombs in England". Because he had been watching a video, Robert had missed the news. He deduced from the over-the-top reaction of the gardaí that there had been a serious explosion with people killed. He came to the conclusion that anyone who had recently been to the UK – as he had been the previous weekend – was being picked up by police in a bid to track down those responsible for the atrocity. Robert became enraged when informed that he was being arrested for possession of explosives. What if something had been planted in the house by gardaí? The possibility of a police stitch-up was uppermost on his mind, particularly after watching the film about the

Guildford Four. He calmed down slightly when he learned that the explosives referred to related to London. Robert was put into a car and driven the short distance to Coolock Garda Station, which was literally located across the road from the Moore family home. It was, he reflects, the worst day of his life. "It started with a swollen jaw and a hangover – then this! I thought to myself: 'Things can't get any worse'."

Meanwhile, gardaí were in the bedrooms upstairs tearing the family's house apart. At one stage they brought down a Garda uniform they had found in the attic and asked Kathy who it belonged to. "I said to them, 'It's hardly mine now, is it?' They knew well it was Tom's. They all knew who he was. But Tom later explained to me that it wouldn't have mattered if he had been their brother – they had a job to do and had to follow procedure. Even though they knew him, they had to make him identify himself for the record."

Tom had to be in work by 7.00 p.m. As he was leaving, he told Kathy to contact Paddy Kennedy, a solicitor friend of his. Kathy knew it would be difficult trying to find a solicitor for Robert after business hours on a Friday evening. As it happened, Kennedy was away on holiday. Tom then suggested Hanahoe's, a prominent law firm in Dublin. She eventually tracked down a solicitor there, who promised to visit Robert later that evening at Coolock Garda Station.

Kathy asked the guards if she could go upstairs to her bedroom and change out of the suit which she had worn to work that day. She noticed that her room had been the least touched; the rest of house was practically ransacked. Outside, gardaí were searching the back garden. Exasperated, Kathy asked DS Fennessey to explain what was going on.

"That's what's going on," he said, pointing to the television. There was a breaking story on Sky News about a foiled bomb attack on London. Six people had been arrested. It all went over Kathy's head. She was trying desperately to contact Elaine on the phone to let her know about Robert's arrest. Failing to reach her at work, Kathy tried Rory Hearty's mobile but couldn't get him either. Then the phone rang – it was solicitor Michael Farrell from Hanahoe's. He said he had been to see Robert in the garda station and asked Kathy if she wanted him to organise a solicitor for Elaine in London. It was only then that the full realisation of what was happening dawned on her.

"Not in a million years did I imagine that Elaine had been arrested," says Kathy. "If I had paid proper attention to Sky News I would have seen Rory sitting beside his car by the side of the road, having just been arrested."

It was Michael Farrell who suggested that Gareth Peirce should represent Elaine. Kathy recognised the name immediately. "I was very alarmed – I associated the name with the Birmingham Six and the Guildford Four. I was worried because I thought that Gareth Peirce just represented political cases and was afraid of Elaine being cast in this light. But Michael Farrell insisted that because of her track record on human rights issues, she would be the best lawyer to deal with this sort of case." He also instructed Kathy not to set foot in the UK under any circumstances. The solicitor warned she could end up "another Annie Maguire", a reference to an aunt of Gerry Conlon – one of the Guildford Four – who had been found guilty of terrorism charges in Britain, despite her innocence. Besides, there would be little possibility of Kathy being allowed to see Elaine in the first place.

Kathy felt helpless and frustrated at not being able to

comfort her daughter. She turned her immediate attention to Robert and was able to visit him that night in the garda station. She was even permitted to bring him over food. "I was very worried about him because he was unable to eat; his mouth was still in a right state from the punch he had received the night before," she remembers.

"The guards were using Elaine against him, saying things like: 'If you want to help your sister, you'll talk'." Throughout the weekend, Kathy couldn't shake the feeling that she, too, was going to be arrested. Any time she visited her son, gardaí would quiz her about Niall and Rory Hearty, who she described as "two lovely lads". She told gardaí she had never heard of or met the other men arrested in London, including Anthony Hyland. Kathy also believed that her nephew, Mark Reilly – who lived in Slough in London – was going to be arrested. Gardaí suggested that he should present himself at a police station and advised Kathy to get her brother, Mark's father, to urgently contact him. As it transpired, Mark Reilly was not arrested.

"Because Elaine and Robert had been arrested, there was probably an element of paranoia on my part," Kathy admits. "I had been over with Elaine in London for the May Bank Holiday weekend and the guards wanted to know everything: where we went, who we had met – that sort of thing. After my children were arrested, I just had a distinct feeling that I was also going to be picked-up and questioned. I kept thinking about the history of Irish people who had been arrested in the UK."

Most of that weekend remains a blur to Kathy. She remembers the house being a hive of activity as friends and relatives rallied round to comfort each other. Not being able to speak to or see Elaine was the worst part. "I was very upset to think of her over there, all alone, and it was frustrating not being able to go over to her. I didn't know what condition she was in; I didn't know how she was being treated – I didn't know anything." As Gareth Peirce had not been immediately available to see Elaine, she was in Paris on business, another solicitor at her law firm, Nigel Leskin, was in touch with Kathy over the weekend and was able to reassure her somewhat about her daughter's state-of-mind.

Robert claims that throughout his detention at Coolock Garda Station, the behaviour of some of the detectives who interviewed him was, at best, questionable; at worst, downright appalling. He was repeatedly taunted about Elaine, with one detective openly speculating that she would be going down for 40 years. "I knew then that they were just trying to get a rise out of me," says Robert today. "There was no way that she could possibly be given that length of sentence. My total belief in my sister's innocence – coupled with their blatant exaggeration – helped calm me down. It made me realise that they were just trying to scare me." His solicitor had warned Robert in advance that police would try to use this tactic. He tried to feign an air of indifference when police would bring people like Sharon or Elaine into their line of questioning. His legal advice had been to simply answer questions about himself. He stresses that the detective who arrested him and the uniformed gardaí at Coolock treated him well at all times. The detectives who interviewed him, however, were variously "underhanded, manipulative and threatening."

On Saturday afternoon, Sharon was released after being questioned at Ballyfermot Garda Station. Michael Farrell warned Robert, however, that he could expect to be held for the full 48-hour period permitted under law. It was later that day before gardaí showed Robert photographs of the other men arrested with Elaine in London, including Anthony Hyland. Robert explained that he had known Hyland from his college days at UCD but hadn't seen him for quite some time, until recently, when he bumped into him in a city centre pub. Since Elaine's move to London, Robert and Sharon had been toying with the idea of following suit. Robert believed he could earn twice as much money doing the same job over there. The couple had given the matter further serious consideration after visiting Elaine in London and sampling her active social scene. Robert believes he discussed his plans with Hyland during what was probably a drink-fuelled conversation. Hyland revealed he would be going over to London for an interview around the same time that Robert and Sharon were planning their next trip. Robert suggested that he contact him through Elaine with a view to them all meeting up and gave Hyland his sister's phone number. It was an innocent gesture that would have dire consequences.

"I repeatedly told the gardaí that Hyland was my friend, not Elaine's," Robert explains. "I also told them that Hyland was one of the nicest blokes you could meet – a nicer bloke than I am. I also tried to show them how circumstances had conspired against us: it was pure coincidence that I had been watching a film about the Guildford Four and was wearing a T-shirt with a tricolour on it at the time of my arrest. It probably looked bad, I admitted, but they had arrested innocent people. The simple fact of the matter was that the gardaí had made a mess of it."

Gardaí were forced to release Robert without charge at approximately 6.30 p.m. on Sunday, 12 July. He was requested to return of his own volition to fine-tune some of his statements, which he did after going home first for a shower and a change of clothes. Despite Robert's release, there was little cause for celebration in the Moore household as they anxiously awaited news about Elaine. Robert was racked with guilt as he thought of the ordeal he had unwittingly put his younger sister through. After all, none of this would have happened if he hadn't given Hyland her phone number. By his own admission, he was of little use to his mother that week. "I have to say, the whole thing with Elaine hit me very badly," he reflects today. "I felt completely responsible for her situation."

Gareth Peirce first made telephone contact with Kathy on Monday, 13 July. She explained that police would have to either release Elaine or charge her within the next two days. Kathy will never forget that Tuesday, 14 July – "a horrendous day" – as they sat waiting for the phone call that would determine Elaine's future.

* * *

Rory Hearty's friendship with Elaine resulted in a weekend he would never forget. A native of Cullyhanna, Co. Armagh, the then twenty-eight-year-old had spent numerous summers working off his college debts in London before finally moving permanently to the city. Rory had studied Irish History and Politics at the University of Ulster, Magee College, Derry, and later went on to achieve a Masters in Irish Politics at Queen's University, Belfast. After years of impoverished student life, London offered an exciting new social scene; and Rory and his friends found themselves with money in their pockets for the first time.

Rory first met Elaine in November 1997, when she visited his brother, Niall, in London. After she moved over to London the following March, the pair became virtually inseparable. "There was just something very easy going about her," he says. "We seemed to instantly hit it off." During her early days in London, Rory helped Elaine settle by showing her around the city and introducing her to his wide circle of friends. Although he didn't know her that long, he trusted her instinctively – so much so that he wrote her a blank cheque in case she was ever short of money. Rory reveals that they were very much part of the expatriate Irish scene. The flat he was renting in Kentish Town was in a house populated solely by young people from Ireland. It was, he says, "a complete open house", particularly when it came to putting up "friends of friends" from home – or even complete strangers. Rory remembers one occasion when the Munster rugby team were playing in the European Cup final at Twickenham. Afterwards, they went to an Australian bar for the post-match analysis. As they were leaving, some lads from Cork – who were fairly drunk after the day's festivities – asked Rory for directions to Croydon. "It would be like someone coming up to you in the centre of Dublin and asking how to get to Kildare late at night," Rory laughs. "The taxi fare would have been ridiculous, so I put them up for the night, even though I didn't know anything about them. It's just something that Irish people do when they're living away from home – they help each other out."

After dropping Elaine off at her office on the morning of 10 July, Rory – who worked as a courier – had spent a typical day driving around gridlocked London in his trusty Vauxhall Astra estate. Before his final delivery, he stopped by his house to pick up his flatmate's girlfriend, who was off work for stress-related reasons at the time. Reluctantly, the young woman agreed to accompany Rory for his last drop of the day, which involved driving from Watford to

Canary Wharf. Being a Friday rush hour, traffic was particularly bad and Rory was glad of the company as they drove at a crawl through Central London. A radio news bulletin reported that there had been an incident in the Holborn area of the city, which had resulted in complete traffic chaos. Hearing this, Rory used his courier's knowledge to his advantage and drove down a side street, where he had a clear run. As they reached Euston Road, he noticed a police car, siren blaring, coming towards them, eventually blocking the path of a taxi in front of them. Rory wondered what the taxi driver had done to fall foul of the police. But it was Rory's car they were interested in. He was instructed to turn off his engine and hand over his keys to the police officer.

"What have I been stopped for?" he asked.

"I don't know," the officer replied.

Just minutes earlier, Rory had been blissfully unaware that police cars had been tailing him as he made his way across London. "I didn't have a clue what was going on and the policeman seemed to be equally baffled," recalls Rory. "All of a sudden, a detective in plain clothes came out of nowhere and started screaming at me to spread-eagle up against the car." Rory noticed that Euston Road, which has three lanes each way, had been entirely sealed off by police.

"I'm arresting you under the Prevention of Terrorism Act – do you understand?" the aggressive detective said.

"No, I don't understand," Rory replied.

"Do you know what the Prevention of Terrorism Act is?" asked the detective.

"Yes," said Rory.

"So do you understand that I am arresting you under the Prevention of Terrorism Act?"

"No."

As he was being ordered to put on a white suit for forensic purposes, Rory caught his female companion's eye for the first time. "She looked at me as if to say: 'What the hell have you got me into?' She didn't know whether to laugh or cry. She half-expected some television presenter to walk out. She thought it was typical of something I'd do; I was always winding people up at every available opportunity."

Rory sat by the side of the road, his hands bound behind his back with cable ties. He noticed the perplexed faces on the growing crowd of onlookers. He was in shock and couldn't believe it when an even more surreal element was added to the terrifying experience when one onlooker started to opportunistically film the unfolding drama. Rory was glad to hear police angrily demand that the man hand over his camcorder. When the man steadfastly refused to hand it over Rory was extremely perturbed. Unfortunately his fears proved warranted when the resulting footage – featuring Rory sitting on the ground beside his car – was later broadcast on numerous television channels. Turning to the policeman who had originally stopped him, Rory again asked if he knew what was happening. "They won't tell me nothing," the officer replied. "But one thing's for certain – I think you're nicked." Given the seriousness of the situation, the remark unintentionally provided some welcome light relief. Rory and the policeman were pictured laughing together in the following day's newspapers.

Rory was brought to Charing Cross Police Station at approximately 7.15 p.m. After an emergency statement was taken, with his full cooperation, he was processed and strip-searched. From his cell he could hear Elaine's induction interview taking place. Only then did he realise that she, too, was somehow caught up in that evening's surreal events. Rory refused to talk to detectives in the absence of a solicitor. He immediately requested that Gareth Peirce be appointed as his solicitor. An old school friend of his, Peter Corrigan, with whom he shared a house in London, had worked for Gareth at Birnberg's. Rory was well aware of the lawyer's work on behalf of Irish people in trouble with the law in Britain.

"I want Gareth Peirce nominated as my solicitor," Rory told a senior detective.

"Who's he?" came the reply. "Is he any good?"

In the event, Gareth Peirce didn't end up representing Rory. With the help of Sr Sarah Clarke – a nun renowned for her work with Irish prisoners in Britain – his brother, Niall, arranged another solicitor, Neil O'May, from Bindman's. Rory was relieved when he met Neil as he was unsure about what to do in the terrifying situation. Rory didn't want to answer any more questions until he had more information about what was going on.

He was interrogated for three days. Before the first interview took place on Saturday, a Northern Irish detective, Phil Johnson, enquired if there was anything Rory wanted to ask him before the tape recorder was switched on. Rory simply asked him about the British Grand Prix, which was being held that weekend. When the tape recording started, Rory replied "no comment" to every question, except to give his name and date of birth. After 30 minutes, the interview ended.

In subsequent interviews during his period of detention Rory did answer questions. He talked to detectives about his academic interest in Irish politics and stressed his support of the peace process and the Good Friday Agreement.

On Monday, 13 July, detectives showed Rory a photograph of 16 rechargeable AA size batteries they had found under his bed. They then showed him a photograph of one of the incendiary devices recovered. Rory was asked to explain how he had come to buy the batteries. He explained that a year earlier, he had been on a health kick and was trying to get fit through exercising regularly. He had simply bought the batteries for his Walkman. Rory remembered buying an eight pack of AA size batteries, which had been on special offer. He reasoned that he must have bought the other batteries in regular packs of four. The detectives then showed him a photograph of an empty eight pack and an empty four pack of batteries, which had been found in a bag in Elaine's flat.

As Rory looked at the packaging on the batteries in the photographs he suddenly realised that the expiry date (January 2002) on the packaging found in Elaine's flat was different to the expiry date (January 2001) on the batteries found in his flat. He pointed out the difference between the two sets of batteries to detectives. To this day, Rory will never forget their surprised reaction to his observation.

The interview was subsequently terminated and Rory was returned to his cell. The Home Office had granted an extension for Rory's detention on Sunday night while the girl arrested with him had been released. It had transpired that police had not intended to arrest her; she had simply been caught up in events by being in Rory's car. On Monday evening, around half an hour after his solicitor had left, a detective entered Rory's cell as he was reading about the Grand Prix and the World Cup final in a newspaper. It was DC Taylor, one of the detectives who had interviewed him over the previous three days. It was unusual for detectives to enter a cell; Rory was worried that he was about to become a victim of police brutality, as had been the experience of numerous high profile Irish prisoners in Britain. "They had been nice so far and I remember thinking that it was about to turn nasty, with another four or five days to go," he says.

"On your bike," the detective said. Rory lay on the bed and didn't move.

"What do you mean?" he asked.

"On your bike – you are free to go," DC Taylor replied.

Rory believed the police were playing mind games with him. He was going nowhere without first speaking to his solicitor. Rory was let out of his cell to make a phone call. He was put through to Neil O'May who asked if everything was all right. Hearing Rory's news, the solicitor assured him that it wasn't some sort of police set-up – he urged him to get out of there immediately. Rory was told to collect his stuff from the cell and a car would be arranged to bring him home. "I was going to tell them to shove it, but I had no money and I knew the traffic was probably chaotic due to a Tube strike that day, so I reluctantly accepted a lift," he says. Half an hour later, police drove Rory home. There was no apology offered, just a curt: "It's just one of those things."

Back home, his flatmate's girlfriend answered the door. "We just stood hugging for a couple of minutes," he remembers. "I think she might have been crying." Later, Rory's friends brought him out for a drink – but he was in no mood to celebrate. "I remember all these bottles of Miller being put in front of me, but I drank maybe only a bottle and a half and just left the pub," he says. "It just hit me there and then that Elaine was still in. I thought: 'What the hell are we celebrating?' I felt guilty; I knew that she was in serious trouble. Bomb making materials had apparently been found in her flat and she was the only one there with Hyland. So you could see how it looked – it was extremely serious."

Chapter Five

GARETH PEIRCE

Elaine Moore's memories of life before 10 July 1998 are mostly happy ones. They were, she reflects, times of joy, independence and great personal achievement. "My family and friends were extremely proud of the life I had built for myself at such a young age. Their faith in me enhanced my ability to strive towards meeting any goal."

Those days now felt like they were part of someone else's life as she awaited her fate in Charing Cross Police Station. Elaine knew that being charged would prolong the nightmare. She dreaded to think about the effect it would have on her mother. There was nothing she could do but wait. Nigel Leskin informed her of three possible outcomes: she would either be released, free to go without charge; charged and remanded on bail; or charged and remanded in custody.

At 5.12 p.m. on Tuesday, 14 July, Elaine was told to leave her cell. As she emerged, accompanied by her solicitor, she was greeted by DC Jones and DC Powell. She was all too familiar with Powell, having been interrogated at length by him for four long days – he was the one she referred to as 'Scar face'. Elaine could feel the temperature rise as she braced herself for the news. She was told to sit on the chair provided. Nigel, standing across from her, never once took his eyes off Elaine. DC Powell "de-arrested" her from the provisions of the Prevention of Terrorism Act. He then immediately re-arrested her for conspiracy to cause explosions and possession of explosives. Both charges were read aloud and recorded by Sergeant Martin Lee as follows:

> 'Elaine Moore, on or before 10 July 1998, within the jurisdiction of the Central Criminal Court, you did conspire with Liam Grogan, Anthony Hyland, Darren Mulholland and a person or persons unknown, to cause by an explosive substance an explosion of a nature likely to endanger life or cause serious injury to property. [This is] contrary to Section 3(1)(a) of the Explosive Substances Act 1883.'

The charge continued:

> 'On and before 10 July 1998, within the jurisdiction of the Central Criminal Court, you unlawfully and maliciously had in your possession an explosive substance, namely Six (6) incendiary devices and an Improvised Explosive Device containing Semtex, with intent by means thereof to endanger life or cause serious injury to property or to enable another to do so. [This is] contrary to Section 3(1)(b) [of the] Explosive Substances Act 1883.'

On hearing the charges, Elaine was overcome with rage. "How fucking stupid are yis?" she roared at the detectives. Nigel Leskin urged her to calm down, reminding her that everything was being recorded. Against the odds, Elaine struggled to compose herself. She was suffering from fatigue and lack of food. "I was just so fed up at that stage," she remembers. "I didn't have the strength to endure even one more day of this sort of treatment. All my energy had been drained by the interrogations."

Nigel Leskin again requested Elaine to remain calm as she was asked if she understood the charges. She replied "yes", but added that she had no knowledge of anything she was accused of. A couple of minutes later, the police read Elaine her rights. This entire episode took place in a corridor adjacent to her cell.

Her solicitor knew there was little point in making a representation for bail at this early stage. He was aware that the Crown Prosecution Service had already made their objections to bail for Elaine known. These objections were based on the "serious nature" of the offence; a fear that Elaine would attempt to abscond; and also because of their belief that the accused had "contacts in Eire" who might help her avoid justice.

Significantly, Anthony Hyland – who was also being held at Charing Cross Police Station – had made a statement to police just hours earlier, in which he had asserted Elaine's innocence. Unlike Elaine, Hyland had refused to cooperate with detectives during the interview sessions. That day, however, he indicated that he wished to make a statement in relation to Elaine Moore. According to police transcripts dated Tuesday, 14 July 1998, he said:

'So far, in relation to these interviews, I have refused to discuss personal details about myself. But at this stage I feel morally compelled to make a statement about Elaine Moore. Elaine Moore knew nothing whatsoever about the contents of my bag and she knew nothing whatsoever of the reasons why I was in London. I firmly regret the trouble I have caused her family; indeed, the trouble and trauma I've caused Elaine and her family. I abused and deceived Elaine to further my own objectives in London. I regret ever having approached her to stay in her house. As I say, she has absolutely no involvement – none whatsoever. She is completely innocent – completely innocent. That is all I have to say.'

At 5.50 p.m., Elaine was brought to have her fingerprints, photographs and a blood sample taken again. It was as if her ordeal at Charing Cross Police Station was beginning all over. This time, however, Elaine was not as sheepish or compliant and didn't cooperate with police in the same manner that she had earlier. She was far more vocal, repeatedly questioning the need for new samples to be taken. Few explanations were forthcoming – it was routine, simple as that. The approach of the police officers also appeared to have become more aggressive. A hair sample was required for forensic evidence, which was tugged sharply from her head. Nigel Leskin was waiting for Elaine in her cell as she was marched back in. He seemed clearly upset for his client but tried to calm her down by offering words of encouragement.

Elaine's fortunes changed dramatically from the moment solicitor Gareth Peirce entered her cell at 6.26 p.m. that evening. The renowned human rights lawyer announced that she would now be representing Elaine. Distraught as she was, she immediately felt a deep sense of relief. She was also glad to learn that Nigel Leskin would still be working closely with them on the case. Elaine had built a relationship based on trust with him since the first night of her detention at Charing Cross. He had been her primary source of comfort and had guided her through the complex and intimidating interrogations. Nigel Leskin was the one person who appeared to understand the circumstances that had led to her arrest. Everyone, apart from her solicitor, happened to view her with deep suspicion. She felt she had bonded with him.

Elaine had good reason to be happy with Gareth Peirce's involvement in her case, given her impeccable track record in highlighting miscarriages of justice and human rights abuses. Born in Yorkshire, Gareth studied at Oxford University before developing an interest in journalism. She moved to New York in the early 1960s where she reported on Martin Luther King's civil rights struggle. It was here she developed the keen sense of social justice that would be the hallmark of her future legal career. Returning to Britain, she studied law at the London School of Economics, graduating in 1973.

During her time at Ben Birnberg's civil liberties law firm, Gareth Peirce has been associated with some of the most high profile human rights cases of the past three decades. She is best known in Ireland as the solicitor who represented the Birmingham Six, the Maguire Seven and the Guildford Four, eventually succeeding in having their dubious convictions overturned. The British actress, Emma Thompson, was nominated for an Oscar for her role as Gareth Peirce in Jim Sheridan's film, 'In the Name of the Father', based on the book by Gerry Conlon of the Guildford Four.

Throughout her notable career as a lawyer, Gareth has challenged the integrity of the British police and highlighted the inadequacies of the appeal system. According to one British newspaper, she is deeply mistrustful of the media and resolutely puts the interests of her clients first. In 1999, Gareth was included in the New Year's Honours List and awarded a CBE (Commander of the British Empire) for 'services to justice'. Having battled against the British criminal justice system for the best part of her career, she apparently saw the irony of becoming a member of the Order of the British Empire. She immediately wrote to 10 Downing Street asking that the award be taken back.

Gareth's initial impact on her young client was almost hypnotic. She reminded Elaine of her mother: kind, caring and reassuring at all times. A tall, slender woman with prominent cheekbones and dark shoulder-length hair, the solicitor struck Elaine as having angelic qualities. Gareth was concerned when she saw Elaine in such a distressed state and did everything in her power to comfort her. They discussed the implications of her being charged. Elaine knew prison was inevitable. It was now time to confront her deepest fear. The more they spoke about it, the more traumatised Elaine became. "I'll never be able to hold my head up again, Gareth, if they send me to prison," she sobbed. "I'll never cope – I know I won't."

Gareth promised Elaine that this would be the "lowest point" of her ordeal. "I felt sure that we could help her in being exonerated," the solicitor recalls. "I told her that she should not feel or believe that this was the end of everything; that it would not inevitably progress to either a conviction or even get to trial . . . I am sure I said to her that this was an extraordinary situation that, to her, must feel devastating, [but I told her] she should not believe that it was going to continue. I thought that this seemed to be a classic case of a completely innocent individual caught in the net of the police, which is like an open-ended trawling. It was by far from the first time that someone who was providing shelter or friendship was being interpreted by police as inevitably being involved in an agreement with other people. The police in this country have been particularly insensitive or incapable of [that] understanding. It was this same net of suspicion that enveloped the Birmingham Six; the fact that you would go to the funeral of a friend who had died and that meant you were in the IRA – it was the same thing."

Apart from the stigma of prison, the horror stories and cruel images from television flooded Elaine's head. She became worried about the frequency of welfare visits and medical examinations she had received. Why were they necessary? The authorities were obviously trying to establish that she had not come to any harm. Why did they need to check her every day? She certainly wouldn't be monitored so closely in prison, she imagined, not to the extent that she had been in the police station cell. Elaine would be just another prisoner – and a "potentially dangerous" one at that. She correctly guessed that Gareth wouldn't be able to visit her in prison as often as Nigel Leskin had at Charing Cross.

Gareth attempted to counsel Elaine about her fears. She explained that the medical checks were really designed to protect the prosecution's case: for instance, to prevent defendants from claiming they had been forced into making a statement by police. They would also have to prove that a prisoner was fit to be detained and interviewed.

Once Elaine had relaxed somewhat, Gareth offered her a frank and honest assessment of what she expected would happen next. Early the next morning, Elaine would leave Charing Cross and be transported to a magistrates' court for a brief remand hearing. After the court appearance, Gareth believed that Elaine would be sent to Holloway, an all-female prison. She personally knew women who were imprisoned there and assured Elaine that she would come to no harm. The worst-case scenario, the solicitor warned, was two months in prison – possibly less – on remand. This would be the maximum amount of time that Elaine would have to stay in jail, Gareth felt. "No way – I couldn't possibly!" was Elaine's response.

Gareth left the cell briefly to collect a few items for Elaine, such as books, cigarettes and £40 cash, which she would be able to spend in the prison shop. She stayed with Elaine for over an hour, constantly trying to assuage her fears. Throughout Elaine's detainment at Charing Cross, Gareth Peirce and Nigel Leskin had been in constant communication with her family back home. Elaine could have spoken on the phone to her family but was worried that it would upset her too much and add to her mother's distress. She had hoped that her first call home would be a celebratory one; to inform her mum that she was being released without charge. That hope had since faded. Gareth now strongly urged Elaine to call home.

As Gareth left for the night, she requested that the wicket, the small hatch in the cell wall, be left open. She was deeply worried about Elaine's state of mind and wanted her closely monitored at all times. There was another welfare visit from the duty officer, who Elaine recognised as being the same one who had recorded the charges against her. The officer seemed genuinely concerned about her and said he would leave the cell door open. She was to call out if she required anything. Elaine asked for a cigarette. She still hadn't eaten.

Reluctantly, Elaine requested permission to make that dreaded phone call home. She tried to remain strong, knowing well that if she started crying now she'd never stop. Stepping out of the cell, she began preparing in her head the approach she would take when talking to her mother. She was escorted to a desk with a telephone on it. At 9.35 p.m. she dialled the number. Her heart sunk when she couldn't get through. After two more attempts, she heard a ringing tone. It was imperative that she stayed composed; she needed to make her family believe she was all right. If she was coping, they, in turn, could cope. Besides, the last thing her mother needed right now was an upsetting call from a distraught daughter.

The phone was finally answered. Elaine heard a woman's voice at the other end of the line.

"Hello Mum," Elaine said.

"Elaine, oh, one minute . . . hold on, I'll get your mum."

Her aunt, Paula, had answered the phone back home in Coolock and seemed to drop it as soon as she heard Elaine's voice. Kathy Moore picked up the receiver almost immediately.

"Hello angel, are you okay?" she asked, not knowing what else to say.

Elaine apologised for not being in touch sooner but explained her reasons. She assured her mother that Gareth Peirce would now be "minding" her, which made her happy and confident that things would work out. Kathy inquired about how her daughter was being treated and wanted to know if she was eating. Elaine felt that, under the circumstances, she had been treated quite well. She explained to her mum about the following day's court appearance, which would probably see her further detained in HMP (Her Majesty's Prison) Holloway. Elaine even quipped that at least she wouldn't have to talk to detectives anymore, which would be "great".

Despite putting on a brave face, Elaine was far from confident inside. Her feeble attempt to make light of her situation was just designed to comfort her mum. Her main priority was her mother's health and mental state-of-mind. Attempting to change the subject, Elaine asked how her brother and dad were keeping. Kathy replied that they were as well as could be expected and said every effort was being made to ensure her safe and speedy return. Everyone back home, family and friends alike, supported her fully and believed she was innocent. This brought Elaine an immediate sense of relief.

Her brother, Robert, came on the phone briefly. Elaine could sense the pain in his trembling voice. She mainly spoke to him about Gareth, as she felt this would help reassure him. She even cracked a joke, determined to remain upbeat against the odds. Her dad then spoke to her, telling Elaine that her mother was holding up well and they were all there for each other. Kathy took back the phone and Elaine promised her she would be in contact again as soon as possible. She reiterated that she was fine and was now focusing on getting through the next few weeks and being reunited with her family.

"I love you Mum," Elaine said before ending the call. "You know that and you know that I'm going to get through this – sure I'm your daughter! You know how resilient I am – I'll be fine."

Looking back, Kathy Moore shudders as she recalls Elaine's first phone call home. "It was awful," she says. "You knew by her that there was a prison officer standing over her as she was talking. She sounded okay but I knew she had to be absolutely shattered."

The phone conversation had lasted 15 minutes. After hanging up, Elaine finally fell apart. Thanking the officers for the use of the phone, she practically ran back to her cell. Elaine was suddenly inconsolable; the pent-up frustrations of the previous five days had been exacerbated by the emotional call home. Her mum, usually the family's pillar of strength, had sounded, for once, powerless and completely at a loss. As she sat in her cell, sobbing, a duty officer approached and asked if she wanted something to eat or drink – she didn't. He informed her that he was going off duty and the replacement officer had instructed that her cell door be closed at all times. Somewhat to Elaine's bemusement, the officer explained that the open door posed a possible threat to her safety. He said that prisoners had been known to use the door and a blanket when attempting to hang themselves. In Elaine's emotional and confused state, it seemed that this officer was being kind to her on one hand by offering her food and drink; then telling her how she could use the open cell door to possibly kill herself. Deliberate or not, she thought it was a bizarre thing for a police officer to say to somebody in her vulnerable state. Not that Elaine was suicidal at this point. Her family were still her main cause of concern and there was no way she was going to cause them further grief by inflicting harm on herself.

A review of Elaine's detainment was scheduled to take place at 2.18 a.m. the following morning but this was brought forward to 11.23 p.m. to allow her to sleep. During the review, an officer reminded her that she was to remain in custody pending a court appearance on the grounds of the seriousness of the charge and the likelihood of her absconding while out on bail. It was all starting to sound quite repetitive.

Once alone in her cell, Elaine lay down and tried to gather her thoughts. Strangely, she felt safer when she was behind locked doors – it acted as a temporary shield between her and the people who were trying to ruin her life. She knew she faced a tough battle to clear herself of these ridiculous charges, which could take a long time. Having somebody as famous as Gareth Peirce represent her also brought to mind other miscarriages of justice at the hands of the British authorities. She was suddenly haunted by the idea of a 20-year prison sentence.

"Jaysus Christ, I'd be 41 by the time I'd be released," she thought. Her parents would be in their sixties by then; her brother and her friends in their forties. Any nieces or nephews she might have in the future would be her age before she'd ever get to meet them. There would be no chance of marriage or having children, only a distinct possibility that she would emerge from prison a raving lunatic. A lot could happen in 20 years: what if she lost members of her family? Certainly all her pets would be dead.

Elaine then thought about the wonderful life that she had before 10 July. She decided ending up in prison could not be an option. She was far too ambitious and determined to ever let that happen. These thoughts brought her some respite as she struggled with her demons in the cell.

"I was not prepared to see mum agonising over me for 20 years," she recalls of her feelings that night. "I felt it would be better for all concerned if I were dead as opposed to rotting in prison. I could not envisage ever settling into a life of incarceration. For me, that was an inconceivable notion. I could really only justify my frame of mind at that time by comparing it to the case of a missing person. The families of such people never have closure until their loved one is found and returned to them. I couldn't entertain the thoughts of mum and my family living a life of torment; never fully knowing how I was or what I was doing. They would always feel guilty if they enjoyed life, knowing where I was and the limitations imposed on my freedom. I just couldn't cope with thoughts of them ageing behind my back. So yes, in a way I did consider ending it all, even though I had decided that I would first fight for my freedom and remain focused and positive over the months ahead. Even now, thinking back on my state of mind at the time, I found a kind of peace just knowing that I would never have to face my worst fear – staying in prison for 20 odd years. I didn't give much thought as to how I would go about it; I just felt a sense of comfort knowing it would never happen. To be honest, I don't think I would ever have gone through with killing myself. That night, though, I found a previously unknown strength that enabled me to cope extremely well with my situation."

Safe in the knowledge that she could retain a degree of control over her own destiny, Elaine fell asleep in the early hours of Wednesday, 15 July. She was awoken for what would be her last welfare visit at Charing Cross. Again, she had no requests or complaints – "I was never one for stating the bleedin' obvious!"

She rose that morning at 7 a.m. While she was showering, her mother phoned from Dublin, only to be told that she couldn't speak to her daughter because of the level of prisoner activity. Elaine was returned to her cell. The door had only been locked for a matter of seconds when it suddenly reopened and two burly detectives entered. Looking up at them from her position, sitting on the bed, seemed to accentuate their towering presence. It was DC Lee and DC Boitel-Gill, who she recognised as the deeply unpleasant detective from her final interrogation. Elaine wondered what they were doing there in the absence of her solicitor. They informed her that they had been authorised by the Crown Prosecution Service to a conduct a 'security of intelligence' interview. Elaine was intimidated by their fixed stares and aggressive tone of questioning. They reminded her of the seriousness of the offences she had been charged with and warned she was facing a possible 20-year prison sentence. DC Lee spoke to her in a patronising manner; DC Boitel-Gill was the "usual ignorant git" she had come to know him for.

"Is there anything further that you can tell us that may be of significance?" DC Lee asked.

"What do you mean?" Elaine replied.

"You know you're in deep trouble," he said.

"There's no need to remind me of that fact," she snapped back.

"This is your last chance," DC Lee continued. "If you cooperate and provide us with information pertaining to the offences of which you are accused and your co-accused, we will speak to the judge on your behalf who may look somewhat more favourably upon you."

"Look, I have been cooperating with everything that has been asked of me – examinations, all lines of questioning," Elaine responded angrily. "I have told you lot everything that I know and yet you still saw fit to press these ridiculous charges against me . . . now you want me to further implicate myself by coming forward with information that I simply don't have. I have been truthful with you lot up to this point. I'm not going to start lying now. I can't help you with your request for information on myself or my co-accused, as you call them."

Appearing dejected and somewhat thrown by Elaine's outburst, the detectives muttered that this was "unfortunate" and left the cell. The incident infuriated her. Her heart was racing. She had seen the true side of what she was dealing with and the behaviour of the detectives confirmed her suspicions that things were about to get worse. Elaine was impressed, nevertheless, at her ability to remain composed during the unexpected visit. If it had been designed to intimidate her, the detectives had failed badly.

Elaine gathered together her meagre belongings: some books, clothing, money and, of course, the vital supply of cigarettes Gareth Peirce had given her. At 8 a.m. the doctor paid her a final visit and routinely checked her body for bruising. Although satisfied that Elaine was fit to appear in court, he seemed concerned that she had continued to refuse food and had consumed limited fluids. According to the 'Prisoner – Custody Risk/Transfer' record, Elaine was 5'6" with shoulder-length blonde hair, blue eyes. She is, in fact, 5'10" with long blonde hair, which at that time hung about eight inches past her shoulders. Her eyes are green, not blue. It was obvious to Elaine that the officer responsible for filling in the report had confused her with the woman who had been arrested with Rory Hearty.

The report continued: "Elaine Moore has been charged with terrorist offences. Would be classed as 'Category A' by prison service. Has used Ventolin and Becotide inhalers while in custody. The lady has eaten very little over the past four days in custody. She has been very quiet over the past 24 hours. May be depressed although no mention of this in custody forms. No specific information relating to escape or rescue attempt."

Any fears expressed by police that Elaine would attempt to escape from custody were ridiculous, in her mind. She recalls one incident during an exercise period when she was handcuffed to a female officer and surrounded by police with guard dogs. As they walked around the yard – for fresh air, more than exercise – Elaine noticed that the handcuff on her left wrist was not secure. She certainly didn't want police thinking that she had tampered with them. In Elaine's view, any sudden movement, such as her becoming free from the cuffs, could easily have prompted a response from the armed guards and have been recorded as 'an incident'. She informed the female officer that one of her handcuffs was not closed properly.

The policewoman, looking somewhat startled, immediately secured the left handcuff. Elaine's honesty was not recorded in any incident report, possibly because it would have made the police officer responsible for her look negligent. She therefore continued to be categorised as a potential escape risk.

Eventually, Elaine was handcuffed and escorted from the main detention block of Charing Cross to a police van. She was ushered into the back of the van and locked into a tiny cell. She noticed another cell to her right. A few minutes later the van door reopened and the vacant cell was occupied by one of Elaine's co-accused – it was Liam Grogan. This was the first time that Elaine ever laid eyes on him, apart from the photograph detectives had shown her during the interrogations.

The van and heavy police escort pulled out of the courtyard, sirens blaring, and made the short journey to Belmarsh Magistrates' Court where Elaine was in for the shock of her life.

Chapter Six

PRISONER AP9372

As soon as the brief hearing had ended, Elaine was returned to a temporary cell located beneath Belmarsh Magistrates' Court. She was escorted from the courtroom by several police guards through a rear exit door, which led out to a flight of stairs. Elaine was placed in a sterile cell containing a hand basin and a concrete slab, which could act as a seat or bed. The heavily reinforced cell door was abruptly closed behind her; the by now all-too-familiar slamming sound echoing down the corridor.

Elaine sat in silence, as though final judgement had already been passed upon her. She tormented herself with life-altering questions, none of which she knew the answers to. Would she be able to cope in prison? Would her family and friends ever hold her in the same regard as they had before? If she ever was set free, could she survive the stigma of prison? Would her life ever be a fraction of its former self? Had she lost all of her possessions forever?

Elaine slowly came to grips with the fact that she no longer had control of her own life. Her future was a luxury she could not take for granted. Her sentimental personal items: books, photographs, letters, items of jewellery – had been plundered by police. The strip-searches had robbed her of any remaining dignity. She began to question her own sanity. But tormenting herself about the prospect of a bleak future was killing her spirit. She needed, above anything else, to focus on restoring her freedom and clearing her name.

Elaine's defences were at an all-time low. Gareth Peirce was her sole source of comfort and Elaine treasured every moment she spent with her. Magistrate David Cooper had remanded her in custody pending a bail hearing, which was scheduled for the following week. Earlier, Elaine had run through her options with her solicitor in the event of her being charged. Gareth felt that, despite the gravity of the charges against her, there was a good chance of bail. However, she wanted to make the strongest possible application so did not apply for bail at the first remand hearing. "I wanted to set the scene that first morning in court and say to the magistrates that we were deliberately not making a bail application today because we have a very strong one to make," Gareth recalls. "We didn't have sureties that day and we didn't have all of the information. She had only been charged a few hours before. Rather than wasting an opportunity, that seemed the appropriate thing to do." At that first hearing, Gareth also took the opportunity to declare Elaine's innocence in front of the magistrates and the media.

From the court's holding cell, Elaine was led into the back of a secure police van, surrounded by three armed detectives. None of them spoke to her; she was merely the prisoner – and a 'high risk, highly dangerous' one at that. Once in the rear of the van, Elaine was encased in a single-seated cell. She remembers the curious sensation of feeling somewhat safer once the cage had been locked.

"Inhumane as it was, at least it separated me from them [the police] and sheltered me from their glare. I was looking at them and thinking how big they were – in width as well as height – in comparison to me. It made me question their bizarre logic: did I really pose such a threat to warrant these ludicrous security measures?"

Sitting handcuffed in the tiny police van cell, Elaine

felt disorientated and uncomfortable, both emotionally and physically. She was still deeply traumatised from the events of the day before, when she was told she had been charged with terrorist offences. It had been the worst 24 hours of Elaine's ordeal so far. But it was her uncertain fate that terrified her the most. She began to feel contempt for the police officers guarding her. Their condescending stares, which previously would have sent her into a state of panic, now merely infuriated her.

"I remember retaliating by staring back and mirroring their looks of disgust. I was thinking about what sort of people they must be, which was probably what they were thinking as they stared and judged me. I had never so much as harmed a fly in my life and, if anything, had always done my best to assist those who needed help. Could these people staring at me say the same? I doubted it. There was a certain injustice to it all."

The police officers accompanying her in the back of the van were big and sweaty. In fact, they weren't even that effective when it came to guarding 'dangerous' prisoners such as Elaine – one of them actually fell asleep in the back of the van. The journey felt like it could possibly be her last and Elaine struggled to catch a final glimpse of the outside world through the darkened windows. She memorised sightings of trees, houses, people, dogs – any image of reality she could store and replay in her mind while she was in prison.

"I didn't know how long it would be before I would see normal things again. If and when I did, what state of mind would I be in? Would I embrace the reality or be terrified by it? Would it all have changed? Would I be able to readapt in a new society?"

During the final minutes of the journey to prison, Elaine struggled with even darker thoughts. Images of brutality flashed through her mind. She thought about the Guildford Four and the cruel treatment meted out to them in a British prison.

"I knew that I would lose my sanity, above all else, if I was subjected to such inhumane treatment. But I was more terrified of being degraded than beaten. I would feel no sense of shame if they beat me, but I would fight at all costs to maintain my dignity."

Although Gareth Peirce had been convinced that Elaine would be remanded in Holloway, which is a prison exclusively reserved for women, the British authorities had other plans for her young client. Instead, the police van passed through the security gates of Woodhill Prison on the outskirts of Milton Keynes in Buckinghamshire. Described by the media as 'Britain's own Alcatraz', the newly opened prison was home to the UK's most violent offenders.

Among them was the notorious Charles Bronson, long considered one of Britain's most dangerous prisoners. Bronson, whose real name is Michael Peterson, had committed more crimes during his initial 25 years behind bars than he had on the outside. According to a BBC News report, Bronson's offences included 20 assaults on warders and 10 counts of taking hostages – one of whom he threatened to eat! Even hardened criminals like Bronson would find the conditions at Woodhill unbearable. In February 2000, Bronson was before a court for taking a prison teacher hostage. Before he was sentenced to life behind bars, Bronson bemoaned his quality of life at Woodhill, describing it as a "living hell". He told the court: "I wake up every morning with a headache from lack of air. Unnatural light . . . my eyes hurt. The first thing I do is go over to that window and stick my lips on the grill and suck in air. That's how I get my air. I have got a toilet in my cell. There is no seat or lid on it. I am living in a sewer. Even the birds don't come to Woodhill – they are frightened by it. Everything is concrete and razor wire. I am in living hell. It is the year 2000 – I hope you understand all that."

Bronson was in good company at Woodhill. Other inmates included the kidnapper Michael Sams and Robert Maudsley – known as 'Hannibal the Cannibal' after the psychopathic character in the film, *Silence of the Lambs*.

Features of the all-male prison include closed-circuit television, intercoms, hi-tech security access codes for doors and electronic locking. Cells are specially designed to prevent prisoners from fashioning weapons or tools. The toilets and sinks are stainless steel and the mirrors are plastic. Tables and chairs at the prison are made of fireproof compressed cardboard and each bed is simply a mattress placed on a concrete plinth.

There is limited contact between prisoners, who have to meet behavioural targets in order to earn even the most basic privileges. The prison's worst offenders are often locked up for up to 23 hours a day and have their meals passed in through a hatch. They are sometimes forced to take their weekly shower or daily exercise inside a wire cage.

As she was helped down from the back of the police van, Elaine was amazed at the excessive security presence arranged in her honour. She could make out at least a dozen prison officers, some with guard dogs. Surely she couldn't possibly pose such a security threat, she thought. Even during her detention period at Charing Cross, Elaine had cooperated at all times. She never even made a fuss about the harsh conditions she had been forced to endure.

Standing at the entrance to HMP Woodhill, Elaine struggled to take in the enormity of her situation. She was anxious, exhausted, bewildered and – above all – terrified.

Elaine was ushered towards a large reception desk, where she was asked a series of questions concerning her name, nationality and religion. She could feel the atmosphere turn icy as she said the words "Irish" and "Catholic". These words alone seemed to confirm her guilt in the eyes of the prison officers, particularly the male guards, who found it difficult to conceal their contempt for Elaine. "This is where we keep the Irish," one of them would later quip as she was led to the isolation wing of the prison.

All of Elaine's possessions: books, cigarettes, a change of clothes, underwear; were displayed on a table for everyone to see, including the male officers. Each item was closely scrutinised before being put through an X-ray machine and labelled. Elaine also had to pass through an X-ray machine, just in case she was concealing any weapons. One of the detectives who had escorted her from court informed the induction officer that Elaine hadn't eaten since her arrest five days earlier. Much to her embarrassment, she was immediately weighed in front of all the officers. Elaine was taken aback when her weight was recorded at 10 stone, seven pounds – she had lost one and a half stone in less than a week. She had put on weight since moving to London, due largely to her busy social life, which quite often evolved around pubs and restaurants. Her body would surely not be able to continue to withstand such rapid weight loss.

Elaine was ordered to proceed into a small room where she would be 'dealt with' shortly. It was time for her first strip-search at Woodhill Prison. She disputed the need for this 'procedure' but wasn't overly vocal in her objections for fear of attracting the attentions of the male prison staff outside the room. The female guards who supervised her strip-search openly admitted that this was an unsavoury aspect of their work. Elaine wondered aloud what type of person would apply for a job that entails locking people in a room and telling them when to eat, sleep or when they can exercise and wash – not to mention forcing them to strip naked. Her attempts at making them feel ashamed were half-hearted and ultimately futile: Elaine knew the guards were merely doing their job.

Following the strip-search, Elaine was issued with prison clothes and ordered to put them on. Remand prisoners are usually allowed to wear their own clothes but Elaine's had been taken by police at Charing Cross for forensic examination. It was now time for her prison mug shot to be taken. Elaine was handed a plaque with a number on it – a number that would replace her identity at Woodhill. From here on in, she was no longer Elaine Moore – she was 'Prisoner AP9372, High Risk, Category A'.

The induction procedure took approximately 45 minutes. Elaine was escorted up a stairwell and along several long corridors. The intensity of the security measures unnerved her. There were closed circuit cameras everywhere and she was surrounded by four prison officers at all times. No keys were in use: the prison wardens simply identified themselves to other guards who monitored and controlled access to all doors.

Elaine was brought into a medical examination room where she was met by a middle-aged male doctor of Asian origin. His kind smile set him apart from the other staff at Woodhill. The doctor asked Elaine a number of by now familiar questions: was she sleeping; had she eaten anything. She told him she had been refusing food for several days but was feeling fine. He queried her asthma condition and Elaine replied that she had been supplied with inhalers at Charing Cross Police Station. Her arms, legs and back were checked for any signs of cuts or bruises, despite Elaine's assurances that she had not sustained any injuries while in custody.

After leaving the doctor's room, Elaine was brought to 'E Wing', a maximum-security section of the prison that had been exclusively reserved for her detention. Not only was she the only occupant of this wing, she later learned that she was the only female prisoner ever remanded in custody at HMP Woodhill. This was because Elaine had been deemed 'High Risk Category A', a status usually afforded to dangerous and violent criminals like Charles Bronson. She was engulfed by a sense of fear and panic.

'E Wing' consisted of six cells, a bathroom, laundry room, TV room, open lounge and meal area, all of which were closely monitored via CCTV from a security control room. This 'containment' unit was stark and bare; the absence of windows added to the sense of desolation.

Elaine was put into the cell where she would sleep for the duration of her incarceration at Woodhill. It was a far cry from her comfortable apartment on Parkhill Road. There was a bed, small table, chair, wardrobe, toilet and hand basin. The only redeeming feature was a tiny window with four thick bars fixed to it. Elaine would look through the window in the hope of catching a glimpse of outside life. Sometimes, she would discretely watch inmates who had been assigned gardening duties, carefully hiding so they would not see her. There were few birds to be heard; just the casual banter of prison guards arriving for their shift.

Elaine felt that her presence was a cause of confusion for prison staff at Woodhill: they seemed unsure how to deal with a 'Category A' female prisoner, one that had to be guarded by up to six officers at all times. High-risk status was usually preserved for vicious rapists and murderers, not a frightened twenty-one-year-old woman. Dinner was cold and unappetising, even to the palate of someone who had not eaten for five days. Elaine later learned that her food was always cold because she was alone in the wing and the other prisoners were served their meals first.

That night, the silence of her cell played havoc with Elaine's mind, keeping her awake until the early hours of morning. The sky was her only clock as she eventually fell into a restless sleep. After sleeping for just three or four hours, the spy hatch on the cell door slid open and Elaine was abruptly ordered to rise for breakfast. She was already awake but clearly exhausted. "I remember not wanting to get up. I didn't have the energy as I had not eaten properly or slept for several days. I also didn't want to venture beyond the cell door because, by doing so, I felt I would be accepting a regimented new way of life."

Elaine glanced at the few belongings she had been permitted to bring into her cell, which were neatly stacked on the desk provided and in the childlike wardrobe. Gareth Peirce had not been permitted access to any of Elaine's possessions – police had confiscated the entire contents of her apartment. As she arose to get dressed, Elaine was careful to move to a position away from the spy hatch. She had always been incredibly self-conscious about being even semi-naked in front of others. Even when she was younger, Elaine would never shower with her school friends after swimming lessons. It was just the way she was.

Surprisingly, the clothes provided at Woodhill didn't look institutional in the least. She was issued with wine or grey tracksuit bottoms and casual T-shirts. Throughout

her time in prison, Elaine always requested extra large –
she didn't want to look in any way feminine.

Just 15 minutes had passed since her wake-up call. An
officer again appeared at the hatch and opened the door.
Reluctantly, Elaine emerged from her cell. Six female
prison officers were standing outside, casually chatting
among themselves. Elaine was told she could eat her
breakfast in the general purposes area of the wing but
chose to bring it back to her cell away from the prying
eyes of the prison staff. Elaine had a phobia about eating
in front of people, a condition that would be exacerbated
by her experiences in prison where she was always the
focus of unwanted attention. She made a beeline for her
cell and the door was locked behind her. She didn't want
to be mixing with the prison officers. Being on her own
made the whole experience somewhat less real.

Elaine made a half-hearted attempt to eat her breakfast
and returned her tray before entering the TV room for a
few hours of ineffective escapism. Some of the prison
officers tried to make small talk with her, although they
seemed initially cautious about approaching her. Elaine
was surprised by their calm, nonchalant manner. They
seemed to be unaware of the specific reasons for Elaine's
detention, but knew she had been arrested under the
Prevention of Terrorism Act. They didn't probe Elaine
for information; she didn't volunteer any.

Elaine was asked if she wanted to take a shower,
followed by an hour's exercise in the yard. She accepted
both offers. She glanced around the shower area nervously.
It was overlooked by a control room, which was usually
manned by a male officer. Elaine was apprehensive. From
what she could gather, he would be able to see her from
the shoulders up while she showered. Even that would
be a serious invasion of her privacy. Elaine asked if she

could take a bath instead, first seeking an assurance that the door would be locked behind her. She could have a bath but the door was to remain unlocked. The officer promised that no one would be allowed to gain access while she was in there. As she ran the bath, Elaine laced it with generous dollops of shower gel, hoping that the excessive bubbles would further shield her modesty. Despite the fact that she was on 'suicide watch', she had earlier been allowed to purchase a safety razor. She was only permitted to use the razor when showering and had to hand it back to the prison officer in the control room immediately afterwards.

Once dressed, Elaine felt a lot more refreshed. She was taken from 'E Wing' out through a rear exit door and down three flights of stairs, with secure iron gates on each level. Entering the prison courtyard, she passed through a gate, which was then locked behind her. Elaine was relieved when she realised she was being left on her own. A high wall with barbed wire and floodlights running along its entire length surrounded the perimeter of the yard. Although in no mood to exercise, Elaine appreciated the opportunity to breathe in some fresh air and distance herself from the prison guards. Her environment was far from perfect – but at least she wasn't handcuffed. Elaine had learned to be grateful for small mercies.

Chapter Seven

THE 'IRA MODEL'

Although Elaine Moore's name and face would not become known to the public for some weeks after her arrest, the media in Ireland and Britain were quick to praise the joint Garda/Scotland Yard operation that had reportedly averted widespread carnage on the streets of London.

'London Tube Bombs Foiled' was the *Daily Mail* headline on Saturday, 11 July, which led with the story on its front page. 'A plot to blow up Tube commuters and bring terror back to the streets of central London was foiled last night with only minutes to spare,' the paper declared. 'Anti-terrorist squad detectives seized three men, understood to be Irish students, as they were about to explode the devices at the height of the rush-hour.' The article said three more people had been arrested later, including a woman on Oxford Street, a reference to Elaine Moore.

Another woman and a man had been arrested near the British Library on Euston Road. The paper reported that the arrests were a result of a month-long joint undercover operation involving police, MI5 and the Irish Garda, following fears that hard-line IRA splinter groups – 'implacably opposed to the Ulster peace deal' – were about to launch a 'spectacular'.

The London arrests had resulted in scenes of chaos on the evening of Friday, 10 July, as terrified commuters were ordered by police to leave Tube stations. Major roads around central London had also been sealed off, causing widespread traffic chaos and leaving many people trapped in offices and shops. A controlled explosion carried out on one device near Chancery Lane Tube station by bomb squad officers added to the sense of panic. Newspapers revealed that two men had been arrested within yards of each other in Thomas Doyle Street, near Elephant and Castle, at 4.30 p.m. A third man had been detained at Gower Street, near Holborn, and was thought to be going into a University College building.

Scotland Yard's Deputy Assistant Commissioner, John Grieve, head of the Anti-Terrorist Squad, told reporters: "We believe these devices were intended to be used in London within minutes." He added: "This evening's arrests are the result of prolonged investigation into dissident criminal Irish republican terrorist groups and a successful surveillance operation."

The British Prime Minister, Tony Blair, was widely quoted in the media as saying: "This has been a very important and successful operation and further reflects the close cooperation that exists between the security forces in the UK and Ireland as together we defeat terrorism wherever it may exist."

Apart from the initial coverage of the London and Dublin arrests on 10 July, the UK press were prohibited from reporting any details of Elaine's case as it was *sub judice*. Despite the media blackout, one English television channel later accidentally breached the ban when it broadcast a photograph of Elaine. However, the restrictions placed on journalists didn't extend to Irish newspapers, which were widely available throughout Britain.

In Ireland, news of the arrests made all the front pages on Saturday, 11 July. 'IRA student bombers seized in swoop' ran the *Irish Independent* headline. The paper's security editor, Tom Brady, reported that the suspects

were all university students from Dublin, Naas and
Dundalk. They had arrived in London earlier in the week
and had booked flights back to Dublin for the evening of
Friday, 10 July. As part of the same operation, gardaí had
arrested a man and a woman in Dublin, another man in
Dundalk and a further suspect in Wexford. According to
the article, two shotguns and electrical switches had been
found in a raid on a flat in Dundalk.

Senior Garda officers told the paper they were satisfied
that the mastermind for the bombing campaign was the
former Provisional IRA Quartermaster who had resigned
the previous October following a stormy army convention
in Donegal. They believed he had since formed his own
terrorist organisation opposed to the Northern Ireland
peace process, styling itself 'Oglaigh na hÉireann'. The
Irish Independent said that two of the students arrested in
London had been attending University College Dublin,
while the third was based at Queen's University in Belfast.
According to gardaí, all three had been associating with
republican groups.

The Irish Times reported that the bomb attack on
London had been planned by republican dissidents
associated with the Sinn Féin breakaway group, the 32
County Sovereignty Committee. 'Gardaí believe those
behind the alleged terrorist operation intended to launch
a campaign to exacerbate the current problems in the
North,' the paper said. However, gardaí admitted that
several of those arrested were 'new faces' with no
significant prior connections with republican terrorism.
One man arrested in Dundalk was said to have INLA
links. The arrests had followed a major Garda Special
Branch operation into the activities of the group calling
itself the 'Real IRA', which supports the 32 County
Sovereignty Committee. Gardaí had detected cooperation

between this group and other dissident elements, including the INLA. According to *The Irish Times* report, the Taoiseach, Bertie Ahern, had complimented the gardai and praised the "effective cooperation" of both security forces.

On 12 July 1998, the *Sunday Independent* claimed that a new republican terror group had developed a ruthless strategy of recruiting middle-class university students to carry out a bombing campaign in London's high profile shopping streets. 'The tactic of specifically targeting students is seen as a cynical exploitation of under-graduate naivety by the former IRA Quartermaster-general and its former head of engineering, who have established a breakaway terrorist group modelled on the IRA,' the article stated.

By Monday, 13 July, Garda anti-terrorist officers were in the process of building up a massive dossier on the two men who masterminded the foiled bomb attacks in London, according to the *Irish Independent*. 'Detectives have gathered vital new information about their splinter organisation as a result of the 10 arrests here and in London following the seizure of six incendiary devices and a small bomb as they were about to be planted at the targets,' wrote Tom Brady. This particular article, however, contained some glaring – albeit unintentional – inaccuracies. Although Elaine Moore was not named in the piece, it stated that the Coolock woman arrested by Scotland Yard detectives was the 'owner of the flat where the students were staying'. Just one of the three students arrested, Anthony Hyland, had stayed at the flat. Furthermore, Elaine did not own the flat and was simply a tenant there.

The article also stated that the woman's 'boyfriend', a reference to Rory Hearty, and a 'girlfriend' had been arrested in London but released without charge. Elaine's relationship with Rory was based solely on friendship.

Elaine Moore's name featured in media reports for the first time on Thursday, 16 July, the day after her initial appearance at Belmarsh Magistrates' Court. *The Irish Times* reported that four people had been before a London court charged in relation to the previous Friday's alleged terrorist bomb plot. The three men and one woman had been remanded in custody until 23 July. No application for bail had been made. They were named as Mr Anthony Hyland (25), whose address was not given; Mr Darren Mulholland (19), Dundalk, Co. Louth; Ms Elaine Moore (21), of Parkhill Road, Hampstead, north-west London; and Mr Liam Patrick Grogan (21), of Naas, Co. Kildare. They had all been charged with conspiracy to cause explosions.

A week later Elaine's family were eventually tracked down in Coolock and relentlessly hounded by journalists. Kathy Moore dreaded the prospect of such publicity. She became a virtual recluse in her home, afraid to venture outdoors for fear of encountering a barrage of photographers and reporters. On Wednesday, 22 July, exactly one week after Elaine was charged, Kathy's partner, Tom, insisted that she get out of the house for a few hours. He urged Kathy to spend the day at the B & B and get some rest. The guests would be out during the day, which would give her an opportunity of spending some time alone without the incessant ringing of the telephone. Reluctantly, Kathy agreed to go. Tom had promised to pick her up at around 7 p.m. and Kathy was furious when he failed to show up on time. "By this stage the guests had started to arrive back and I was becoming increasingly unnerved, unable to fathom a reason for him not showing up," Kathy recalls.

At around 9 p.m. Kathy's mobile phone rang – it was Tom. He said he couldn't get out of the house because the place was crawling with reporters. Earlier, Tom had innocently answered the door where he was met by a reporter from the *Irish Independent*. He simply closed the door but, suddenly, journalists and photographers started appearing out of nowhere and converged on the house. Over the telephone, Kathy could hear the constant sound of her doorbell ringing. Other reporters were knocking on her neighbours' doors, desperately fishing for any morsel of information about Elaine. Fortunately, the houses on either side of the Moores were rented and the tenants living there were new to the area and didn't know Elaine.

"Everybody keeps to themselves on our road," explains Kathy. "We'd know each other to see and say hello to, but I wouldn't even know their names. Most of them didn't know any of my family's business and were gracious enough not to speak to the newspapers."

Robert's arrival home caused a ripple of excitement through the gathered media. He remained silent as reporters fired questions at him about his sister. Despite their persistence, the journalists would return to their newsrooms that night devoid of decent copy. The Moores were not giving any interviews. Tom didn't want the newspapers to find out about his business, fearing a media circus, so was afraid to drive there to pick Kathy up. He had no doubt that he would be followed if he attempted to leave the house. He urged Kathy to stay put until 5 a.m. the following morning, at which stage she could get a taxi home. That day, Kathy purchased every single newspaper available. After frantically scanning page after page, she was relieved not to find a single word written about Elaine.

Kathy's relief was short-lived. In the early hours of

the following morning, Friday, 24 July, she was awoken by the sound of her doorbell. Glancing out her bedroom window, she was glad to see her brother-in-law's taxi parked outside. She assumed that Brian Herron had just called to see how she was holding up. Nervously, he handed her a copy of *The Star*. 'Model on bomb charges' screamed the headline on the 'exclusive' story by the paper's crime correspondent, Barry O'Kelly. 'A stunning Irish model is one of the four suspected republicans charged with trying to bomb London,' he wrote. The paper revealed that Elaine had worked for a leading Irish model agency. Her photograph was blown-up to cover the entire front page and showed her wearing her gold necklace with a pendant in the shape of a map of Ireland – the one British police believed symbolised her membership of the 32 County Sovereignty Committee. "I sat in stunned disbelief; I couldn't believe it," says Kathy.

The origin of the photograph in *The Star* has eluded Elaine to this day. Its publication was the start of a three-month-long tabloid feeding frenzy. Coming in the middle of the so-called 'silly season', when slow news days are common, the Elaine Moore story was every editor's dream. Not only did it make great copy, but the main protagonist was photogenic to boot; certainly not your stereotypical hard-line terrorist suspect. Cue a plethora of crass headlines, such as the *Evening Herald*'s 'Elaine goes from the catwalk to the cells'.

Given her limited experience of life on the catwalk, Elaine was slightly bemused – and somewhat embarrassed – by her media moniker as the 'IRA model'. In fact, her reported modelling career never really got started. Her mother had introduced her to Grace O'Shaughnessy – a top Irish model back in the '60s and '70s – who encouraged Elaine to give it a go. With her high, prominent cheekbones and 5' 10" stature, O'Shaughnessy believed the attractive eighteen-year-old would be offered modelling assignments if she signed up to an agency. Elaine was dubious but decided to arrange for a screening anyway. Polaroids were taken and Elaine had a portfolio created to show prospective clients. Unfamiliar with the modelling world, Elaine neglected to maintain contact with the Assets agency to inform them of her availability for work. When she phoned up one day to inquire about her portfolio, she was asked why she hadn't been checking in on a weekly basis and if indeed she was interested in work. Her one and only assignment for Assets was a photo shoot for University College Galway to promote a recruitment drive. Soon after, Elaine attended a screening but quickly decided that the world of modelling wasn't her scene. But the model tag remained thanks to the fertile imaginations of the tabloid press.

Despite Kathy's refusal to answer the door to reporters, she knew deep down that it was only a matter of time before she would have to speak to them. "Tom said that although it would be a hard thing to do, he felt I should talk to them," she says. "He thought it would be better to get my side of the story out and let them know what Elaine was like, rather than them making up their own stuff." The publication of *The Star* article that morning had led to a renewed media assault on the Moore household. Kathy even pretended to be somebody else when confronted by a reporter from the *Evening Herald,* as nobody knew what she looked like at that stage. Kathy had been monitoring the various comings and goings of journalists from the safe distance of her bedroom all morning. She heard the gate opening, followed by a voice speaking on a mobile telephone. The doorbell never rang. Instead, something was shoved through her letterbox.

Peering out through the curtains, Kathy saw a man drive away in a black Mercedes. She went downstairs and read the letter – it was from an RTÉ researcher working for the 'Today With Pat Kenny' radio show. It read: 'I am sure that this is a very difficult time for you and your family, but I understand from newspaper reports that your daughter, Elaine, intends to plead not guilty to the charges against her. I wonder if you feel it would be a good time to talk in public about the situation.'

Kathy felt that the request for the interview had been handled sensitively. With Tom's encouragement, she eventually phoned Pat Kenny on the direct line number given in the letter. After speaking with him for around one hour, he gently urged her to go on his radio show the following Monday. "He really felt that we needed all the support we could get for Elaine," she says. "He said that people should know what type of person Elaine was and what sort of family she came from. Pat gave me so much confidence because he was so understanding, so sensitive and so nice to me. He made me think: 'Maybe not everyone's out to get us after all'."

Kathy was worried that she might freeze up live on air. Some days she couldn't put two words together due to the stress of the ordeal; at other times she would be all business-like and practical. She rang Pat Kenny back and asked if he could pre-record the interview. He agreed and conducted the interview with Kathy over the telephone that afternoon. It was broadcast on his show on RTÉ Radio 1 the following Monday, 27 July. Speaking on the programme, Kathy declared that her daughter was simply the victim of a dreadful mistake. She described the experience of arriving home on 10 July to find her house full of gardaí. Within minutes, her son, Robert, had been arrested. "I think I went into total shock at the stage,"

Kathy told Pat Kenny. She also explained how British police were using Elaine's "amazing interest" in Michael Collins against her, as well as the discovery of the gold pendant in the shape of a map of Ireland. "There is absolutely no evidence against her," Kathy added.

The reaction to the Pat Kenny interview was phenomenal. Kathy – and Elaine – literally received hundreds of letters of support after the broadcast. The show's researchers had given out Elaine's prison address. Some letters arrived, despite being simply addressed to 'Elaine and Kathy Moore, Dublin'. The programme received a flood of calls from listeners who wanted to express their outrage at Elaine's ongoing detention in a British prison. Kathy feels that Pat Kenny's interest in the case largely influenced the public – and media – perception of Elaine. Every day after the interview, Pat Kenny had one of his staff phone Kathy to see how she was doing. She says she will never forget his kindness during those difficult months of 1998.

The radio experience made it easier for Kathy to deal with the media and she began giving interviews to newspaper reporters, even inviting them into her home. Some journalists crossed the line between intrusiveness and resourcefulness. Details of a personal letter sent to Kathy from Elaine while she was in Woodhill prison appeared in *The Star*.

Elaine continued to have mixed experiences with the Irish media. While many journalists and broadcasters, most notably, Pat Kenny, were extremely helpful in the campaign to secure her release by constantly highlighting her case, Elaine was hugely sensitive over even minor inaccuracies in newspaper reports. She was later forced to initiate legal action against two major Irish publications in a bid to defend her good name and reputation.

Chapter Eight

A HARSH REGIME

The monotonous drudgery of everyday prison life hit Elaine hard. Each day was virtually indistinguishable from the next; set apart only by the occasional visit from her solicitor and the routine strip-searches that were part and parcel of such privileges at Woodhill. A typical day went as follows:

8.00 a.m.	Breakfast call, shower, exercise or TV
10.30 a.m.	Lock-up (Mondays, Wednesday and Fridays)
11.30 a.m.	Lock-up (Tuesdays, Thursdays, Saturdays and Sundays)
1.00 p.m.	Lunch
4.30 p.m.	Lock-up until morning
5.00 p.m.	Dinner
7.30 p.m.	Hot water or tea

The conditions at Woodhill were very draconian with prisoners locked up in their cells for up to 21 hours a day. During her early days at the prison, Elaine sometimes spent as long as 19 hours at a time locked up. This punitive regime may have been par for the course for Woodhill's vicious killers, but it was particularly harsh on a young woman on remand who had yet to be found guilty of any crime.

On the morning of Friday, 17 July, exactly one week since her arrest, Elaine awoke dreading the monotony of the day ahead. She couldn't make up her mind if she was merely feeling acutely fed-up or experiencing the onset of depression. Her choices were far from varied: breakfast, bath, exercise and television. Elaine was heartened when she learned she was to receive a visit that day. Some time later, it was confirmed that it would be from Gareth Peirce. She was delighted at the prospect of seeing a friendly face and – possibly – receiving some positive news.

Before her solicitor arrived, Elaine was briefed on visit procedures. Escorted by four guards, she was brought through the labyrinth of corridors that eventually led to the visitors' area. Elaine was ushered into a room and bluntly told that a strip-search would have to be carried out in advance of the visit from Gareth. Noticing her reluctance, Elaine was informed by the female officers that the sooner they got started, the quicker it would be over. Sure weren't they all women? It was nothing they hadn't seen before. This gave Elaine cold comfort and she remained unconvinced. "It may be routine to you lot but it's a sinister, malicious act in my eyes and I'll never conform to your way of thinking," Elaine retorted. Much to her annoyance, her remark was met with blank indifference by the officers who proceeded with the search regardless. She had little choice but to comply, as failure to do so would have resulted in her right to a visit from Gareth being revoked and an incident report being filed against her which could have further restricted her already limited 'privileges'.

She was instructed to wait in the visitors' area, a large open room sparsely furnished with several chairs and tables. The prison officers guarding Elaine seemed confused and flustered, as if they were unsure of how to deal with her. As she sat waiting, they huddled together and talked in hushed, urgent tones as walkie-talkies crackled aggressively. Elaine was then led into a room that was divided equally by a glass partition. Thoughts of Hannibal Lector encaged behind glass crossed her mind. This was to be a 'closed visit', with no contact allowed between Elaine and her solicitor. She sat staring through the glass into the other identical half of the room, willing Gareth to walk through the door. She was feeling dejected after the search followed by the humiliation of being treated like a dangerous animal. She became aware of a slightly raised voice emanating from outside the room and soon recognised it as Gareth's. The solicitor seemed furious and was remonstrating loudly with prison guards about her client's rights, informing them that she would be forced to take action unless the situation was rectified. Gareth entered the room in a flurry and sat on the opposite side of the glass, her eyes wide with horror. She was clearly outraged, apologising profusely at the manner in which Elaine was being treated at Woodhill. As she gathered some papers together, Gareth endeavoured to bring this "outrageous episode" to a speedy conclusion and refused to commence the legal briefing.

After a few minutes, a guard sheepishly entered Gareth's side of the room and informed her that her request for an 'open visit' had been granted. As Elaine was led from the room, her solicitor quipped that she looked like a Nike model in her casual attire. Given the intensity of the situation, Gareth's stance followed by her comment shattered the monster facade that had been placed on her client. "She was incredible that afternoon as she had complete control," Elaine recalls. "The guards dispersed throughout the room, and stood idly like chastised children. She had reinforced their lack of professionalism and had threatened them with disciplinary action. They had now been forced to comply with my solicitor's instructions and faced possible incident reports being filed against them, which felt great." Elaine and Gareth were brought from the closed visit section and directed towards a more private, less clinical room. The door was closed behind them. Finally, they were alone. Still apologising for the appalling conditions at Woodhill, Gareth explained that it had taken her a few days to find out which prison Elaine had been taken to. Much to her frustration, neither the police nor the prosecution had been forthcoming with this information. She had contacted Holloway to arrange a visit with Elaine, only to be informed that she hadn't arrived there. Gareth was horrified when she learned that Elaine had been detained in an all-male maximum-security unit at the infamous Milton Keynes prison. "It was completely ridiculous," Gareth remembers. "I'm not sure if I was shocked – I had been shocked before and one never ceases to be amazed at the cruelty and stupidity of the prison department in this country. It rises on each occasion to a new level. This was yet another example."

Gareth assured Elaine that every effort would be made to have her transferred to the all-women's prison at Holloway. She was determined to go to court immediately to pursue the matter. Although disturbed that she was in an all-male prison, Elaine took some solace from the fact that she didn't have to mix with other prisoners. Her induction into Woodhill had deeply disturbed her. She felt she wouldn't be able to withstand another upheaval. She urged Gareth not to make any representations to have her transferred to Holloway, a place where she would surely have to blend in with real criminals. The solicitor seemed taken aback by Elaine's reluctance to move from Woodhill but gradually came to understand the method in her madness. She would respect Elaine's wishes, peculiar as they seemed. There were other downsides to Woodhill, too, given the distance Elaine's legal team had to travel to visit her. It didn't matter. A fear of the unknown had always been Elaine's Achilles' heal. She preferred to stay put.

Gareth Peirce was probably never fully aware of the calming effect she had on Elaine. "Her mere presence instilled me with a sense of peace," she says. "Her word was gospel, even though a lot of the time those words were not what I had hoped to hear. The consistent accuracy of her predictions never ceased to amaze me."

Before the visit was terminated, they discussed the bail hearing, which was scheduled to take place on Thursday, 23 July. Elaine complained about the humiliating strip-searches but Gareth was unable to offer any reassurance in this regard. Unfortunately, a maximum-security unit meant maximum-security procedures. After the visit, Elaine was forced to undergo a further strip-search, which shattered any confidence she had gleaned from her legal consultation. Gareth had given her hope; the prison guards had stripped her of it. Dejected, Elaine returned to her cell and was locked up for the evening.

That morning, Elaine had been given a 1,500-piece jigsaw by prison staff depicting the trial of William Wallace, the Scottish nationalist immortalised by Mel Gibson in the Oscar winning film, *Braveheart*. Ordinarily, Elaine would never have even attempted to take on such a mammoth project due to time constraints and her general lack of interest in puzzles. But now, time was all she had. The jigsaw would help take her mind off things and while away the long hours. She thought about the *Braveheart* movie and how strange it was that she should be given such an appropriately themed puzzle.

Elaine had previously filled in four forms specifying the details of people she wished to contact. Stringent security checks would first have to be run on those named before she could phone them. The following day, Elaine received clearance to phone her mother's number only. Each prisoner was allowed a quota of telephone cards and Elaine had purchased some earlier. However, because she was a foreign national making overseas calls, the phone cards would only last her a few minutes. Elaine was delighted to get through to her mum and assured her that she was bored but otherwise fine; her surroundings were clean; and the guards were mostly female and treating her well. Apart from telling Kathy about Gareth's visit the previous day, Elaine mostly enquired about her loved ones back home.

That evening, Elaine was furious when her ration of cigarettes failed to arrive. A heavy smoker by any standard, they were her one constant source of strength in prison. Elaine suspected that the cigarettes were purposely being withheld from her. She was right. Rory Hearty had sent them earlier but they simply weren't passed on to her. Mercifully, one prison officer brought her some tobacco. But Elaine's luck was out — she had no matches or lighter. She would have to improvise and learn some prison tricks-of-the-trade. The female officer handed in two long strands from a mop and lit one end – it would smoulder for several hours that night. Elaine was not allowed to have a lighter unsupervised in her cell. As a novice, she hadn't ordered any matches from the prison shop and would be unable to do so until the following week.

The next morning, Elaine received matches and two men's magazines from a prison guard. A male prisoner had sent them to her. Although grateful for the matches, Elaine was unnerved that other prisoners were aware of her presence at Woodhill. The only explanation was that an officer had discussed Elaine with them. Later that night, word of Elaine appeared to have spread throughout Woodhill. The prisoners took turns calling out her name and beckoning her to come to the window. Their words echoed throughout the block, sending a chill through Elaine as she sat alone in her cell. Although the other prisoners were locked-up, too, the fact that they knew about Elaine unsettled and troubled her deeply. She was sick to her stomach with worry and ignored their repeated invitations by remaining silent, never once responding to them. The prisoners loudly continued to openly discuss her with each other through the bars of their respective cells. One prisoner informed the others that she was an IRA prisoner. The banter continued for many hours. Periodically it would steer away from her. They were intrigued by how strange it was that she was the sole female prisoner at Woodhill and speculated about the reasons for her detention. Elaine mentioned her concerns to a guard, who replied that the prisoners had been made aware of her by visitors. Elaine, the officer admitted, had become the major topic of conversation among the prisoners. She was urged not to reply to their taunts.

Disturbingly, the prisoners located below Elaine were also in the 'high risk' category. According to one officer, they were in prison for a multitude of crimes: armed robbery, murder, rape . . . some had even offended while in custody, assaulting fellow inmates or prison officers. Elaine wondered why the officer was telling her all this? Was it some form of psychological warfare? Intentional or not, it was frightening the life out of her. Night after night, Elaine lay restless in her bed, unable to block out the voices that called up to her, pleading with her to talk to them. She knew that even replying once would signal the end of any peace she might have. When the calls subsided, even a cough or a sneeze on her part would trigger their cries. "It was truly terrifying," she recalls. "My movements throughout the day were dictated by the officers and were further restricted by the prisoners in the evening. I was already suffering from insomnia and their taunts just made any prospect of sleep near impossible."

On Monday, 20 July, Elaine was subjected to a 'monthly cell turnover'. Two female officers conducted the cell search before turning their attentions to Elaine. She disputed the validity of the search only to be informed that it was standard procedure that all Category A prisoners were subjected to one every four weeks. All items of clothing were removed and checked. This form of strip-search felt more sinister because it was conducted in her cell, normally Elaine's sole sanctuary from prison staff. Regaining her composure, she could make no sense of the urgency for such a search. After all, she had been on 'E Wing' for five days and was the only prisoner located there.

Elaine was unnerved by a visit from the prison's educational department representative. It seemed to imply that she would be there for a long time, something she didn't want to consider. That said, she was bored and needed to keep her mind stimulated. Elaine decided to use the time to improve her knowledge of the Irish language and also opted to study psychology, a subject she had enjoyed at college. From the prison library she ordered a copy of Tim Pat Coogan's biography of Michael Collins. Given the fact that the police had made so much of her fascination with Collins, Elaine believed that choosing such a book would further show that she had nothing to hide. That evening, her cigarettes – 60 in all – finally arrived.

That night the nightmares began. Elaine regularly woke up in a cold sweat and in tears. The nightmares usually related specifically to her loved ones. In the loneliness of the night, Elaine would document and analyse each bad dream until it drove her close to despair. If unable to return to sleep, she would sit up into the early hours of the morning trying to concentrate on the jigsaw.

On the morning of 21 July, at 10 a.m., Elaine was informed of a visit from a Mr Mulligan of the Irish Embassy. She was strip-searched twice in honour of the occasion. Mr Mulligan conceded that there was very little he could do to help Elaine. His primary objective was to ascertain whether or not her human rights were being violated in any way. He simply wanted to know how she was being treated. Mr Mulligan could identify with Elaine's plight to some degree. He explained that 20 years earlier, police had detained him for one day in Wales for no reason. He had also been to visit Elaine's 'co-accused' at Belmarsh where they were all being kept together. Elaine, on the other hand, was in solitary confinement. Mr Mulligan spoke about the media attention Elaine was generating back in Ireland, where there was growing interest in her case. He stressed that the services of the Irish Embassy would be available to her should any of her rights be violated while in custody. There was, possibly, one way in which he could assist her. Elaine explained that she wanted her phone card quota increased on the grounds that she needed to make overseas calls. Mr Mulligan promised to make some inquiries in this regard and she later had extra phone cards allotted to her.

There were three things a prisoner could look forward to at Woodhill and all three were marred by procedure: visits from legal representatives and relatives necessitated strip- searches; phone calls were monitored at all times;

and all letters were screened and edited with words censored or sentences obscured by thick black marker without explanation. That evening, Elaine decided to document her prison experiences by making descriptive diary entries. Gareth Peirce had urged her to keep a diary, telling her it would be something she could show her grandchildren in later years. Elaine feared that the diary would be scrutinised by prison guards – and she was right. But she had come to care less and less about what they thought. Besides, maybe it was time for them to know exactly how she felt about her treatment at Woodhill.

In an entry in her diary on 21 July 1998, Elaine wrote:

> I really feel as though I have been kidnapped but, strangely, everyone knows where I am. No one can help. I must be patient and allow myself to be locked away and degraded by this prison's cruel regime until someone says I'm free to go or a price is put on my freedom. Since I've been labelled as a High Risk Category 'A' prisoner, placed in solitary confinement in an all-male prison, surely no amount of money offered to secure bail will be accepted. Am I really considered that much of a danger that only this prison is capable and secure enough to hold me? What a load of nonsense! I've been stereotyped to add to the hype. When and how can this possibly end?

Chapter Nine

THE GOLD PENDANT

On Wednesday, 22 July, the eve of her initial bail application, Elaine received a visit from Nigel Leskin. Although the meeting with Nigel was important, Elaine's mind was elsewhere. She was preoccupied with thoughts of the strip-search that would await her after her solicitor left. She had already gone through one such ordeal prior to his arrival at Woodhill. Elaine struggled to amass some benefit from Nigel's visit, as he spoke in enthusiastic tones about her bail prospects.

Elaine perked up slightly as Nigel showed her a newspaper article that was largely supportive of her plight. It even suggested that there was a sense of public outrage back home in Ireland over Elaine's treatment by the UK authorities. A photograph of her Parkhill Road apartment accompanied the article. Rory Hearty had given the paper an interview, in which he revealed that the police had destroyed his car. This saddened Elaine – she knew how much Rory loved that car and fondly recalled the many driving lessons she had received in it. Rory never found out what exactly happened to his car.

One explanation offered to him by police was that it was flooded with chemicals as part of a forensic exam-ination to find traces of explosives. He heard that it had subsequently been blown up as it was unfit for use. Police later compensated him for the loss of his car, but in the short-term it resulted in his inability to return to work as a courier as he had no transport. His employers were very supportive of his plight and held his position open indefinitely.

Elaine received letters from Rory almost on a daily basis. Having spent three days locked up in a cell himself, he knew how much she would appreciate regular contact with the outside world. That day, he had informed her of his uncle's death. Elaine was deeply upset for her friend. He had already been through so much over the previous 12 days and she knew the bereavement would have a profound affect on Rory and his family. Things just seemed to be getting progressively worse. After the funeral in Armagh, Rory had met up with Elaine's mother in Dublin Airport before catching his flight back to London. Kathy wanted to give Rory a suit to bring over to Elaine for her court appearance. As they sat chatting over a coffee in the airport, Rory and Kathy were engulfed by a sense of paranoia. "Rory kept pointing to people, wondering if they were undercover detectives," recalls Kathy. "We just couldn't relax. We felt there was a real possibility that we were being watched." There was good reason for Kathy to feel paranoid. When her son had been arrested, Irish detectives had repeatedly suggested to him that Rory and Niall Hearty were somehow involved. They had related this theory to Kathy and quizzed her at great lengths about her own visits to London.

That evening, Elaine received a package from her brother, which contained a Walkman, tapes, some books and a letter. Robert, as usual, had put a lot of thought into the parcel's contents and Elaine could attach some significance to every item. Even the choice of music on the tapes seemed to contain a message from Robert. Elaine knew he would be desperately worried about his little sister. She had been reassured by both her mother and Gareth that Robert had coped extremely well with his arrest and had come to no harm. But Elaine knew that her ordeal would have hurt him considerably. They had always been incredibly close. Elaine recalls a time in her childhood when Robert visited the dentist and was accompanied by his sister and his mum. Even though he was the one who had a tooth extracted that day, it was Elaine who needed consoling. She wept openly at the thoughts of what her brother was going through. Elaine and Robert had always been conscious of each other's pain: no more so than now.

On the morning of her bail application, Thursday, 23 July, Elaine was taken from her cell and brought down to the prison's reception area. After being strip-searched, she was handcuffed and seated in the back of a police van. Inside, she was placed in a small cell that separated her from the prison officers and her handcuffs were removed. From the limited view she had through the obscured window, Elaine noticed that the van never stopped once after leaving Woodhill until reaching its final destination. Members of the public watched, transfixed, as the van sped through the streets of London, sirens blaring, mounting pavements when necessary and breaking every red light in its path.

Arriving at Belmarsh Magistrates' Court, Elaine was again handcuffed and escorted from the van under heavy-armed guard. There seemed to be machine gun toting police officers everywhere. The sight of them terrified her. Elaine was brought into a holding cell, where a female officer searched her. She was given her tailor-made cream suit that her mother had sent over. However, Kathy had neglected to include a top that Elaine could wear under it. Elaine politely turned down her solicitor's offer of a top. This had instilled a sense of relief in Rory when Gareth relayed the tale to him. He later wrote to Elaine that he knew that prison had not changed her and quoted her in the letter as saying: "Oh no, Mrs Peirce, I couldn't wear that – it doesn't go with the suit." Elaine had to position the suit carefully so it wouldn't be too revealing. The last thing she needed was to be inappropriately dressed before the magistrate.

Leaving the cell, Elaine was brought to the bottom of the stairs which led into the courtroom. Here, she noticed her three co-accused – Anthony Hyland, Darren Mulholland and Liam Grogan – each one guarded by up to three men. She was careful not to make eye contact with any of them. Together, they all stood in silence until ordered to proceed up the stairs. Each prisoner was assigned a specific seat in the dock with officers strategically placed on all sides. Elaine fixed her gaze on Gareth Peirce, who smiled benignly back at her.

The magistrate was David Cooper, who had presided over the initial court hearing the day after Elaine had been charged. Cooper asked if there were to be representations made for bail on behalf of the four defendants. Gareth Peirce responded that only her client was seeking bail at that stage. The Crown Prosecution Service, in objecting to bail, believed that Elaine would abscond in an attempt to avoid justice. The prosecution unveiled their grounds for contention, placing heavy emphasis on Elaine's gold pendant in the shape of a map of Ireland. This, it was claimed, was a symbol of membership of the 32 County Sovereignty Committee. Reference was also made to a tricolour flag and photographs of Michael Collins – and 'other' known terrorists – found in Elaine's apartment. Surprisingly, there was less emphasis put on the alleged contents of the bag recovered from her room. The implication was that Elaine must have seen the bag and known what was in it. Gareth told the court that, as a mother of sons, there had been countless rucksacks in her house, "no doubt filled with dirty socks and God knows what". She could not have been expected to check their contents every time they spent the night.

Gareth revealed that the gold pendant had, in fact, been purchased almost four years earlier by Elaine's brother, Robert, as a Christmas present for her sister. She produced a receipt to verify this claim. Dismissively, Gareth highlighted the fact that the chain had obviously been purchased some years before the formation of the dissident republican organisation referred to by the prosecution. Pendants such as this one were widely available in most Irish gift shops. If the prosecution's contention were to stand, then surely, Gareth asserted, a vast majority of American tourists – and, indeed, herself – must be viewed with the same suspicion, as they also owned similar pendants. The tricolour, the court heard, had simply been purchased in Camden Market. It was similar to ones that hung freely and openly in pubs and homes throughout London. The 'other' known republican terrorists who adorned her wall were actually members of the Irish Government featured in a picture of the first Dáil Éireann.

Although Magistrate Cooper rejected bail, Elaine and her legal team were encouraged by the poor quality of evidence that had been put forward against her by the Crown Prosecution. Gareth had always felt that bail was unlikely to be granted on such a serious charge on the first attempt. On the surface, the prosecution's evidence was flimsy, circumstantial and could not possibly be allowed to stand alone in the case against her client. To Elaine, the magistrate seemed unhappy with the case put forward, particularly when he asked if the prosecution had anything more to add. They didn't, but assured

Magistrate Cooper that this was because their investigation was still at an early stage. Despite stating that he was not particularly impressed by the case against Elaine, the magistrate again remanded her in custody to Woodhill prison pending a further court appearance the following Thursday. Cooper warned the Crown Prosecution Service to have their case more prepared by then.

Elaine noticed the heavy media presence in the court's press area. Rory was also there, sitting in the public gallery above where Elaine was standing in the dock. After the hearing, she was removed to a cell, which reminded her of a dungeon, for a 'closed' legal consultation with her solicitor. Speaking to Elaine through a glass panel, Gareth was in optimistic form after the hearing. They discussed tactics and what was likely to happen next. Elaine had been dazzled by Gareth's performance in court. "It was an incredible feeling sitting in that dock, just watching Gareth represent me," she says. "She was so sharp and defiant in her approach as she dissected the prosecution's case. At times I would drift off and almost enjoy watching her until the cold realisation as to why she was there kicked in. As the only applicant for bail, I appeared to be the sole focus of proceedings, which added to my sense of paranoia."

Gareth said she would be travelling to Dublin shortly to meet Elaine's mother. Apart from gathering vital background information about Elaine, she would use the visit to attempt to allay any of Kathy's fears surrounding the case. After the consultation, Elaine was immediately strip-searched. Afterwards, she overheard some of the prison guards, who had been present in court, discussing her. They commented on the flimsy nature of the prosecution's case and seemed genuinely baffled as to why bail had been denied. From this point on, their attitude towards Elaine became more sympathetic. Even on the journey back to Woodhill, the officers continued to openly talk about Elaine's case. Her mood was more upbeat now; the adrenaline still pumping. Elaine could finally hold her head up in defiance – she felt somewhat vindicated.

Looking through the small window, Elaine could see that the armoured van in which she was travelling was accompanied by at least four squad cars. It took up to 17 armed guards and police – all wearing bullet-proof vests – to escort her. She had been informed that such measures were in anticipation of a possible rescue attempt. "Given the erratic speeds of the van it crossed my mind that if there was an accident I would be in serious trouble. I was handcuffed and locked in a cell within the van. What chance would I have had?"

Arriving back at Woodhill, Elaine was strip-searched and returned to her cell on 'E Wing'. She phoned her mother and spoke enthusiastically about that day's court appearance, neglecting to mention the repeated strip-searches and armed escort. Elaine was oblivious to the fact that her mother was well aware of the undignified manner in which she was being paraded to and from court. The world was watching thanks to the many TV cameras outside.

Lying in her cell that night, Elaine went through the day's events in her mind. If the judge had merely stated that she did not pose a threat, she would have simply walked free from the court. But he hadn't said that – and now she was back in prison. Although Elaine had been in buoyant form earlier, she now felt worn down and demoralised by the four strip-searches she had been subjected to. She couldn't understand why the magistrate, on one hand, seemed unimpressed by the prosecution's evidence, but still refused to release her on bail. It was as though light had been shed on her plight and yet she was still subjected to the humiliation of life as a Category A prisoner.

Elaine awoke in a foul mood on the morning of Friday, 24 July. The fleeting highs and lows of the previous day had now been replaced by a sense of desperation. Just thinking about her bail refusal infuriated her. As a Catholic and in line with her religious rights, Elaine had requested that she receive Mass each Sunday from the prison chaplain, Fr O'Connell. He would say Mass in the TV room and also visited her sporadically during the week. On that particular day, his timing was impeccable. Elaine welcomed the opportunity to be able to talk openly about the court ruling and vent her frustration about the soul-destroying strip-searches. The priest comforted her as best he could. Afterwards, Elaine declined an opportunity to exercise in the yard. She just wanted to be left alone to wallow in her misery. Instead of adjusting to prison life, Elaine was finding it increasingly difficult to settle into it.

The fact that Elaine's next bail hearing was set for 30 July was ominous in itself. The date coincided with the first anniversary of the death of her aunt and godmother, Evelyn. Elaine reflected on what had been an extremely difficult year for her family, putting particular strain on her mother. Evelyn had died suddenly and without warning at the age of 41. Kathy had not only lost her sister, but her closest friend. Prior to Evelyn's passing, the Reilly side of Elaine's family, comprising of seven girls and one boy, were unaware that they had a medical history of aneurysms of the brain. This hereditary defect had devastating consequences. Elaine's grandfather, Paddy Reilly, had died suddenly at the age of 46 in 1969, as he drove towards the family home in Nobber, Co. Meath. The cause of death was recorded at the time as a cerebral haemorrhage, but it would later emerge that it was, in fact, an aneurysm. His wife, Eileen, later survived three brain haemorrhages and underwent brain surgery in 1976 and 1977.

On 28 July 1997, Evelyn awoke with a pain in her ear and complained to her husband about it. As Thomas was urging her to see a doctor, she collapsed in his arms. Evelyn never regained consciousness and remained on a life-support machine in Beaumont Hospital until 30 July when a decision was made by the neurosurgeon to switch it off. The death stunned the family. Evelyn had enjoyed excellent health throughout her life. There was some comfort for her loved ones when her husband agreed to donate her organs, allowing Evelyn to live on, in a way, through others.

Evelyn's death would affect the lives of her sisters and brother in other ways. Hospital consultants now firmly believed that aneurysms were a hereditary condition. As a result, all of her siblings had to undergo angiograms, a painful surgical procedure that carried the risk of a stroke. The Reilly family were also affected by a history of polycystic disease, another hereditary condition for which they also were tested. Thankfully, the results of the tests revealed that Kathy Moore was free from both diseases. However, two of her sisters, Paula and Anna, were not so fortunate and had to undergo brain surgery to clamp their aneurysms. Much to the family's relief, both operations were a success. The past year had been a trying one for Elaine's family. She prayed that her second attempt at securing bail would be successful, as she wanted to be there to comfort her mother on the first anniversary of Evelyn's death.

A phone call to her mother on Saturday, 25 July cheered

Elaine up no end. Kathy was in optimistic form. Due to media interest in her case, there was a groundswell of support for Elaine back home. Newspapers had even commented on the lack of evidence against her. Kathy expressed confidence that Elaine would be released soon. For the remainder of the day, Elaine clung to her mother's words of hope. She had little control of her roller coaster of emotions, which ranged from deep depression to overwhelming confidence. She started to do her own laundry and began to exercise more regularly in her cell – it was important that she stayed strong and focused. Elaine met with Fr O'Connell and asked if he would organise a Mass in memory of Evelyn, which gave her a small sense of achievement. Later that day, Elaine had to sign a disclaimer in relation to items belonging to Niall Hearty that she had collected from him in Oxford the night before her arrest. She had promised to keep them safe for him while he was in America for the summer. Niall was now due back at college in Oxford to re-sit exams and desperately needed the books and notes that were now in police possession.

Elaine had experienced great difficulty sleeping since the night of her arrest. It would usually take her hours to fall asleep, as her mind was constantly plagued by negative thoughts and the taunting voices of prisoners below. When she did eventually drift off into an uneasy slumber, vivid nightmares wreaked havoc with her mind. This left her exhausted the next day. Elaine began eating less and less as each day passed. She was fast reaching breaking point.

On Monday, 27 July Elaine was sitting in the TV room when a prison officer approached with her mail. She broke down in tears as she read a card sent from her mother, telling Elaine how proud she was of her and how much she loved her. At the end of the card Kathy inscribed

21 kisses, 'one for every year of happiness you have given me.' Weeping uncontrollably, Elaine left the room for the sanctuary of her cell. The prison officers seemed surprised by her distressed state as she had rarely expressed emotions in their presence.

There was more trauma that day in the form of two strip-searches as Elaine was granted a legal visit. Two particular prison officers appeared uncomfortable at times when conducting the searches. They deployed a method of trying to make the ritual more discreet by shielding Elaine with a towel and breaking the search into two sections. Their efforts, while appreciated by Elaine, were thwarted by another officer who strenuously objected to such a lapse in procedure and demanded that the searches be carried out by the book. Elaine responded angrily, letting this officer know a few home truths. "I told her she was a sad old cow with nothing better to be doing."

Another female officer tried to calm Elaine by revealing that a discretionary 'closed visit' was to be permitted with her mother. Despite the fact that she missed her mum desperately, Elaine flatly declined the offer. There was no way she was going to be deprived of being able to hug her mother. Elaine could not bear the thoughts of having to communicate with any member of her family through a sheet of glass. Kathy would have been devastated if she had seen her daughter under such restrictive conditions. Elaine knew her mother would understand her reason for turning down the visit.

The legal visit was from a young lawyer, Alistair Lyon, who was there on Gareth Peirce's behalf; she was in Dublin that day meeting with Elaine's mother. Alistair handed Elaine two large brown envelopes, which contained character references from her family, friends, former employers, teachers, politicians – basically anyone she had ever known. He also showed her the front-page picture that had appeared the previous Friday in *The Star*. Although she had been made aware of the article, it didn't seem real now that she was finally reading it. Alistair tried to prepare Elaine for Thursday's upcoming bail hearing, again warning that there was little chance of it succeeding. Outwardly, Elaine accepted this but secretly refused to believe that it would be anything but successful. Her confidence was unfounded but she desperately needed to believe that an end to her ordeal was near.

That night, as Elaine lay awake in bed, a male officer knocked on her cell door and then spoke to her through the hatch. Calling her by her first name, he said he had heard about her distressed condition earlier that day; she was to call him if she needed anything. Elaine wasn't afraid of this particular guard; he had seemed friendly on the few occasions she had met him. There were others, however, who she deeply feared. Elaine was always uncomfortable being alone in the wing with a male officer. She realised that if a guard ever decided to enter her cell, the only people she would be able to alert to her dilemma were the prisoners in the cells below her.

On Tuesday, 28 July Elaine finally snapped. After been strip-searched twice the previous day for her legal visit, she was informed that another 'cell turnover' was required, despite the fact that this was supposed to be just a monthly ritual. Elaine became enraged and launched an expletive-riddled verbal attack on the female officers assigned to the task.

"Are you lot making up procedures as you go along?" she asked angrily. "The information I have is that cell turnovers are carried out once a month. I haven't been here two full weeks and you're saying I have to be subjected to this lark again – no fucking way!" The guards replied that due to her high-risk category status, the prison warden deemed the impromptu search necessary. Elaine could not be mollified as she continued her tirade against the prison officers. "What is it with you people? Do you not trust each other? The only person who could pass something through to me is one of you lot. Every time I blink I'm searched. It's unnecessary and in violation of my rights. Do you get a kick out of degrading me in this way? I bet you don't treat the murderers and every other type in this kip as poorly as you treat me. I hope you can't sleep at night – I know I certainly can't."

One of the officers apologised to Elaine, saying they would put her in another cell while they carried out the search. "Don't touch that fucking jigsaw," she yelled at them. "I've spent hours working on it. If you're going to break it, tell me now and I'll do you the honour – but don't you touch it!" They didn't dare. As the strip-search commenced, Elaine aggressively threw her T-shirt at the officers. Her outburst was clearly out of character. She could not recall such intense feelings of anger before. Conscious of Elaine's fragile state, the prison officers didn't conduct a full search and tried to get out of her way as quickly as possible. Once inside the sterile cell and out of their view, she broke down. Slowly but surely, the regime at Woodhill was breaking her spirit. When she was allowed back into her cell, Elaine noticed that everything had been put back neatly in its original position; the jigsaw appeared untouched. "You can close that fucking door on your way out," she snapped at the departing prison officers.

On Wednesday, 29 July, the eve of her second bail application, Elaine wrote in her diary:

> I feel that I am the person that has been
> most deeply affected by this whole mess.

Elaine had every right to feel hard done by. Her whole career and life had been destroyed as a result of her being arrested, charged and detained in prison. Even if she had been granted bail, she would not have been able to return to her flat – it had been sealed off by police and destroyed by chemical treatments carried out as part of their forensic examinations. Everything she possessed in London: clothes, jewellery, personal keepsakes; had been seized by detectives, desperate for evidence against her. She would almost certainly lose her job at Netlink. People she loved had also been affected by the events of 10 July: her brother and his girlfriend were still recovering from the ordeal of their arrests in Dublin, as were Rory Hearty and the young woman detained with him. Back home, Elaine knew the media focus was on her. Although the publicity would highlight the apparent injustice of her situation, Elaine worried about the effect on her mother and the thoughts of being recognised in public if and when she eventually returned to Ireland. Would she be stigmatised by prison for the rest of her life? As she pondered those thoughts, the copy of the Michael Collins biography she had ordered from the prison library finally arrived which helped to improve her mood slightly.

Chapter Ten

BURDEN OF INNOCENCE

Apart from the determined efforts of her friends and family, there was also high-profile political support for Elaine back home in Ireland. Although it went virtually unacknowledged at the time, the Irish Government – a coalition between Fianna Fáil and the Progressive Democrats, led by Taoiseach Bertie Ahern – was actively involved in behind-the-scenes diplomatic efforts to secure Elaine's release.

On the night of Elaine's arrest, Kathy Moore frantically phoned every politician she could think of. As it was a Friday night, she was unable to make contact with any of them but left urgent messages on their answering machines. Mary Banotti, the Fine Gael MEP (Member of European Parliament) for Dublin, was the first public representative to call Kathy back and would become closely associated with Elaine's case.

Kathy Moore had been involved with the Fine Gael party for almost 20 years and had stood as a Dublin Corporation local election candidate in the Artane ward in 1991. Elaine had been a member of Young Fine Gael and had helped out with her mother's election campaign as a teenager. "She was a bit apprehensive about me running," laughs Kathy. "She said she would go mad if she saw my face on an election poster with a moustache drawn on it, or something."

Robert Moore, on the other hand, was a member of Fianna Fáil and had been the secretary of a local Cumann during his UCD student years. He was also acquainted with Cyprian Brady, a close aide of the Taoiseach who worked in Bertie Ahern's constituency office. Elaine's father, Martin, and her mother's partner, Tom, were both Fianna Fáilers.

A sister of former Minister for Justice, Nora Owen – and, coincidentally, a grandniece of Michael Collins – Mary Banotti had known the Moores for many years. In fact, both Kathy and Elaine had canvassed for Mary during her unsuccessful bid for the Irish presidency in 1997. Offering any assistance she could, Mary asked Kathy if she knew for sure that Elaine was not involved in the previous day's events in London. Kathy didn't blame Mary for asking such a question but assured her that there was "no way on earth" that her daughter could be engaged in terrorist activity. "She [Mary Banotti] had met Elaine but you couldn't say she really knew her – she knew me well," says Kathy. "You don't blame people for wanting to check everything out. I wouldn't put my neck on the line unless I was convinced. And I am eternally grateful to her for that."

Kathy never had a shred of doubt about Elaine's innocence. "People always say they know their children and I know that, deep down, you can never speak for anyone except yourself," she explains, "but I don't believe there has ever been a mother and daughter as close as we are. I always knew exactly who her friends were and exactly where she was going. She was never allowed out on street corners, only in friends' houses. Mainly they would always be in my house. We are best friends as well as mother and daughter. We would talk about everything and anything. She also had great interest in my work [at the women's refuge] and violence was something that she abhorred. She would be absolutely appalled at the things that men would do to women. I knew she wasn't capable of being involved in anything like that."

While she was happy to take Kathy's word, Mary Banotti phoned Gareth Peirce to seek further advice before getting involved in the campaign to free Elaine. The solicitor assured her that Elaine was "totally innocent". As a mother herself, the MEP empathised with Kathy's situation. "I suppose we all had children who might put someone up," Mary reflects, "and I think that was a resonance with a lot of people at the time." The fact that she is a grandniece of Michael Collins was "hugely significant", in Mary's view, as he was being referred to as a well-known Irish terrorist by the prosecution.

Mary Banotti was the first politician to publicly assert Elaine's innocence. On Saturday, 25 July she told *The Star* newspaper: "I know this woman is absolutely innocent. I feel totally confident that Elaine is innocent of the charges." She went on to describe Elaine as "a very warm, open person". When interviewed for this book, Mary wanted it made clear that she never went to the media with Elaine's story. She said her European Parliament office in Dublin was like a pressroom that summer, with journalists constantly looking for the Moore family's phone number. "Nobody ever got their phone number out of us," Mary says.

As the second bail hearing approached, Mary Banotti fully immersed herself in the campaign to have Elaine released. She was in daily contact with Kathy Moore and spoke regularly on the phone to Gareth Peirce. The politician's intervention was deeply appreciated by the Moore family, particularly when she offered to put up £20,000 of her own money towards Elaine's bail, which was expected to be substantial. She had also written a glowing character reference for Elaine, which would be presented to the magistrate for the bail hearing. On one occasion, however, the MEP's input proved counter-productive. Gareth Peirce flew to Dublin on Monday, 27 July for what Kathy expected would be a private meeting with the family. She was somewhat taken aback when Mary Banotti phoned to say she would be turning up. As Kathy and Tom were going through the case with Gareth in their living room, Mary arrived, accompanied by her daughter. According to Tom and Kathy's version of events, Mary then dropped a bombshell by innocently asking Gareth about strip-searches. Unfortunately, Mary couldn't have known that this was the one thing that Elaine had deliberately kept from Kathy, knowing how deeply it would upset her.

"It nearly killed me when I heard that, because it hadn't crossed my mind," admits Kathy today. "I'd heard about other Irish prisoners being strip-searched in Britain in the past. Elaine had obviously been trying to protect me by not telling me. It just wiped me out. I mean, it was bad enough just having to think of Elaine being there and locked up for as long as 19 hours a day, but to think about strip-searches was just too much. Elaine was a very modest girl. She wouldn't even strip off in front of me. Just to think of her going through that ordeal was more than I could cope with."

Gareth Peirce explained that Elaine had asked for a reduction in her legal visits because she couldn't face being strip-searched every time. Tom was furious that Kathy had to find out about the strip-searches in this way but didn't express his anger to Mary at the time. He remembers Kathy being inconsolable for three days after the meeting. It was as though she had just given up. Elaine was later horrified at the manner in which her mother had heard the news.

Mary Banotti, for her part, has absolutely no recollection of bringing up the issue of strip-searches that day. She insists that her only knowledge of Elaine being strip-searched would have been from what she had read in the newspapers. However, Elaine's prison ordeal had yet to emerge in the media at the time of the meeting in Kathy Moore's house. When it was put to her that she may have innocently asked Gareth Peirce a question about strip-searches, generally, Mary replied: "I can't even comment on that, simply because I don't know. I have no recollection of Kathy being appalled or anything. I went there; Gareth came from the airport; we were both in a hurry; I saw her [Elaine's] bedroom and spoke to Kathy and her partner . . . it was all very quick. I was there to meet Gareth, essentially . . . we can't have been there for more than 10 minutes."

Further high profile support for Elaine came from Peter Barry, the former Tánaiste and Minister for Foreign Affairs. When it emerged that Elaine's bail could be set as high as £200,000 sterling, Peter Barry publicly offered to put up £50,000. Quoted in *The Examiner* on Thursday, 30 July 1998, he felt Elaine's case was "a clear miscarriage of justice" and said he was willing to provide money and a character reference to help her. "I am convinced this girl is innocent," he said. "Every now and then the British judicial or security system seems to have a fit of amnesia and puts people like Elaine Moore and the Birmingham Six in prison without ever investigating whether there is any evidence against her [*sic*]. Even a cursory examination would show that this girl is innocent." Mr Barry declined to be interviewed for this book about his role in Elaine's case.

* * *

Left:
Martin Moore pictured with Elaine (three years old) and Robert (five years old) in Dublin, 1979.

Below:
Kathy Moore with Elaine in her bedroom in Coolock, Dublin.
"… I don't believe there has ever been a mother and daughter as close as we are … We are best friends as well as mother and daughter."

Above: The 'IRA Model' –
Elaine pictured for her
Assets modelling portfolio,
aged nineteen.
Left: Elaine's apartment on
Parkhill Road, London.
(© Nigel Barklie)

Above: Rory Hearty, Elaine's best friend and confidant, pictured with Elaine in a London pub.

Below: Settling in on Elaine's first night in the Irish Chaplaincy, Tollington Park, London.

Entering Belmarsh Magistrates' Court for a remand hearing, 27 August 1998. (© Nigel Barklie)

ove: Elaine is released from Holloway Prison, 29 August 1998.

elow: Elaine outside the retreat house on Reddington Road after her release
om Holloway.

Above: Elaine's twenty-second birthday in Rory Hearty's flat.

Below: Independence Day, 8 October 1998 – celebrating with friends in London.

*ove: Elaine's press conference, Dublin Airport, 10 October 1998. (© Collins
oto Agency)

*low: Radio and television presenter Pat Kenny with Elaine after Ireland's soccer
tch against Malta, 14 October 1998.

Elaine with her niece, Saoire, 2001.

Elaine on holiday in Crete with Paul, 2001.

Meanwhile, back in Woodhill prison, Elaine struggled to emotionally prepare herself for her second bail hearing. She awoke early on the morning of Thursday, 30 July with a nauseating sensation in the pit of her stomach. Despite being warned by her legal team to brace herself for another disappointment, Elaine clung desperately to the hope that the magistrate would grant bail this time round. A further refusal would result in her being subjected to four strip-searches that day. She feared that above anything else; even the soul wrenching disappointment of being denied bail would be easier to take.

Just after breakfast, two female guards entered Elaine's cell to perform the 'prison exiting' search. For the first time, this included examinations of her hair, mouth and ears. Even though there was only a slim chance of Elaine being released that day, she was instructed to gather her belongings, just in case. The prison had misplaced her sports bag. Elaine wondered what she would look like leaving court with her few belongings displayed for all to see through the transparent bag she had been given, with the words 'HMP WOODHILL' printed in bold letters on it.

A senior officer entered the cell and started to make idle chitchat with her, possibly in an attempt to assess her mental state. Elaine was having none of it and simply ignored her. The officer seemed unperturbed by Elaine's rudeness, commenting that, in all her years in the prison service, she had never seen a bed so neatly made. Elaine was a tidy person by nature and always kept her cell neat. But as soon as the officer uttered that comment, Elaine took a mental note to never make her bed so neatly again. Petty as it seemed, she didn't want the Woodhill staff to think she was settling in and conforming to prison life.

For some reason, Elaine got the feeling she was being

treated more harshly that day. It was as if the prison officers and police alike had been told to put the pressure on. Not only had she been subjected to a more thorough and probing body search, but even the handcuffs seemed to be fastened tighter, leaving prominent red marks around her wrists when eventually unlocked. This time, the handcuffs were not removed while Elaine travelled to court in the back of the police van, as had been the case for the previous bail hearing. The prison officers were more reluctant than usual to talk to her. Maybe someone had got his or her wrists slapped for being too friendly towards her. After all, the prison officers at Woodhill wouldn't necessarily have been used to guarding women, particularly one of 'High Risk' status. Some of them had previously chatted openly with Elaine and even tried to comfort her when she was feeling down.

The police van roared through the suburbs of London. Elaine looked out the window enviously as people walked freely down the streets, as though they didn't have a care in the world. She thought about how lazy she had been in the past, always using taxis and buses to get around. If she was ever released, she vowed to appreciate all aspects of life more fully.

Continuous changes in security procedures were having a profound psychological effect on Elaine. She was the first prisoner to enter the courtroom. Elaine noticed that three police officers had been placed in a triangular position to specifically guard her. When her three co-accused finally entered, she realised that they only had five officers in total assigned to them. This, she felt, would cast her in an unfavourable light in the eyes of the magistrate and the media by implying that she presented the greatest escape risk or – worse still – was potentially more dangerous than the others. The court was packed with journalists, which added to Elaine's sense of shame and embarrassment.

The prosecution's case against Elaine relied upon the implicit suggestion that if Anthony Hyland, the man allegedly found in possession of illegal items, had stayed in her flat, then she must have known about his intentions. Police had implied that Elaine's flat was, in effect, a 'safe house'; that she must have been aware of what had been left in the bag found in her room. However, Gareth Peirce insisted that police inquiries would have supported the following background:

- The defendant who had stayed at Elaine's flat [Hyland] had known her brother, though not well, at university in Ireland some years before. He had made contact with Elaine having obtained her telephone number via her brother;

- her brother and his girlfriend had been visiting Elaine in London at the time of the first of two visits by Hyland. They had stayed at her flat that first weekend. Also present on that occasion had been Elaine's former flat mate, Paul Walsh, and his girlfriend;

- on the occasion of the second overnight stay by Hyland, police surveillance would show that he had arrived at Elaine's flat clearly unannounced. He had been compelled to leave and wait until Elaine arrived home from work;

- surveillance would show that Hyland was in the flat when Elaine's landlord, his wife and her future lodger were also there;

- Elaine had left for the evening with a friend [Rory Hearty] to go to Oxford and did not return until the early hours of the following morning;

- police would also be able to confirm that on the night before the arrests, when Hyland had stayed at the flat, Elaine had been about to take on a second lodger, as Paul Walsh had since left. Consequently, there was an empty room available that night;

- observation would lastly confirm that Elaine had left early for work on the morning of the arrests. Hyland had been left in the flat on his own. Police evidence presented in court made mention of him going into a travel agent to arrange a flight back to Ireland for the next day.

The Crown Prosecution Service had very little new evidence against Elaine to introduce to the court. Once again, Magistrate Cooper seemed unimpressed with the strength of the case against her. He urged the prosecution to ensure that evidence be gathered in an expedient manner. Just as Cooper appeared to be toying with the notion of granting Elaine bail, he rejected her application and further remanded her in custody to Woodhill until 27 August. He said he was quite sure that Elaine Moore was "honourable, idealistic and altruistic" but could not grant bail at this time. Gareth recalls that the magistrate had given the distinct impression that he had been impressed by the strength of Elaine's bail application.

"He listened very carefully and appeared to be agreeing that the whole thing was ludicrous," she says. "I certainly recall him nodding; I think Elaine would too. When it came to the part about those pictures of Michael Collins on the walls representing paid-up membership of a paramilitary organisation, he seemed to actually agree [with us]. He seemed to be laughing at the prosecution."

Back in the dungeon-type cell below the courtroom, Elaine was raging. The length of the remand period was outrageous – four more weeks of soul-destroying isolation. She was disgusted that Cooper had, in her opinion, lacked the conviction to grant her bail even though he appeared to agree that the case against her was weak. She requested that she be allowed to remain in her suit for the return journey to prison; after all, she was supposedly on remand. One prison officer said she wasn't sure if this would be permitted; another emphatically rejected her request. Elaine threw another uncharacteristic temper tantrum. "Why not?" she screamed. "Whatever happened to innocent until proven guilty? I'm dressed up like a convict, forced to wear prison-issued clothes, handcuffed like an animal and surrounded by armed guards. It's your man Cooper who needs locking up, not me."

On the journey back to prison, Elaine stubbornly refused to make eye contact with any of the police officers guarding her. She resented the very sight of their uniforms, which had become a symbol of their power over her. She may have known nothing about them personally, but at that point in time held each and every one of them in utter contempt.

Back at Woodhill, Elaine continued to rant and rave as the prison officers carried out their final strip-search of the day. Lying in bed later that night, she tried to draw encouragement from her earlier consultation with Gareth, who felt there had been positive elements to the court hearing.

The fact that two bail applications had been rejected by the magistrates' court now paved the way for a hearing at the Old Bailey, possibly the next day. Gareth had always contended that this would be their route to success. "The crown court is the trial court," she explains. "The Old Bailey is like the central criminal court. If there is a case to go to trial, it gets committed up from the magistrates' court to the crown court. You have a right to appeal to the crown court if you are refused by the magistrate."

But even Gareth's optimism could not lift Elaine's spirits that night. The fact that she had been unable to comfort her mother on the first anniversary of her Aunt Evelyn's death caused her great upset. Furthermore, her confidence in British justice had been shattered by her two failed bail applications. She was sick of being a handcuffed prisoner, caged in the back of a police van. It was time to take control. She would do so by embarking on a hunger strike.

Elaine had finally cracked.

Chapter Eleven

THE GATES OPEN

Back in Dublin, Elaine's family were getting desperate. Frustratingly, Kathy was unable to travel to London for the Old Bailey hearing on Friday, 31 July. She needed to stay at home in case Elaine's latest bail application in the crown court was successful. Even if granted, bail was expected to be substantial – at least (Stg)£200,000 – and Kathy would have to raise the money in Ireland and arrange for its transfer to Britain. Up until now, there had been no point even attempting to visit her daughter in prison. Elaine had made it clear that she didn't want her mother to see her in Woodhill as only a 'closed visit' would be granted. On top of that, Elaine wanted to minimise the number of strip-searches she was being subjected to by restricting visits.

Speaking to *The Examiner*, Kathy called for the Irish Prime Minister, Taoiseach Bertie Ahern, to urgently intervene in Elaine's case. She said the conditions under which her daughter was being held were appalling. Other women held as 'Category A' prisoners had suffered nervous breakdowns, Kathy claimed, a fact that was later supported by Gareth. A spokesperson for the Department of Foreign Affairs said they were doing everything they could and a representative from the Irish Embassy in London would be attending the latest bail hearing in the Old Bailey. "I feel so helpless, so powerless," Kathy told the newspaper.

"All parents want to do everything they can for their children, and I can't even visit her." In a further article in *The Examiner* that morning, Pat Brosan wrote: 'The British legal system is heading down the road to another gross miscarriage of justice and in the most spurious of circumstances.'

The hundreds of letters of support Elaine received from complete strangers while in Woodhill had been a constant source of encouragement. Public interest in her case back in Ireland was approaching fever pitch as a result of blanket media coverage. Kathy Moore's emotional interview with Pat Kenny, in particular, seemed to have struck a national chord. As addresses were often omitted from the letters and Elaine had limited resources, it was not always possible for her to reply to everyone. But she cherished each and every letter sent to her and took refuge in their warm sentiments. Every correspondence helped restore Elaine's belief in kindness and basic humanity.

She was sent a hand-written, scroll-like note from a large group calling itself the 'Ring of Kerry Michael Collins Adherents'. Eoin Ryan, a Fianna Fáil TD, wrote to Elaine in Woodhill, offering his sympathy and help. He said he would ask the Minister for Foreign Affairs to look into her case and raise it with the British Government. One separated mother-of-five had been moved to write to Elaine after hearing Kathy on Pat Kenny's radio show. 'Firstly, let me say that there are a lot of people, including myself, who believe in your innocence,' she wrote. 'You have the best defender in Gareth Peirce. You will come out of this and your innocence will be proved. Always have faith in yourself and you will have the strength to cope. Always remember that your family and friends will leave nothing unturned to bring you home. The Government in this country, I am sure, will also do their best to clear up this terrible mess. They have a duty to their citizens.'

Young Fine Gael set up a special email address for its

members to send messages of support to Elaine. The following email illustrates the anti-British sentiment often provoked by Elaine's arrest – even within the usually conservative ranks of Fine Gael supporters: 'Why not extend the peace process to what the British call "the mainland"? The most draconian laws in Britain are solely for the Irish PTA (Prevention of Terrorism Act). It cannot be considered the act of a friendly country [when] our citizens are harassed, arrested and detained, without charge, by British police – supported by British legislators of all parties – purely because they are Irish. It is indicative of the British attitude that even a former Tánaiste [Peter Barry], a leading figure in trying to bring peace to these islands, is treated as just another Paddy. It's time that we ask the British the question – is the war over.'

However, in Woodhill that morning, Elaine was feeling drained after another sleepless night. The rosary beads that Fr O'Connell had given to her had helped a little. He had joked that saying a few decades of the rosary was a sure-fire way of nodding off. Elaine was determined to commence her hunger strike and refused to eat any breakfast. She probably wouldn't have been able to hold down food anyway as she felt extremely nauseous. The drama of the previous day's court hearing had left her in a highly vulnerable state.

Although she didn't have to personally attend court that day, Elaine was starting to get anxious about the Old Bailey hearing. Sometimes not knowing what's going on can be more terrifying. Gareth had informed Elaine that Mary Banotti was travelling to London to personally offer a character reference to the court on her behalf. Mary would be appearing in the capacity of family friend and as a member of the European Parliament. Gareth felt that the appearance in court of a prominent Irish politician would prove most helpful. The Fine Gael politician, among others, had submitted a written reference that had been presented to Belmarsh Magistrates' Court at the previous day's bail hearing. It read:

> 'I wish to state that I have known Elaine Moore and her family for many years. I know her family to be warm and hospitable and of high personal calibre. Her mother, Ms Kathy Moore, was a candidate for the Fine Gael Party in the local elections and I personally canvassed for her, as she and Elaine have done for me, for many years in every election. Elaine is a highly intelligent, highly motivated young woman. For the record, I am also aware of her great historical interest in Michael Collins, who was my great-uncle. I feel totally confident that Elaine Moore is innocent of the charges and that her involvement was random and innocent. I am also confident that, if granted bail, she would respect the direction of the court.'

Gareth had received numerous character references that painted a clear picture of Elaine's hospitable nature. One friend of her brother's wrote:

> 'Having stayed at Robert's house, and he having stayed in mine, it comes as no surprise to me that his sister would let even a casual acquaintance of hers stay at her house. Indeed, Robert had invited me to stay at Elaine's when I am scheduled to go to London later in the year, despite the fact that I have only met

Elaine on a handful of occasions. I know the
judge will grasp the Irish tradition of hospitality
and having an open door. This is even more
true [of] people in college who have little
money for accommodation, and the close-knit
community of Irish abroad.'

Elaine was glad that her mother would not be in London
for the hearing. She didn't savour the thoughts of Kathy
having to endure the ordeal of court or being paraded in
front of the media in an emotional state. She was initially
concerned to learn that her bail application would not be
made by Gareth this time, but by the highly respected
QC (Queen's Counsel), Michael Mansfield. Her fears were
based on her lack of knowledge of the British judicial
system. Elaine was also unaware of Mr Mansfield's
formidable track record as a legal civil rights activist. Her
concerns were to be unfounded. The renowned barrister
had been fully briefed on her case by Gareth and would
represent Elaine that day with the same degree of
professionalism, passion and determination. At the hearing,
which was held in chambers, Mary Banotti made an
impassioned plea on Elaine's behalf to the Recorder of
London, Judge Michael Hyam.

As she waited for news back in Woodhill, Elaine
carefully studied the facial expressions of the prison
officers, hoping to extract clues about the outcome of the
court hearing. They certainly weren't going to volunteer
information and she was too proud to ask them anything.
While Elaine sat nervously watching television, word finally
came through that she was to phone Gareth's office. She
returned to her cell, trying desperately to compose herself
for the moment she had been trying to block out of her
head all morning. For Elaine, there was a certain finality

about this phone call: either she had been granted bail or would be staying at Woodhill for another four weeks. They were the only two possible options. The hunger strike she had just started could end up lasting a lot longer than one day. Elaine tried to act as nonchalantly as possible as she left her cell and made her way to the phone. She promised herself that she would do her utmost to conceal her disappointment in front of the prison staff if the decision had gone against her and that she would carry on her hunger strike.

The prison guards gathered around a long table to her left as Elaine approached the telephone. As she lifted the receiver, one officer offered her some words of encouragement, while others smiled supportively. She dialled the number and was put through to Gareth's office immediately.

"Hello Gareth, it's Elaine," she said, only to be greeted by an unfamiliar voice, which totally confused her. She was still unsure what exactly was going on when the voice exclaimed: "Congratulations Elaine . . . Mary Banotti here."

She wondered why the MEP was congratulating her. Mary continued speaking to her as if Elaine already knew what had happened. Still reluctant to let down her guard, Elaine remained sceptical until she heard the familiar, warm voice of Gareth, who informed her that bail had been granted. Oblivious to the presence of the prison staff who surrounded her, Elaine let out a shriek of pure, unadulterated joy. "I don't believe it – thank you all so much! When do I get out?"

But things weren't as simple as that, as Gareth began an in-depth explanation of what had transpired in court that morning. At the previous two hearings at Belmarsh Magistrates' Court, the only objection to bail raised by the prosecution was that Elaine might abscond – not that she would commit further offences. Bail had been set at (Stg) £190,000 to provide a guarantee against any possible attempt by Elaine to evade the judicial process. Bail money had come from Peter Barry (£50,000), Mary Banotti (£20,000) and through Elaine's family and friends, who raised a further £50,000. In addition, three sureties living in London agreed to enter into a bail commitment of £40,000, £20,000 and £10,000 respectively to ensure Elaine's future attendance in court. She would not be free to return home to Ireland. A further condition of bail was that she reside at an address provided by the Irish Chaplaincy in London until her remand hearing on 27 August. Explaining his decision to grant bail, the judge had described Elaine as "a young woman of high standing". He also commented that the case against her did not seem particularly strong.

Speaking to reporters outside the Old Bailey, Gareth Peirce said: "We were sure that with all the facts – or lack of facts – before him, that any judge would grant bail, so in a sense we were predicting it. But on a charge like this there's always a doubt as to whether anyone who deserves bail will necessarily get it."

With great sensitivity, Gareth informed Elaine that she would most probably remain in prison until all the bail money had been lodged into a special account that was being set up. However, there was a hitch. It was a Bank Holiday weekend in Ireland. This meant it would not be possibly to arrange for the transfer of the money from Dublin until at least Tuesday. Surprisingly, Elaine took the news well and didn't seem too fazed by the prospect of a few more days in prison. Gareth revealed that they had been waiting for Elaine's phone call for quite some time. Immediately after bail was granted,

Gareth had contacted Woodhill with a message for Elaine to phone her office. It was at least two hours before prison staff conveyed this information to her. Also taking part in the three-way phone conversation with Elaine from Gareth's office was Rory Hearty. Still reeling from the news, Elaine was feeling dazed and confused and initially didn't recognise her friend's voice. Rory would later note in a letter to Elaine that she sounded sceptical and suspicious when he spoke to her that day. Ending the call, Gareth urged Elaine to get in touch with her mum in Dublin.

Kathy was ready to collapse from exhaustion but had somehow found the energy to see her through the previous few days – she was always more focused during a crisis. Due to the frenetic activity in the Moore household, Elaine was unable to get through to her mother on the phone, which had been tied up all day by journalists, friends, relatives and various well-wishers. Grateful as she was for the support, Kathy asked most callers to free up the line as she was expecting her daughter to phone. After dialling unsuccessfully for around half an hour, Elaine was ecstatic when she finally heard her mother's voice. Celebrations were already underway in Dublin as news of Elaine's impending release had been confirmed a few hours earlier. In a bizarre sequence of events that began at 8.15 a.m. that morning, Kathy claims she unofficially received information from an official source that Elaine was almost certain to get bail. This was despite the fact that the Old Bailey application had yet to be heard. Although encouraged by the political tip-off, Kathy refused to get excited until she heard the news directly from Gareth Peirce. The incident does suggest, however, that clandestine talks relating to Elaine's case had taken place between Irish and UK government officials.

Over the phone, Elaine could tell there was a full house back in Dublin. Members of her family and friends had been waiting for some news with her mum. She listened to the excited voices buzzing in the background. Mother and daughter could hardly contain themselves as they expressed their love for each other. Elaine was on a pure high after putting down the phone and even spoke to the prison officers who had been sympathetic to her earlier. They genuinely seemed pleased for her. Compared to her depression the night before and the long, anxious day, Elaine now felt re-energised as if she had suddenly rediscovered the joys of life. She had started her hunger strike that day, firmly committed to sticking to it for as long as it seemed necessary, but the court's decision meant that she would soon have control of her own life back for good. Elaine wanted to run outside and scream with delight, but her enthusiasm was tempered by her restricted environment. In her diary entry that night, she wrote:

> Words cannot express how I'm feeling, having been granted my right to bail. Freedom, though limited, is just around the corner. Mum was overjoyed; Gareth (love her) is so happy; everyone is celebrating – except me. It kind of feels like having the most important occasion in your life celebrated without you.

In light of the serious charges against her, Gareth Peirce doesn't believe they had any great difficulty in securing bail for Elaine. "It certainly appeared difficult to Elaine, but in terms of the allegation – conspiracy to cause explosion – it is very rare to get bail on a charge like that, although some people have in the past."

* * *

Back in Ireland, there was a broad welcome for Elaine's bail. The Taoiseach, Bertie Ahern, said the Government was pleased that the bail application was successful. 'We have been monitoring the case of Elaine Moore and the others that were arrested since it happened through the London Embassy,' he told RTÉ. 'We have had close contact within the prison since it happened and with their legal advisors. I've had a number of conversations as well with the Attorney General on this particular matter . . . but we were awaiting the outcome of today's case and while, naturally, I can't comment on a case that is still before a British court, we are pleased with the result of today.'

Peter Barry, who had pledged £50,000 towards the bail, told *The Irish Times* he would have preferred if Elaine had been released altogether. "The idea of a young girl like that in prison, in isolation, with those charges laid against her – there is no case against her," he said. "I just thought it was so ludicrous when I read the initial reports of her case."

Elaine's case was also causing growing concern in Westminster. Peter Temple-Morris, the Labour MP, declared: "She deserves to be out on bail . . . I think that putting her in prison, in custody, at this time was an unnecessary suffering."

Most Irish newspapers had been quick to jump on the miscarriage of justice bandwagon that followed the bail hearings. Elaine Moore was no longer just a news story. Court details of her appalling treatment in Woodhill, along with the flimsy nature of the Crown Prosecutor's evidence against her, had convinced most journalists of her innocence. In the eyes of the media, at least, Elaine had been transformed from suspected terrorist to wrongly accused woman.

'Everyone will share the unrestrained joy of Elaine Moore's family over the decision to grant the twenty-one-year-old Dublin girl bail and release her from prison,' read an editorial in *The Examiner* on Saturday, 1 August. '. . . the sheer enormity of the bail sum, set at almost £200,000 by an Old Bailey judge, is an indication of the gravity of the terrorism case in which she has, unwittingly, become ensnared . . . Based on the flimsy evidence put forward so far by the police, the public is convinced that Elaine Moore is totally innocent of charges connecting her with an alleged terrorist bombing plot. Tragically, even if she survives this regrettable incident, it will change her life forever.'

On the same day, the *Irish Independent* declared: 'Elaine Moore is guilty . . . guilty of being full of the natural Irish generosity which ensures that our young emigrants abroad look after each other. Observing that tradition of unquestioning hospitality has cost her dear. It has put her through three weeks of hell, an experience that must make every Irish person who travels to London regularly shudder with apprehension.'

Best-selling author Cathy Kelly expressed similar sentiments in her *Sunday World* column on 2 August 1998. 'Her naivety put her in the wrong place at the wrong time and she has been paying a terrible price for it . . . when we go abroad, the legendary friendliness of the Irish is magnified. Maybe it's missing home or longing for the company of people with the same sense of humour, but one Irish accent in a sea of Estuary English pulls the heartstrings faster than a blast of 'Riverdance'. That proved to be lethal for Coolock girl Elaine. Innocents abroad like her are easy prey for cynical, manipulative people.'

A *Sunday World* editorial comment called for the immediate release, without charge, of Elaine Moore.

'Many innocent people, with no link whatever to the Troubles in the North, have been killed in the most cruel, cynical manner. The victims have included children. So it comes as no surprise that the British authorities are sometimes paranoid when it comes to dealing with the Irish people suspected of bomb offences. But in their understandable zeal to catch the fascist idiots who want to bomb Britain, the UK authorities will also have to distinguish between the guilty and the innocent. We have no doubt at all about the innocence of Elaine Moore, the young Dublin woman pulled in when a number of bomb suspects were arrested recently.'

Elaine received a boost from an unlikely source that weekend in the form of a statement from the 'Real' IRA, the dissident group linked to the foiled bombing attack on London. Sources within the paramilitary organisation told the *Ireland on Sunday* newspaper that Elaine Moore was not on 'active service' and was innocent of the charges levelled against her. 'Guerrillas move with the innocent,' one source was quoted as saying. 'The (Real) IRA does not send active service units over to stay with known republicans. This is a war situation and innocent people get caught up in it.' Another source told the newspaper: 'Moore is not a volunteer with Oghlaigh na hÉireann. She is not one of ours.' In the same article, a source in the Provisional IRA confirmed that Moore was 'definitely not a member'. These statements sparked further calls for charges to be dropped against Elaine.

Prior to her successful bail application, the *Sunday Independent* warned that Elaine faced 'an incredibly tough fight' to clear her name and could face a possible 20-year jail sentence. This was despite the fact that senior anti-

terrorist gardaí had informed Scotland Yard that they
had never heard of her until the day before her arrest. A
highly placed garda source told the newspaper: 'It was a
joint operation between the British and us which undoubtedly prevented a bombing tragedy in the centre of
London. But the British were responsible for implementing
the operational side of it. We provided the intelligence
and she [Elaine] didn't come anywhere into it until the
day before her arrest when [Anthony] Hyland arrived
over at the flat. It will be an incredibly tough fight for
her and it is going to be very difficult for her to clear her
name.'

This same article, written by crime correspondent Liz
Allen, also contained a serious inaccuracy. The senior
garda source was quoted as saying: 'The attitude of the
British is that the explosives were found in her flat. She
had moved the bag, so her fingerprints are going to be all
over it anyway.' Elaine had always insisted that at no
stage did she touch Anthony Hyland's rucksack, in which
Semtex had allegedly been found by police. This was the
beginning of a volatile relationship between Elaine and
the *Sunday Independent*. An article by the same journalist
a week later would have a profound psychological effect
on Elaine and lead to her taking a libel action against the
newspaper.

The publicity surrounding the case led to an outpouring
of public sympathy for Elaine. On the rare occasion that
she felt up to leaving the house, Kathy Moore was
constantly approached by well-wishers offering their
support and, in some cases, asking if they could start a
petition for Elaine. Although bail was expected to be
high, Kathy nearly fainted when informed by Gareth on
the phone that it had been set at (Stg)£190,000. Tom
assured her that raising the money would be no problem

and he went into the city to meet Elaine's brother and father. Within an hour they had raised more money than they needed. "The phone never stopped ringing with friends, even people you wouldn't even think of, offering money," says Kathy. "In the end, we could have raised the bail money five times over if we had needed to. It was like that all weekend – people were absolutely amazing."

Paddy Hill, one of the Birmingham Six, later generously offered to act as a surety for Elaine, by that stage however, other arrangements had been put in place.

* * *

The fact that Elaine's release on bail was now just a formality added to her anguish that weekend. She felt extremely down on the morning of Saturday, 1 August after yet another night of disturbed sleep. Usually on a Saturday, her 'out of cell' period was extended by an hour and a half. That day, however, she found herself locked in her cell during breakfast. When Elaine questioned prison staff about this, she was told that there weren't enough officers on duty to guard her. This struck her as ridiculous: why did she need up to five or six guards assigned to her when she had been granted bail? Even though she was expected to be released the following Tuesday, Elaine found herself spending even more hours than usual, 21 in total, locked up in her cell. It seemed ludicrous to her.

Out of sheer frustration, Elaine lashed out at the carefully stocked books on her shelf, scattering them all over the cell. She badly needed a reassuring talk with the people who mattered most to her. It would be Monday before she could speak to Gareth again. Time seemed to drag by more slowly than ever. Sunday was the same:

early lock up, monotony, loneliness and cold food. Maybe her mind was playing tricks on her, but Elaine got the distinct impression that the prison officers were now deliberately trying to wind her up. There was no way in the world that she would be able to survive for much longer in prison.

Even before Elaine was granted bail, the prison authorities were coming under increasing pressure to move her from Woodhill. Elaine's incarceration with all male prisoners at Woodhill had been a cause of major concern to British Irish Rights Watch, who brought the matter to the attention of the European Committee for the Prevention of Torture. Jane Winter, the organisation's director, stated in her 1998 report: 'We understand that there are serious doubts about the extent of her involvement in the alleged crime, but whether she is guilty or not, there can never be any excuse for holding women in male prisons.' Apparently the authorities contended that plans had been hatched for the wing to be populated by women in the near future. It was around this time that Gareth became aware of a rumour through the legal grapevine that consideration was been given to the transfer of the serial killer, Rosemary West, to the wing.

Over the years, Gareth Peirce had observed the psychological and physical damage caused to 'Category A' prisoners placed in solitary confinement. Some of her former clients had been held in similar conditions. In one particular case, psychiatric and psychological reports showed that a woman prisoner went from having a high IQ to being borderline sub-normal. The experience of being imprisoned in isolation was considered to be a major factor in her decline. Her condition dramatically improved when she was eventually moved to another prison and allowed to mix with convicted offenders. Due to her fear of the unknown, Elaine had instructed her solicitor not to make representations to have her moved to Holloway women's prison. In Gareth's view, there was a serious risk that Elaine would suffer irreparable long-term damage to her mental and physical health if she remained in isolation at Woodhill. She had lost an alarming amount of weight and showed obvious signs of sleep deprivation. There was no doubt in her mind that had Elaine continued to be detained in these conditions up to her trial, she would not be in an appropriate state to do justice to her defence. According to Gareth, even the anxiety caused by being arrested and charged can have a permanent effect on a defendant.

"Elaine was obviously still the same intelligent, strong, young woman – one could see that," says Gareth. "But so had the other 'Category A' women I had seen and prison had a bad effect on them. I certainly didn't want that to happen to Elaine – I was not going to let that happen. The best way of avoiding it was to get her bail."

Gareth's fears were further compounded on Monday, 3 August when Elaine told her she was "cracking up". The brutal regime at Woodhill now seemed more harsh than usual. Gareth explained that although bail had been granted, Elaine would continue to be treated as a prisoner until the Woodhill authorities had received the relevant documentation. Elaine understood what Gareth was saying, but still found it difficult to accept. But at least she only had one day left.

Gareth assured her that every effort was being made to ensure her release as soon as possible. Once the bail money had been transferred from a bank in Dublin, release papers would be sent via fax or courier to the prison and Elaine would be released. Gareth urged her to be patient and to remain calm.

After the phone conversation with Gareth, Elaine convinced herself that there was light at the end of the tunnel and spent the rest of the day thinking about being reunited with her family and friends. She wondered what life would be like as a remand prisoner out on bail. Although aware that she would not be able to return to her flat, due to the legalised vandalism carried out on it by forensic police officers, Elaine was hopeful of being able to stay at Rory's house. She was bitterly disappointed when Gareth outlined the conditions of her bail which required Elaine to reside with an Irish religious community in London. But at least she would be out of prison; free to spend time with the person she cherished most: her mother. Elaine couldn't wait to hug her.

Elaine felt proud of herself when Tuesday morning finally arrived. Somehow, she had survived Woodhill. With a slight spring in her step, she left the cell and went to take a bath. It was important that she looked good today. During her time at Woodhill, the only request she had made was for a tweezers. It took two weeks for this request to be denied — it apparently constituted a safety hazard. Elaine was surprised that the razor she had been issued with was deemed safer. Feeling self-conscious in the bathroom, she went back to her cell, but neglected to return the razor. Once inside, she attempted to re-shape her eyebrows with the razor. The results were pretty impressive, considering. She later approached the officer in the control room who had given her the razor some 30 minutes earlier, loudly announcing that he had forgotten to retrieve it from her. Much to Elaine's delight, he seemed noticeably flustered — his neglect could have caused a serious breach of security. A prisoner with a razor in a cell had the ability to inflict serious injury on themselves or others. "So much for procedures, eh?" Elaine said mockingly as she returned to her cell, with a smile on her face.

Later, as she sat watching TV, Elaine heard the words she had been waiting for all morning. "Time to pack your bags, darlin'," said an officer with a gruff, northern accent. "Thank God for that!" Elaine exclaimed. She went immediately to her cell and started packing. Without supervision, Elaine put on the cream suit she had worn during her bail hearings, along with a pair of high-heeled sandals. For the first time in almost a month, she began to feel like something resembling her old self. She rejoiced at the thoughts of life without strip-searches.

Elaine's good mood seemed to have rubbed off on the prison officers, who were noticeably more cheerful than usual. She was informed that the prison had been notified of her impending release. As she stood in 'E Wing' with her belongings, Elaine was pleased to see Fr O'Connell approach. The priest was more than aware of the effect that prison life was having on her and was delighted to learn of her successful bail application. He told her that the prison was buzzing as word of her release reached the other inmates. Elaine was escorted to the reception area where – to her absolute horror – she was informed of the necessity of an exit strip-search. "It really took the wind out of my sails," she remembers. "There I was, just about to be released, yet forced to endure such a completely unwarranted intrusion." The look of hope had been drained from her face.

After the search, Elaine's belongings were scanned in the X-ray machine and she was led to the reception desk to finalise paperwork and answer some routine questions. It was during the exiting procedures that Elaine first realised that something was not quite right. She was concerned to learn that a fax to confirm her release had not yet been received by the prison. A decision was shortly taken to return Elaine to 'E Wing' where she would have to await further news: after all, she was still technically a prisoner. Frantically, she attempted to speak to Gareth on the phone, but only managed to get through to her secretary, Tracy. Elaine asked her what the hold up was. Tracy explained that the necessary documentation had not yet been processed. Apparently, an administrative delay had resulted in the bail money not being transferred in time from a bank in Dublin to an account in London. Gareth's secretary could not understand how the authorities at Woodhill had presided over such a farcical situation. Why had they prematurely processed her release in advance of receiving the relevant documentation? Elaine could only conclude that the powers-that-be were playing mind games with her.

Back in 'E Wing', some of the prison officers apologised to Elaine for the confusion. They had opened a cell for her, close to the exit, where she could sit while she waited for the necessary documentation to arrive. They were optimistic that the matter would be sorted out in no time, but Elaine sensed that time was running out. The officers were forced to lock her up when they were suddenly assigned to other duties. Having come so close to tasting freedom, she now found herself alone again in a bare cell. She knew she had been a victim of 'Murphy's Law' – anything that could possibly go wrong, did go wrong. She paced the cell repeatedly, losing hope with each passing minute. When the officers returned they still had no positive news for her. She resigned herself to another night in prison.

As the evening arrived, Elaine was informed that time had run out – the situation could not be resolved until the following day. "Why the hell was I paraded to reception?" she screamed furiously. She was returned to the cell she had been kept locked up in for the previous three weeks. It felt like Groundhog Day. Elaine had been tantalisingly close to freedom, only to have it ruthlessly snatched from her. "It was dangled in my face and taken from me in the cruellest, most sinister manner," she feels today.

Overcome with rage, Elaine hurled her bag of belongings against the cell wall. Because she had been scheduled to leave prison, no officers had been assigned to guard her. This resulted in Elaine having to spend the remainder of the day in her cell. It was the worst possible punishment imaginable. She was convinced that somebody had orchestrated the entire fiasco to push her over the edge. She couldn't accept that anyone could be so incompetent. It was not the extra day in prison that hurt Elaine most – it was the shattered expectation. "There was no need for drama. Had the day merely elapsed as Gareth had pointed out that it might, I would have been fine. It was the unnecessary search conducted on the promise of freedom that really got to me. To top things off I was returned to a bare cell and locked up for the remainder of the day. It was like the induction into prison all over again."

Meanwhile, Kathy and Tom had arrived in London. They spent most of the Tuesday with Rory Hearty sitting in the beer garden of a pub awaiting confirmation of Elaine's release. "All I remember is wanting to be there for her as soon as she walked through those gates," says Kathy. "We waited and waited for news all day. Then Gareth called to say that the money had not arrived in the special account set up for the bail. She said Elaine would have to spend another night in prison until it was sorted out. I didn't realise at the time that Elaine had been waiting to be released in the prison's reception area and then was told to go back to her cell. It was awful."

It was the longest night of Elaine's life as she lay awake attempting to make sense of the day's events. As usual, the other prisoners loudly discussed her, declaring that she must be innocent because she got bail on terrorist charges, but they did not call up as they thought she had already been released.

The next morning she was told she would have to eat breakfast in her cell. A female officer explained in a sarcastic tone that because staff numbers were down, Elaine would have to remain in her cell. At least five officers were required to be on duty in the wing before she could be allowed out. Later, when the door was eventually unlocked, Elaine was still fuming and blanked the officers as she walked past them. One guard commented that her sandals posed a safety hazard – Elaine told her to "go to hell".

Sitting in the TV room, Elaine stared blankly at the screen, unable to get excited about her imminent release. She had created a barrier in her mind; she expected nothing. A female officer, who Elaine found incredibly annoying, entered the room.

"I have good news and bad news for ya," she said light-heartedly.

Elaine glared at her, willing the ground to open up and swallow the officer. "Just tell me," she snapped.

"Well," she replied, "the bad news is that I'm walking you out; the good news is that you're free to go."

Elaine displayed no emotion. She was brought down to a room near the reception area and subjected to one more strip-search. "Haven't you bastards put me through enough?" she sighed wearily. This time, all the documents appeared to have arrived in time for the exit procedure.

Elaine was desperate for a cigarette but was too stubborn to ask the prison officers.

Finally, she was free to go. Elaine's release had been officially granted. A prison warden offered to carry her belongings as far as the gate for her. But even her walk towards freedom was marred by the wolf-whistles and sexist remarks of hundreds of male prisoners, who heckled Elaine from the exercise yard. A male officer approached her just before she reached the large steel gate. He informed her that there was a slight hitch – there was no one there to collect her.

"I'll wait outside," Elaine told him.

"That's up to you," the officer replied, "but as soon as that gate goes back, you will be mobbed by dozens of photographers and journalists. As soon as that gate opens you will be released and it will be closed behind you. To be honest, those reporters can be like animals. They'll surround you and even if you refuse to comment, they'll antagonise you until you are forced to say something you might regret. But you can leave if you want – it's up to you."

Gareth had warned Elaine about the possibility of a strong media presence outside Woodhill. In fact, she had encouraged her to say a few words to journalists as a way of expressing her gratitude for all the support she had received back home in Ireland. But Elaine was a shy person under normal circumstances and couldn't face doing media interviews so soon. She felt emotionless. A media circus was the last thing she needed, particularly the mob-scene scenario that had been painted for her.

The prison officer told Elaine they had had difficulty getting in touch with her mother. She had recently been contacted and was now on her way to Woodhill, although she was still some distance away. Elaine couldn't believe that her mum wasn't waiting outside. She asked the officer if she could stay where she was until Kathy arrived. This could not be permitted for security reasons. Elaine had two stark choices: go outside and be mobbed by the assembled media; or return to the reception area to wait for her mother to arrive. Reluctantly, she chose the latter option. She stood in stunned silence unable to believe that her release had been further delayed.

Elaine returned to the reception area, avoiding eye contact with any of the officers and ignoring the taunts of the prisoners in the exercise yard. After about 20 minutes word reached her that her mother had arrived. Elaine stood up and left without uttering a word. As the electronic gate opened slowly, Elaine braced herself for the media onslaught. But there was no aggressive mob awaiting her outside. There was a strong posse of journalists and photographers all right, but they were waiting patiently, some distance away from the gate. 'The bastard!' she thought, suspecting that the prison officer had intentionally misled her. There had been no reason why she couldn't have waited outside. She had always imagined that her release from prison would be a time of great joy and excitement. But twice it had turned out to be a depressing, anti-climatic experience.

It was with intense relief that Elaine walked through the gates and caught sight of her mum, who had come to take her away from the madness of HMP Woodhill.

Chapter Twelve

A STRANGE KIND OF FREEDOM

Kathy was bursting with happiness as she ran towards her daughter. She vividly recalls seeing Elaine walking out through the prison gate. "It was an unbelievable feeling," she says. "I was just totally overwhelmed – it was too good to be true." While exclaiming how beautiful Elaine looked, Kathy was taken aback by her daughter's fragile appearance. She had lost a worrying amount of weight, was pale and had dark circles under her eyes. As they embraced each other, Elaine was enveloped by the warmth that only a mother can provide. Turning to Rory, she was surprised to notice a lone tear trickle down his face. The enthusiasm of his hug almost crushed her delicate body. Tom also seemed on the verge of tears. He, too, was immediately concerned by her dramatic weight loss. At that very moment, Tom was stung on the nose by a bee, lending a surreal, albeit comic, feel to the moment. They all laughed at the ironic timing of the bee's attack. One disaster after another seemed to befall anyone associated with Elaine in those days.

Even though Elaine was in no frame of mind to talk to the media, Gareth felt it would be helpful if Kathy said a few words to the awaiting journalists and camera crews gathered outside. After all, media coverage of Elaine's case – particularly in Ireland – had been overwhelmingly positive. Earlier, Kathy had approached the reporters –

who had been waiting outside the prison for two days at that stage – and thanked them for all their support. "We are delighted that this part of the ordeal is over," she told them. "I will never be able to thank you, the media, enough and all the supporters back home in Ireland for the support that they have given us throughout this time." When asked about a comment attributed to a garda source that Elaine would face a tough battle to clear her name and could spend 20 years in prison if convicted, Kathy responded: "I am 100 per cent certain that Elaine will clear her name. I know about the circumstances surrounding her arrest. We are in no doubt the court will see fit to free her. We are certainly hoping the charges will be dropped before it comes to trial. We just have to keep our fingers crossed." Kathy was inundated with requests for a photograph of herself and Elaine leaving the prison. She reminded them that her daughter had been through a harrowing experience and was feeling very fragile – but she would ask Elaine for them anyway.

After the emotional reunion, Kathy broached the subject of the photograph request with Elaine. She wouldn't have to give any interviews, she stressed. The media just wanted her to walk towards them so they could get some pictures. After Kathy explained how positive the newspaper coverage had been back in Ireland, Elaine was eventually persuaded to accede to the request. True to their word, the media kept their distance from Elaine as she walked away from the prison entrance with her mother; Rory and Tom stayed in the background.

"It's great to see you, Elaine," one reporter shouted. "Give us a wave for the camera," said another. Elaine just smiled and mouthed the words "thank you" at the sea of clicking cameras. As a result of a newspaper article published after the successful bail hearing, Elaine's address at the chaplaincy had been revealed. Kathy pleaded with the journalists not to follow them there, as they needed some privacy. They agreed to respect her wishes. Despite the notorious reputation of the press, Elaine and Kathy both agree that the media behaved impeccably towards them that day.

"They were anything but intrusive," Elaine says. "I really admired and appreciated the way they handled the situation."

Leaving the prison grounds, Elaine noticed the battered old car that Rory was driving and playfully teased him about it. "Where on earth did you get this thing, Hearty?" she mocked. The police had destroyed Rory's car, so Gareth Peirce had lent him her old Honda for the day. Elaine stopped slagging the car as soon as she heard it was Gareth's. She felt honoured that the solicitor had given them the car to pick her up from prison. Was there anything that this woman wouldn't do for her? "The car was an old model and a little worse for wear," admits Rory, laughing. "It was hard to believe that it belonged to one of the top lawyers in the country."

Before heading back into London, they stopped off for a drink at a little bar in Milton Keynes. They brought their drinks outside to a seated area beside a river and basked in the warm glow of the August sunshine. Elaine ordered a pint of Budweiser – there was none on draft so she asked for two bottles and a pint glass. "I see you're as determined as ever," Kathy quipped. Elaine's mood was extremely upbeat, almost celebratory. Rory was deeply concerned at her complacent manner, fearing it represented the proverbial calm before the storm. "Elaine was in fantastic form – she was absolutely flying; laughing and joking about everything and wanting to find out all that had happened while she was locked up. She was very positive. I remember thinking how hyper she was. It was as if she had just returned from her holidays, the way she was talking." Looking back today, Elaine believes that her naive enthusiasm was simply a manifestation of her deep sense of relief.

Elaine seemed to marvel at everything around her as she sat outside the pub. In her head, she recited the words of her favourite Pogues's song, 'A Pair of Brown Eyes'. " . . . and the birds were whistling in the trees, where wind was gently laughing." It was one of those songs that summed up the moment perfectly. Before leaving, Elaine phoned her father. She had only spoken to him once since her arrest, the night she first phoned home, when he just happened to be in her mother's house. Apart from her solicitor, Kathy's number was the only one she had been authorised to call from prison. Martin was thrilled to hear his daughter's voice, although disappointed not to be there for her release. Robert was also unable to travel to London to see his sister. Even though gardaí had assured him that he would not be arrested if he went to Britain, Gareth Peirce felt it would be best if he didn't take any chances. On the drive back to London, Elaine asked Rory to stop the car. After 26 days locked up in a cell, she wanted to experience the feeling of being able to walk freely and unaccompanied. She emerged from the car like a wide-eyed child. It felt as if there were endless possibilities brimming on the horizon.

But true to Rory's instincts, Elaine was not holding up as well as she appeared to be. As they approached London, she asked Rory if they could go to her favourite, local pub. Rory's heart sank. He couldn't bear to tell Elaine that he felt that they couldn't go to the pub. Relations between Rory and the couple who ran the pub had been badly damaged by the events of 10 July. He had been on friendly terms with the landlord. Elaine was also a well-known regular there. She had even helped the barman out of a fix at one stage by putting up two friends of his – the Belfast couple.

When Rory learned that Elaine had been charged, he had immediately contacted Gareth Peirce and asked what he could do to help her. She told him to collect as many character references as possible from people who knew Elaine, which could be presented as evidence in court. Rory took the task seriously, even giving up alcohol so he could stay focused on the campaign to have his friend released. "I knew that I would need a clear head every day if I was going to be of any use to Elaine," he explains. "It would have been too easy to just hit the bottle and drown my sorrows as I wasn't working and had very little to do." Rory was particularly keen to get a reference from the barman, who would have been able to testify as to Elaine's hospitable nature. He had also hoped to obtain a reference from the Belfast couple, which Gareth felt would be important. If anything, Elaine should have been more wary of letting two strangers from Northern Ireland stay in her flat than a well-mannered academic from Dublin such as Anthony Hyland. Numerous promises to deliver the references to Rory were subsequently broken and he finally realised that he was being fobbed off.

Rory tried to dissuade Elaine from going to the pub on the day of her release, instead suggesting a meal at the Spaghetti House in Piccadilly, which was a favourite restaurant of hers. When Kathy also urged that they go elsewhere, Elaine became suspicious and even more adamant about visiting her friends in the pub. "Why not just for one drink?" she asked, becoming increasingly perplexed. "We're supposed to be celebrating, for God's sake." There was no other option – Rory was forced to tell her that he felt that they couldn't go there because they wouldn't be welcome.

Ordinarily, Elaine would have shrugged off such an incident or dismissed it as insignificant. Now, however, it was an indication of the prejudices she could be subjected to as a result of being in prison. While in Woodhill, Elaine had received many letters of encouragement, none of them judgmental or negative. This led her to believe that no one she knew had formed any unjust opinions of her. Now she was getting the impression that certain things had been kept from her by family and friends. For the first time since her release, she became extremely upset. Rory stopped the car and Elaine jumped out and ran off. Rory quickly caught up with her. "She just completely broke down," he recalls. "I was kind of glad that she did, because I had been worried about how relaxed she had been earlier – it was unnerving, in a way. It was good that she broke down and got it out of her system."

Elaine attached considerable significance to feeling that she couldn't go to her favourite pub. To her, it now seemed that she was being viewed with the same contempt and suspicion by her supposed friends as she had been by the police and prison authorities. It wasn't simply a case that she didn't know who to trust; more importantly, she didn't know who trusted her. What else, she wondered, were her family and friends keeping from her?

Kathy eventually caught up with Rory and Elaine as they stood talking in the middle of the street. She reminded her daughter of the many positive references that had been written by the people who mattered. Then there were those complete strangers whose lives had been touched by her story. Elaine drew some comfort from her mother's words and agreed to get back in the car. They drove through an area Elaine was familiar with, close to her former apartment on Parkhill Road, before arriving at the Italian restaurant. Elaine's mood had improved considerably by the time they sat down to eat in the Spaghetti House and the atmosphere was mostly jovial as they swapped humorous experiences over dinner.

Elaine reluctantly asked her mother about conditions at the Irish Chaplaincy, where she had agreed to reside each night as part of her bail conditions. Kathy and Tom, unable to find accommodation in the vicinity of the chaplaincy, had already been staying there at the invitation of two kind-hearted priests, Fr Val Noon and Fr Joe Brown. They spoke in glowing terms about the hospitality they had received over the previous few days, stressing that Elaine could not possibly find nicer people to stay with. As they approached the chaplaincy, Elaine glanced out anxiously at the dark, imposing building, which resembled an old cathedral. Dozens of steps led up to a tall church with wooden doors, surrounded by pillars. St Mellitus's Church at Tollington Park was located in a somewhat dreary, run-down part of London; a far cry from the upmarket Hampstead area where Elaine had lived. She first met Fr Joe and Fr Val, whose warm and gentle manner helped put her at ease. Elaine was then introduced to a number of other priests, who were all extremely welcoming, before being shown to her temporary new home. She would be staying at Fr Gerry French's place, which was located at the far end of the church grounds. The priest was away at the time and had kindly offered Elaine unrestricted use of his large apartment, complete with living area, kitchen bathroom and bedroom. She was astounded by such generosity. For the first time in almost a month, she would be able to live with a degree of privacy and independence.

Having her mother with her gave Elaine a false sense of security as she settled in to her new surroundings. She knew she would be terrified living in the apartment on her own after Kathy and Tom returned to Dublin the following Sunday but, typical of Elaine, she tried to stave off the inevitable by not thinking about it. She had become adept at mentally blocking out negative thoughts when they entered her mind – it was her way of coping. Tom and Kathy had been given a room in a separate part of the building but, at Elaine's behest, stayed at her apartment for the rest of the week. Elaine and Rory set up camp for the night on the living room floor where they talked and giggled into the early hours of the next morning. As she drifted off to sleep, Elaine felt safe in the knowledge that it would be her mum waking her up the next morning, cup of tea in hand; not a faceless prison officer.

Elaine's outlook on life was positive when she awoke the next morning on Thursday, 6 August; a semi-free young woman with her mother by her side. Kathy was eager for Elaine to participate in a telephone interview with Pat Kenny for his radio show. Although Elaine had been advised by Gareth not to speak to the media – except to express her gratitude to her supporters – she made an exception for Pat Kenny after hearing from Kathy how helpful he had been in highlighting her case. For legal reasons, she was careful not to comment on the circumstances surrounding her arrest and simply used the interview as an opportunity to thank the Irish people for all their support. That morning, Elaine had been introduced to Carmel, a bubbly, talkative woman who worked in the Irish Commission for Prisoners Overseas office, which was based at the chaplaincy. Elaine was wary of her at first, but grew to appreciate Carmel's support and considerable kindness, especially after her mother returned to Ireland. She cautiously ventured out into the grounds of the chaplaincy, concerned about the possibility of a media or police presence outside. She had yet to learn of the full details of her bail conditions. Normally, it was standard practice for somebody in her position, or even on lesser charges, to sign-on at a designated police station every day. Strangely, this was not a condition of Elaine's bail, despite the fact that the prosecution had repeatedly expressed fears that she would abscond. This led her to believe that her every move was being watched from a distance by undercover police. Even Gareth Peirce agreed that Elaine's fears were probably justifiable.

Kathy has no doubt that they were all under constant surveillance. "Even though they were in plain clothes, they were very conspicuous," she explains. "We would move, then they would move. They followed us everywhere, even to restaurants and pubs. Everyone knew who they were." Their suspicions were well founded. Two friends of Robert's were staying overnight in London before catching a plane to Prague the next day and spent an evening in Scruffy Murphy's pub with Elaine and her friends. As they left the pub that night, the taxi in which they were travelling was immediately pulled over by police and they were searched and questioned. Furthermore, police never once contacted the chaplaincy to check if Elaine was adhering to her bail conditions. "They knew she was staying there, simply because they were watching her," Kathy maintains.

The day after her release, Kathy brought Elaine on a shopping spree. Usually every girl's dream day out, this expedition was more out of necessity than anything else. Police had seized every item that Elaine possessed in London when they raided her flat. Kathy remembers spending around £1,000 on the most basic items for her daughter. She had no clothes to wear, except for the cream business suit sent over for her bail hearings. Elaine needed an entire new wardrobe: everything from shoes to a coat. First stop was Oxford Street, which was just a short distance from where Elaine had been arrested at work. It was also uncomfortably close to Charing Cross Police Station, where she had subsequently been detained for five days. Unusually for her, Elaine was not relishing the shopping experience. Kathy noticed her daughter was constantly lagging behind and appeared tense. Having spent weeks in virtual isolation, the presence of large crowds now panicked Elaine. Her fear was compounded by an acute sense of paranoia as she scanned the faces of all those around her. She became highly sensitive to the presence of security men and CCTV cameras in the shops, with all their connotations of prison. Elaine asked her mother if they could abandon the shopping trip, which they did after hastily purchasing some essentials.

After meeting up with Rory and Tom for dinner, they decided to end the evening with a drink in O'Neill's pub in Covent Garden. Being an Irish pub, Elaine was afraid she might be recognised or even verbally abused by people who just had a rudimentary grasp of her case. Aware of Elaine's fears, Rory protectively scanned the pub for any hint of hostility. To his horror, he noticed a prominently displayed copy of the *Irish Independent*, featuring a large photograph of Elaine and Kathy as they left Woodhill prison. She was still wearing the same cream suit as the one pictured in the newspaper, making her even more recognisable to those around her in the pub. Elaine felt she stood out from the crowd. Rory grabbed the copy of the newspaper from the display rack and put it under his arm. Feeling self-conscious and uncomfortable, Elaine requested that they finish their drinks and leave. So far, life on bail had been a mixed experience. She dreaded to think how she would cope outside the protective shell of her family and friends. Hopefully, in time, she would learn to adjust.

In the days following her release, Elaine paid a visit to Gareth Peirce accompanied by Kathy. She warmly hugged the woman she considered her saviour. After chatting informally for a while, they soon got down to the serious business of discussing the case. Top of the agenda was Elaine's bail conditions. The judge had simply ordered her to reside at the chaplaincy and did not specify a time for her to return there each night. However, Gareth felt it would be prudent if Elaine adhered to a self-imposed curfew of midnight. This would prevent the prosecution from accusing Elaine of abusing her bail conditions, which could lead to the imposition of a strict curfew at the next remand hearing. Elaine was due to appear before the magistrates again on 27 August, where bail was expected to be renewed without difficulty.

While Elaine was in prison, Gareth had made numerous unsuccessful attempts to get in contact with her employers at Netlink to establish if her job was still available. Not one to be fobbed off lightly, the solicitor, after leaving numerous messages, finally got to speak to her manager. He had bad news: Elaine's job was gone. Due to the importance of the America On-Line account that she had managed, her position needed to be filled immediately. He said there was also uncertainty as to when Elaine would be available to return to work. Although she understood Netlink's reasons for replacing her, Elaine felt hurt at the manner in which she had been informed of the decision. Furthermore, Gareth had told the company that the granting of bail was imminent and assured them that her client had no case to answer. Elaine had pinned her hopes on returning to work, which would have instilled some sense of normality in her life. It also would have been helpful in her bail application if her solicitor had been able to tell the magistrate that Elaine had a steady job to return to. On a personal level, she had also forged some close friendships during her short time at Netlink. Then there were the financial implications of losing her job to consider. Even from a young age, Elaine had always felt a need to earn her own living and she treasured her independence. Now, it seemed, prison had robbed her of everything she once held dear about London: her freedom, her apartment, her career and fledgling new friendships. Elaine's dismissal from Netlink was widely reported by the Irish media. According to *The Examiner*, the company's position was that it had not been kept informed about her case – a claim strenuously denied by her solicitor. The paper pointed out that Elaine was now unemployed in London and barred from leaving the country while charges were pending against her. Speaking to the *Evening Herald*, Kathy said that, once again, her daughter had been "further victimised".

Despite receiving confirmation of her dismissal, the meeting with Gareth had put Elaine in a positive frame of mind and she left the solicitor's office feeling reassured and confident. She was now looking forward to catching up with some friends later that evening in Scruffy Murphy's. As Kathy and Elaine got ready to go out for the night, Carmel from the office dropped in some letters and messages for Elaine. Scanning through the mail, she noticed a Netlink headed envelope, which she opened with apprehension, half expecting to find her P45 inside. To her absolute delight, it was a letter of support from her former colleagues. It read:

'Dear Elaine,

Not sure how to start this letter, except with the biggest question: how are you coping? We are missing you immensely and cannot believe what you are being put through. We just wish we could do something to help; something to show that it is all a complete mistake and that we want you back with us. Support is probably all that we can offer, for we know what a lovely young lady you are; someone who has been a good friend and a kind and caring person. Please do not let this get you down; shortly we will be sitting down having a good laugh, drinking beer (well, better than the Guinness served in the Oarsman). I am sorry if this letter sounds bleak, but presently we are too shocked and stumped over the whole situation to know what to say. Is there anything we can do? Just name it. In the meantime, whatever you do, please don't lose touch with us. We've tried leaving messages on your solicitor's mobile phone before but have not had any response in the past. Can't say we have anything to moan about, for there is a beautiful young gal to look after. You may not want to call the office. Drop me a note to say you're ok at my home address. Either home or office, whichever is more convenient for you. If there is a possibility we can meet, please let me know.

Lots of love and best wishes – Shaf, Debbie, Nick and William.'

Spurred on by the letter, Elaine immediately phoned Shaf at the office. He seemed delighted to hear from her and gathered other excited colleagues around to share in the call.

"You have no idea how desperately worried we've all been," Shaf told her.

"I'm fine – I was just concerned that you lot would think the worst of me," she replied.

Elaine made arrangements to meet up with her Netlink work mates the next day. She was elated as she ended the call. That evening, Elaine felt a strong sense of anticipation as she met Rory's circle of friends for the first time since her release, including the young woman who had been arrested with him on 10 July. Also in the pub was a cousin of Rory's, Tyrone Falls, from Northern Ireland who had acted as one of the sureties for Elaine's bail. Her initial feeling of anxiety quickly dissipated as she was embraced by everyone she met. Elaine was notably more at ease and happier than she had been for quite some time – she was in a familiar place, surrounded by familiar faces. Finally, a semblance of normality had been restored to her life. It was exactly what she needed.

After breakfast the next morning, Elaine set out to meet her former Netlink colleagues. When she entered the pub, a deafening cheer erupted. Elaine was gobsmacked by the enthusiasm of their welcome; she was mobbed by Nick, Will and Shaf, all asking questions at the same time. After the initial excitement of the reunion died down, the mood turned sombre as they quizzed her about her prison ordeal. They sat in silence as Elaine told them about life in Woodhill, although she consciously peppered the conversation with snippets of humorous anecdotes. She was deeply touched to learn that after her arrest, staff at Netlink had scanned the Internet for information about her; they had even started buying Irish newspapers. Elaine admitted that had they not tracked her down at the chaplaincy, she probably wouldn't have had the nerve to get in touch with them for fear of rejection. One friend, Will, admitted to Elaine that he had been deeply troubled by the allegations made against her. The lack of information surrounding her arrest, coupled with his ignorance of the political situation in Northern Ireland, had added to his sense of confusion. After speaking to his mother about her, Will eventually came to the conclusion that, even if Elaine had somehow been involved, she must have had good reason. "You're some Muppet, Will," she responded, although she was touched by the generosity of the sentiment. Meeting up with her old Netlink buddies had lifted Elaine's spirits no end. When she rejoined her mum, Tom and Rory, she talked enthusiastically about how well the lunch had gone.

As the days progressed, however, Elaine began to find herself in a detached, semi-conscious state of mind. She spent her days and nights trying to get used to her changed circumstances and setting up a new sense of structure in her life. Her family and friends tried to keep her positive making sure to tell her about all the many supportive media reports relating to her case. At that time, they were aware that not all reports shed positive light on Elaine's situation. When Kathy saw how upset her daughter became when she found out they couldn't go to her once favourite pub, she wanted more than ever to protect her. Kathy felt it was essential to shield Elaine from any further negativity. She was concerned about the possible adverse effect negative media coverage would have on her daughter's already precarious state-of-mind.

A prime example of this was when on 9 August 1998 the *Sunday Independent* published an extraordinary article about Elaine's case. The article was headlined: 'Vital evidence held back in terror case'. The most potentially damaging revelation in the story was an assertion that British anti-terrorist officers intended to reveal more evidence in court which, they claimed, would implicate Elaine with the Real IRA. An unnamed police source was quoted as saying: 'There is a lot of scepticism from the Irish media about this woman's arrest. Do we need to say that we did not show our full hand in court? It would be daylight stupidity for us to have gone to court and given all the details of our intentions with regard to the prosecution which we intend to pursue.' The source added: 'Since when do prosecutors present all of their facts to the defence at the outset? We are charging this woman with a specific crime and we did not do so without having hard evidence. There are other circumstances which we won't be going into. Suffice to say we have a case to present and she will be dealt with in the courts. As far as we are concerned, the woman has a case to answer. I am letting you know that.'

The article went on to quote an unnamed Irish Government source, who considered it 'very unlikely' that charges against Elaine would be dropped before her case got to court. 'The understanding we have is that the British police say they have enough to bring a case against her,' the source said. Finally, a garda source quoted – again unnamed – pointed out that the former National Quartermaster of the IRA was now believed to be in control of the Real IRA. 'The question must be asked: "How would a man of his experience send an operative to London for such a job if a safe house was not guaranteed?"' the article concluded.

Elaine's family and friends were horrified when they read the article and went to great lengths to hide it from her. Even though the *Sunday Independent* is an Irish newspaper, it is widely available for sale throughout London. A week earlier, on 2 August, the same journalist had written a piece that was also kept from Elaine. It had incorrectly claimed that Elaine had handled the bag found in her room and implied that her fingerprints would have been all over it. Kathy emphatically told Rory that under no circumstances was her daughter to be shown either article.

* * *

Elaine's newfound confidence began to wane as soon as her mother and Tom returned to Ireland that weekend. There were heartbreaking scenes at the chaplaincy as Elaine and Kathy hugged each other goodbye. Elaine desperately wanted to be getting on that plane with them. She stopped herself from begging her mother to stay, knowing that Robert needed her back home. Kathy also had to return to work at the women's refuge, if anything, just to keep her mind occupied.

Despite her best efforts, Elaine had great difficulty settling in at the chaplaincy. Without her mother staying there, she felt isolated and imprisoned. The apartment was located at the rear of the church and was accessed via a poorly-lit laneway. Inside, there was a series of doors, one of which led directly to the altar. As she climbed the many steps leading up to her apartment, an ominous creaking sound would reverberate throughout the old building. Even when inside the apartment, Elaine had more fears to conquer, heightened by the fact that there was no key to lock the main door. A fragile door latch was all that separated her from the outside world. It was quite common for homeless people to wander around the grounds of the chaplaincy at night in search of food or shelter. It made her feel vulnerable. Elaine had gone from maximum to minimum security. It was, she reflected, a strange type of freedom. The apartment itself, while comfortable, took on an eerie atmosphere at night thanks to its stain-glassed windows. Rory made her promise that she would not leave or enter the apartment on her own after dark.

Elaine recalls one occasion when she enjoyed a night out on the town with her cousins, Louise and Mandy, who had travelled over from Dublin especially to see her. The three of them had grown up together and Elaine spent many a summer out in her Aunt May's house as a child. They passed a memorable day together in London as they reminisced about old times. Reluctantly, Elaine said goodbye to her cousins in the pub that night as her self-imposed curfew of midnight approached. She insisted that they stay on and enjoy themselves. Sitting in the back of a taxi, Elaine was struck with the sudden realisation that she would have to enter the chaplaincy alone. She thought of phoning Rory but, as it was late, decided against disturbing him. Arriving at the chaplaincy, Elaine pretended to be talking on her mobile phone as she walked frantically and nervously down the dark laneway. With a trembling hand, she struggled to get the key in the main door before dashing up the series of stairs. She was traumatised by the time she closed the door of the apartment behind her. She sat up watching the BBC World News Service on television until it began to get bright. Only then did she fall asleep.

To comfort her on other sleepless nights, Rory often sat up talking with Elaine until daylight arrived. He would only leave when he was sure she was finally asleep. This was just another example of Rory's unflinching devotion towards Elaine; he went to extraordinary lengths to look after her. During the day, it was easy for Elaine to steer clear of conversations about the battles that lay ahead. At night, however, as she talked through the early hours of the morning with Rory, Elaine was forced to open up to him about the harsh realities facing her. Her first priority was to get out of the Irish Chaplaincy, which had become another form of prison for Elaine. She asked Gareth to make an application for a change of address at her upcoming remand hearing. Privately, she felt guilty for making such a request, particularly as the priests and staff at the chaplaincy had treated her so kindly. Fr Gerry, whose apartment she was living in, was due to return in September, but a room on the opposite side of the chaplaincy was to be made available to her. Thankfully, the priests sympathised with Elaine's situation and assisted her in finding alternative accommodation. A particular incident vindicated her desire to leave. Late one night, she answered the intercom in the apartment to hear a strange man requesting to be let in. She was panic stricken, but calmly directed him to the other end of the building where he could speak with one of the priests. Sandwiches, soup and tea were regularly dispensed to London's less fortunate citizens by the kind-hearted staff at the chaplaincy. The man trying to gain access to Elaine's apartment had no sinister motive – he was probably just looking for food. He had scared her witless, nonetheless.

A few weeks after her release, Elaine was thrilled to learn that her father would be visiting her. Her dad's fear of flying resulted in him having to travel by ferry from Dublin to Holyhead and then catch a train to London. Elaine was excited at the prospect of seeing her father for the first time since her ordeal began as she awaited his arrival at Euston train station. She excitedly made her way to the platform as the arrival of her father's train was announced. Her joyous expression quickly turned to one of disbelief when she saw Martin step down from the carriage. He had lost an incredible amount of weight and looked seriously ill. "Are you all right, Dad?" Elaine asked nervously. He assured her that he was fine, but had not been able to eat a thing since learning of his daughter's arrest. Elaine remained sceptical. She hadn't been eating properly either but didn't look in any way as bad as her father did – he had the appearance of a terminally ill man. A heavy smoker all his life, she feared that he had cancer and her family had shielded her from the bad news because of what she was going through. But Martin explained that he had gone for a check-up and the doctor had diagnosed him as suffering from a stress-related eating disorder. Elaine wasn't convinced initially, but, to this day, her dad has not recovered from the condition and still suffers from his nerves.

Elaine also had an emotional reunion with Rory's brother, Niall, when he returned from a six-week-long working holiday in America. He had spent the summer in Wildwood, New Jersey, where Elaine had first met him two years previously. While there, he had written an important character reference, which Gareth later showed to an Old Bailey judge as part of their application for bail. Crucially, it explained the background to how Elaine had come to live in London in the first place. It showed that contrary to the prosecution's claim, she had not arrived with any political agenda.

Unfortunately, Niall had also been caught up in the bizarre events of 10 July. Earlier that day, Niall had arrived in London from Oxford. His inability to contact either Rory or Elaine caused him concern. He made his way to his brother's house where he was greeted by Rory's flatmate. He had also been unable to contact Rory or indeed his own girlfriend. As neither had a key they decided to make their way to a nearby pub, agreeing to check Elaine's apartment, which was en route.

As they turned the corner on to Parkhill Road, they were shocked by a vast police presence directly outside Elaine's apartment. Niall feared that there had been an accident or worse still, that she had been attacked. This fear was compounded by the sight of police wearing forensic suits. They proceeded in the direction of her apartment where detectives approached them and demanded that they identify themselves. Both men were taken into the lobby of the apartment block where they were questioned and searched. During that time police were removing large quantities of furniture from the apartment. Niall's continuous requests for information concerning his brother and his friend were ignored. Amidst all the commotion, Niall overheard a detective on a mobile phone asking whether or not they should hold them. Eventually police disclosed that Elaine had been arrested but refused to comment on Rory. They were then told that they were free to go. Later that evening Niall discovered his brother's fate in a very surreal way: he watched Rory's arrest on the news.

Niall continued to feel the effects of Elaine and Rory's arrest long after that day. A postgraduate, legal studies student at the Oxford Institute of Legal Practice, Niall had returned from America to re-sit some of his final exams. His studies, and, by extension, his aspiring career as an attorney in law, had been placed in jeopardy when police seized his study notes and books from Elaine's apartment. Niall had meticulously planned the trip around the exams. The arrest of his older brother had forced him to delay his departure to America in the first place.

Rory had assured him that he would relentlessly pursue Scotland Yard to have his notes returned and would forward them to Niall in the States. However, attempts to retrieve the items from Scotland Yard had proved a bureaucratic nightmare.

Elaine worried about the strain this must have put on Niall. She felt she had undermined their friendship in some way and was apprehensive about meeting him. She needn't have worried. As she entered Rory's living room, Niall jumped up and threw his arms around her. Elaine was thrilled to receive such a heartfelt welcome from a man to whom she had such a strong attachment.

For reasons, which remain unknown, his notes and books were not released until Saturday, 20 September. He was scheduled to re-sit his exams that Monday. After four years of legal studies, Niall's career prospects depended on the results of the exams. It would be several months before Rory could bring himself to tell Elaine that Niall failed the exams by only a few percent. This meant that he would be forced to repeat the entire year at the Oxford Institute; without the practitioner's certificate, his career as a lawyer could never fully materialise. Niall sensitively played down the significance of the notes, but Elaine knew too well the extra pressure it must have placed him under. As far as she was concerned, he had already been seriously inconvenienced by her situation. She was devastated for her friend and felt directly to blame for this major setback.

* * *

Elaine didn't wake up until 2 p.m. in the afternoon of Saturday, 15 August 1998, having only succumbed to sleep a few hours earlier. Rory called round to the apartment and they discussed plans for an informal meal out that evening. It would be a casual affair: just 12 friends enjoying each other's company in a relaxed atmosphere over some fine food. The dinner would be followed by a visit to Scuffy Murphy's, which Elaine was looking forward to. Rory told Elaine that he had a few errands to run first and would be back to her within the hour. An hour passed and there was still no sign of Rory. She tried to distract herself by turning on the television but was becoming increasingly concerned about her friend; it was unlike him to be late. Elaine phoned his mobile but there was no response. 'What if the police had stopped him again?' she thought, conscious that her every move was being monitored. Anytime she spoke on her phone she could hear a clicking sound, which led Elaine to believe that police had tapped the line. Suddenly, there was a rap on her door. It was Rory, hidden behind an enormous bunch of lilies – Elaine's favourite flowers. He hadn't been able to find lilies anywhere, which was what had delayed him. Not wanting to ruin the surprise, he had deliberately ignored her phone call. Sensing Elaine's relief, Rory promised there would be no more surprises, no matter how well intentioned.

Shortly after 6 p.m., Rory went home to get ready so Elaine settled down to watch some TV. As she channel hopped, scenes of unimaginable carnage flashed on the screen before her. A car bomb had been detonated in the heart of a busy shopping district in the Northern Irish town of Omagh, Co. Tyrone. Each updated report brought news of an increasing death toll. The atrocity, which was immediately attributed to dissident republicans, would eventually claim 29 lives – including a woman seven months pregnant with twins; hundreds more were injured, maimed and scarred. Rory returned a few hours later to find Elaine staring, transfixed, at the television. He had desperately hoped she hadn't heard about the tragic events in Omagh, knowing how much it would affect her. Elaine was inconsolable and he had great difficulty convincing her to leave the apartment and join her friends for dinner. At the restaurant, the atmosphere was strained as her friends noticeably avoided any mention of the subject. Fighting back tears, Elaine excused herself and went to the ladies' room where she cried in private. The sheer scale of the casualties and devastation in Omagh appalled her. Twenty-nine lives senselessly lost – it was simply beyond her comprehension.

The so-called Real IRA later claimed responsibility for the Omagh atrocity. There was little comfort for the victims and their families when the group apologised for the casualties. A statement issued by Oglaigh na hÉireann (IRA) read: 'Despite media reports, it was not our intention at any time to kill any civilian. It was a commercial target, part of an ongoing war against the Brits. We offer apologies to the civilians.' The statement – which had reportedly been telephoned to a newspaper by a caller using a recognised code word – was met with widespread revulsion. The then Secretary of State for Northern Ireland, Mo Mowlam, condemned the admission as 'a pathetic attempt to apologise for and excuse mass murder.' Seamus Mallon, the North's Deputy First Minister, said the statement was an attempt to 'excuse the inexcusable'. In what was hailed as a watershed in the peace process, Sinn Féin President, Gerry Adams, said he condemned the attack without equivocation. Meanwhile, the Irish and British Governments announced the drafting of strict new anti-terrorist legislation in a bid to catch the killers.

The Omagh atrocity had a strong psychological impact on Elaine. She was deeply troubled by the fact that in the minds of the victims' families, she could be associated with the people responsible for such an appalling loss of human life. It was the antitheses of everything she believed in. Rory sensed a distinct change in Elaine after Omagh. Up to that point, her case was based on a foiled bomb plot. Now, however, the organisation she was accused of conspiring with had caused untold devastation. The fact that people had been killed made everything more sinister. Her impending remand hearing now took on a greater significance and weighed heavily on her mind. She became more reluctant to talk than usual when asked about her case and eventually refused to discuss it, even with close friends and family. "It wasn't even a case of: 'If we don't talk about it, it will go away'," Elaine explains. "It was more that I was sick to death of the whole sorry episode. I made every effort to speak about anything other than 'the case'. I just needed to escape from it."

Rory, however, believed she was in denial and constantly challenged Elaine about her reluctance to discuss her case. He was actively involved in the campaign to have the charges against her dropped. There were several influential people who could possibly help her; he just needed Elaine to contact them personally. She refused, arguing that she was never one for asking for help. Rory wouldn't drop the subject and became more determined than ever to get Elaine on board the campaign. "He knew what was best for my case but not necessarily what was best for my mind," she believes. "Selfishly, I often forgot about the ordeal he had been through. On reflection, my unwillingness to cooperate must have caused him a great deal of strain. I'm still amazed by the amount of grief he put up with from me. I suppose he knew, however, that he was my confidant; the one person I could express my genuine fears to. He was probably aware that if he closed the door on me, I would have been lost without him. But the problem was that the only way I could cope, in a sense, was by not coping at all. I craved normality. What I really needed from Rory was for him not to change; to be the same outgoing, fun loving guy he had previously been. That would have meant him conforming to my somewhat irrational perception of things – but that's what I needed. I didn't have the strength to fight at the time."

But Rory didn't see it that way. Despite the fact that she had the best possible legal team, he feared that her attitude could damage her case. Although they remained inseparable, the strain on Rory and Elaine's friendship was beginning to show.

Chapter Thirteen

A Serious Setback

Just three weeks after her release on bail, Elaine found
herself back in prison after a routine remand hearing
unexpectedly went against her. The entire episode served
to further erode her faith in the British justice system.

The remand hearing was scheduled to take place at
Belmarsh Magistrates' Court at 10 a.m. on Thursday, 27
August. Earlier that week, Elaine was disheartened to
learn that Gareth Peirce would not be available to attend
court. An associate, Tim Greene, had been fully briefed,
however, and was to take Gareth's place at the hearing.
Elaine was apprehensive, despite her solicitor's insistence
that every eventuality had been covered. Her trust in the
British legal system lay solely with Gareth; without her,
the outlook seemed grim. Not wanting to pressurise
Gareth, Elaine kept her concerns to herself.

When Rory arrived at the chaplaincy to pick them up
that morning there was a palpable sense of tension. He
was accompanied by his flatmate, who was one of Elaine's
sureties and had to be in court to re-sign on her behalf.
Together with Kathy and Tom, the five of them drove to
the court in Greenwich. The conversation was kept light
and upbeat to take Elaine's mind off the hearing. There
was talk of a nice lunch after court, followed later by
dinner and a night on the town, to celebrate the inevitable
renewal of her bail. Her nerves played havoc with her
stomach as they approached the courthouse. Elaine
consoled herself with the fact that for the first time since

her arrest, she was being driven to court in a car, surrounded by her family and friends. It was a far cry from
her previous appearances where handcuffs, police vans,
screaming sirens and armed escorts were the order of the
day.

Kathy, who was wearing a large, white eye patch, looked
as though she had been through the wars as she
accompanied her daughter to court. Two weeks earlier
she had been walking past a building site in Dublin when
she felt something fly into her eye. The pain got so bad
that she had to go to the Eye and Ear Hospital, where
they discovered a piece of granite embedded in her pupil.
"During the procedure to remove the fragment, they told
me not to blink or I would be blinded," she recalls. Doctors
were concerned about Kathy's condition and wanted her
to return for a check-up the following morning. However,
as she was flying out that evening to be with Elaine,
arrangements were made for Kathy to attend a London
hospital instead. The eye patch made Kathy feel unsteady
on her feet and more self-conscious than usual as she
faced the full glare of the media outside the court. "When
you have a patch over one eye it affects your whole sense
of balance," she explains. "I couldn't even see the footpaths
– it was awful. To top things off, I had to give interviews
with the press which certainly didn't help."

There was maximum security in and around the court
building. Elaine tried to feign a cool and calm manner in
front of the media and police, not wanting to outwardly
express her true feelings of fear and insecurity. Kathy
remembers that security was noticeably tighter than it
had been for the earlier bail hearings. "It was like going
through an airport," she says. "Every person going in to
the court was scanned and all bags were put through an
X-ray machine. Outside, the police were looking under

every car." Elaine was relieved to walk through the scanning machine without incident – she had dreaded the thought of being subjected to a physical search. As she entered the courthouse shortly before 10 a.m., she was photographed looking pale, strained and anxious. The picture appeared in the following day's newspapers. "I'll never forget that day. That image perfectly captures how I was feeling that morning."

Kathy will never forget sitting in the waiting room with Elaine before her case was called. "We were surrounded by armed guards, with their guns trained on us – it was really intimidating. I just kept looking at my little girl, who had no involvement in anything. You could tell by the look on the faces of the police that they held us in contempt. They saw me as the mother of a terrorist. I remember thinking: 'One slip of the finger and we're gone'. I felt they were just waiting for a chance to open fire – that's how nervous I was. It reinforced my fears about what Elaine must have been subjected to. It all became too much and I had to go out and get some fresh air."

Gareth had expected that Elaine's bail would be routinely renewed in a matter of minutes. In advance of the hearing, the prosecution had been advised that one of Elaine's sureties, Lynn Solomon, a film producer, would not be available that day to re-sign. She had booked a holiday to America well before Elaine had been arrested. Gareth had suggested that a further £20,000 could be lodged with the court until the surety returned two days later. The Crown Prosecution Service had already indicated that this proposal was acceptable to them.

However, as the hearing got underway before Magistrate David Cooper, it quickly became apparent that renewing Elaine's bail was not going to be as straightforward as originally anticipated. After just five minutes, the three men also accused of terrorist offences were further remanded in custody until 17 September – none of them had made a bail application. As Grogan, Hyland and Mulholland were led handcuffed from the court, Elaine remained in the dock while her solicitor Tim Greene attempted to slightly alter her bail conditions. Things got off to a good start. After evidence from Fr Gerry McFlynn, the magistrate agreed to a change of address for Elaine from the Irish Chaplaincy to a religious retreat house on Reddington Road. Elaine was deeply relieved. She knew Kathy would also rest easier in the knowledge that her daughter would feel more secure at the new address.

But Elaine had been lured into a false sense of security by the magistrate's initial cooperation. The mood in the courtroom seemed to change as Magistrate Cooper suddenly found fault with one of the two sureties who had turned up in court to re-sign. A cousin of Rory's, Tyrone Falls, had put up £10,000 based on his ownership of a property in Northern Ireland. This surety's proof of financial worth had been accepted previously by police and the prosecution when the Recorder of London in the Old Bailey granted Elaine bail on 31 July. Magistrate Cooper indicated that he was unhappy with this surety for two reasons: firstly, he did not have a valuation of the property involved; and secondly, he did not consider property in Northern Ireland to be an acceptable form of proof of worth. Mr Cooper's suggestion that the six counties were outside his jurisdiction reportedly caused offence within the ranks of the North's unionist parties.

Magistrate Cooper also found it improper that the third surety had gone on holiday and he declined to accept the lodgement of an additional £20,000 as a satisfactory substitute. When solicitor Tim Greene asked if this woman was seriously expected to forego her holiday, the magistrate replied: "Why not, if she thinks so much [of Elaine Moore] that she is prepared to put up £20,000." Elaine stared dispassionately at Cooper from the dock. The same magistrate who had denied her bail on two previous occasions seemed, yet again, intent on sending her back to prison. She glanced at the journalists sitting to her right as they frantically took notes and attempted to make sense of what had just transpired in court. Turning again to Cooper, Elaine tried to convince herself that a mere magistrate would not have the authority to overturn a decision by an Old Bailey judge.

Gareth Peirce had never envisaged such difficulties arising. "It was a week in which nothing could have gone wrong – and everything did go wrong," she reflects. "I remember my colleague ringing me from the court and saying: 'You won't believe what has happened'." Gareth was confident she had covered all angles. She had allowed for no margin of error by organising a further £20,000 in lieu of the surety who was away on holiday in America. No one could have envisaged the magistrate objecting to this arrangement because it had already been agreed with the prosecution. As it all started to go pear shaped, Elaine wished, more than anything, for Gareth to whisk into court and put the magistrate in his place. She certainly didn't blame the replacement solicitor for what went wrong that day; she simply felt that Mr Cooper would not have behaved in such an obstinate manner had Gareth been in court.

After instructions were issued to Elaine's legal team, the hearing was adjourned. Previously, she had been escorted from the court by prison guards or police. This time, she was beckoned to approach the far end of the court in the direction of the magistrate. The bailiff let out an exasperated squeal as Elaine simply walked passed Mr Cooper and exited the court. She had inadvertently broken court protocol by leaving before the magistrate did. 'Great,' she thought to herself. 'That will give Cooper something else to moan about.' Tim Greene emerged from court looking slightly worse for wear from his unexpected conflict with the magistrate. Cooper's refusal to accept the adjustments to Elaine's bail terms had even seemed to take the prosecution by surprise. The implications of the magistrate's decision were simple: her solicitor and family would have to come up with other sureties amounting to £30,000 by the end of the day. After the initial shock wore off, Kathy and Tom set about contacting the various people who had originally come forward to put up bail money for Elaine. Their offers had been politely declined after the (Stg)£190,000 was raised within hours of the Old Bailey ruling. Now, however, it was time to fall back on their generosity.

In a nearby waiting area, Elaine overheard journalists voice their confusion about her case. They were sensitive enough not to approach Elaine, instead offering discreet smiles of support from across the room. Turning to Kathy, who was exuding an air of quiet desperation, Elaine nervously asked: "Can we sort this out, Mum?" Her mother replied that they were doing everything in their power. To the casual observer, Elaine appeared disarmingly calm. But having dealt with Magistrate Cooper before, she was well used to setbacks. She sat in silence, trying to figure out the logic of his reasoning. How could he decide that a property in County Antrim was not suitable? Did he not have any knowledge of the conflict in Northern Ireland? The six counties, after all, were still considered by the British Government to be part of the United

Kingdom. Elaine felt the familiar gaze of the armed police officers that stood guard over her. Why were they suddenly necessary again? During the previous three weeks she had been free to walk the streets of London. Now, for some reason, she was once more perceived to be a high security risk.

Elaine's family and solicitor were given until 5 p.m. to comply with the conditions set down by the magistrate. As last ditch efforts were made to find replacement sureties based in London, she resigned herself to the fact that she would be returning to prison. Tim Greene brought Elaine to a waiting room, away from the main general-purpose area, to escape from the prying eyes of the media and casual bystanders. There was an element of comic relief when the armed guards in the room suddenly disappeared shortly before 5 p.m. "They mustn't be getting paid any overtime," Elaine joked, which helped ease the tension. She took a pack of cigarettes from her handbag before handing it to her mother; she then slowly removed her jewellery and did the same. "I'll see you all later," she said, as she moved around the room to hug her mother and her friends. "You won't be getting rid of me for long; I'll be back annoying you all in no time." Elaine channelled all the positive energy she possessed into that farewell. She was to be brought before Cooper for that day's final judgement and she was damned if she was going to let him see her upset.

Walking back towards the courtroom, Elaine and Rory spoke briefly with Mark Lloyd, a Channel 4 news reporter, who offered any possible assistance he could. He appeared to be as baffled by the earlier events in court as they were. Elaine's fate was a foregone conclusion, according to Kathy. "She knew she was going back to prison; she knew that time had run out." When the court reconvened, her solicitor said that a surety of £20,000 was being offered by the owner of a pharmaceutical company based in Northern Ireland, with assets of £0.75 million. However, this proposal fell through when Mr Cooper continued to insist on London-based sureties being found. The magistrate stressed that despite the admirable character references provided for Ms Moore, he had not set the original conditions for her bail. He warned that if the sureties were unacceptable to the clerk of the court, Elaine would be remanded in custody. "No one would be sorrier about this than I am," he declared. Tim Greene pointed out that her case had caused great concern in Ireland. A representative of the Irish Embassy had authorised him to say that it would be viewed with the utmost concern if his client was returned to prison. This remark seemed to clearly irritate the magistrate. Mr Cooper responded that he was aware how "unsatisfactory and distasteful" a return to prison would be, but felt he would be open to all sorts of criticism by setting a crown court order to one side. "An Old Bailey judge is far superior to me," he said. "These are the conditions and I ought to follow suit." The magistrate rejected a suggestion that Elaine be placed under house arrest with her solicitor until the matter was resolved. Tim Greene said he was asking the court "to take what is perhaps a compassionate view and avoid the literal one which the court has imposed so far." The magistrate replied: "Of course I want to do so . . . but I feel I really ought not to allow my heart to rule my head in this matter."

Although terrified deep down of returning to prison, Elaine's face remained emotionless as he remanded her in custody again. Much to her chagrin, Cooper made reference to the recent terrorist atrocity in Omagh when announcing his decision. He had never allowed Elaine to walk free from his court – that day was to be no exception. Kathy Moore continues to hold David Cooper in complete contempt for what he put her daughter through. "I'll never forget his face as he looked down through his glasses at her and sent her back to jail," she remembers. "I actually felt as much hatred for him as I did for the people that involved her. To this day I believe that the way he treated Elaine was just awful."

Elaine felt humiliated as she was led from the court and brought down to that all-too-familiar dungeon. After walking a considerable distance from the courthouse through a maze of corridors, she was placed in a graffiti-covered cell that stank of urine and vomit. As the door slammed behind her, she instinctively took out her packet of cigarettes. She almost had to suppress a laugh when she realised she had forgotten to bring a lighter with her. Elaine was left in the cell for well over an hour. It had apparently been difficult arranging transport for her at such short notice, particularly as it was now rush hour in London. She had no idea what awaited her that evening; nobody saw fit to tell her anything. Because her hearing was due to reconvene the following morning, Elaine felt there was always a possibility that she would be held at Belmarsh overnight. Officers regularly checked on her through the spy hatch in the cell door. Elaine had no requests other than asking them for a light.

Outside the maximum-security courthouse, Elaine's distraught mother spoke of her anger and frustration at the day's bizarre turn of events. "The only thing that is going to help Elaine now is for every politician in Ireland, regardless of party, to use all their might to do something about this situation," she told the *Irish Independent*. "This case has been a nightmare since the beginning but nothing would have prepared me for the nonsense that went on today." Elaine's family did not learn until later that night that she had been brought to Holloway women's prison in London. Kathy told reporters that she had been given "the run-around" by the prison authorities. She described the British criminal justice system as "scandalous and disgusting". Rory, too, was exasperated as he left the court. He sharply criticised the magistrate for not accepting sureties in Northern Ireland.

* * *

Elaine's cell door was eventually unlocked and two prison officers escorted her out of the building. On closer inspection Elaine realised that they were, in fact, both women – she had mistaken one of them for a good-looking man. She braced herself for the usual display of police strength that had characterised her previous journeys to prison. This time, however, the armed guards were noticeable by their absence. Elaine was casually placed in the back of the security van; she was not handcuffed or made to sit inside a cage. The officers told her to buckle up as they jumped into the front of the vehicle. The van left the court grounds and Elaine was baffled when one of the officers cranked up the volume on the stereo, forcing her to listen to techno music for the duration of the trip. The van drove at a steady pace, unlike her earlier experience when the driver had mounted kerbs and broken every red light in his path. There wasn't even a police car escorting them. "It was a surreal experience," according to Elaine. "It was more like being in a taxi than a prison van. The officers couldn't have cared less about their prisoner. They joked, laughed and sang all the way there. It made an absolute mockery of their heavy-handed treatment of me on the previous occasions – it proved that it had been overly harsh and completely unnecessary."

The van finally came to a halt in a prison courtyard that Elaine didn't recognise. She had expected to be returned to Woodhill but had instead been sent to HMP Holloway, an all-women's prison in north London.

First opened in 1851, Holloway was designed to hold up to 532 prisoners at any one time. It became an all-female prison in 1903 and has been home to Britain's most infamous mass murderers, including Rosemary West, who received 10 life sentences for her part in a series of sexual killings with her husband, Fred. Former inmates at Holloway have told harrowing stories of sex attacks, bullying and intimidation – and not just at the hands of other prisoners. Nine female prison officers were transferred to other duties in controversial circumstances in March 2002. This followed a five-month inquiry into claims that a group of officers at Holloway had sexually harassed new female recruits and intimidated male colleagues. Thankfully, Elaine was blissfully unaware of Holloway's reputation and knew nothing of the inmates it housed.

As Elaine was led in to Holloway's reception area other prisoners emerged from police vans parked in the courtyard. She noticed they were all carrying their belongings with them. Obviously, they were more prepared for a stay in prison than she had been. As the induction process commenced, a middle-aged female officer commented on the fact that Elaine had no jewellery or personal items to hand over.

"I see you came prepared for this evening's visit, Ms Moore," the officer said sarcastically.

"Do I honestly look like I'm prepared to be here, you idiot?" Elaine rudely retorted. She was still dressed in the suit she had worn to court that day – hardly suitable prison attire. Her sole possession was a packet of cigarettes.

Although she had braced herself for a soul-destroying strip-search, Elaine was relieved to be subjected to a far more sensitive procedure than what she had experienced at Woodhill. She entered a dressing room where she simply had to pass out her clothes to a guard. "That's fine, Moore, you can get dressed now," she was told. She wasn't issued with any prison clothes so Elaine put her suit and high-heeled boots back on and proceeded to the medical room. A nurse spoke to Elaine in a pleasant, polite tone while she took down her details. However, her friendly disposition changed as soon as she read the charges against her. With a look of disgust, she turned to Elaine and snapped: "You certainly wouldn't think you were a terrorist to look at you. My God, what is the world coming to?" Elaine pointed out that she was on remand and had been found guilty of nothing. "But that doesn't matter to you lot, does it? I'd appreciate if you could keep your opinions to yourself." Out in the waiting area, there was disorganised chaos as prisoners were served inedible looking microwave dinners. Elaine flatly declined an offer of food. As they ate, the women chatted amongst themselves, mainly about the reasons for their arrest. One was doing time for the attempted murder of her boyfriend; another for manslaughter; and a third was in for theft. Only Elaine and two women sitting to her immediate right stayed out of the conversation. She cringed as she listened to their bravado; she had spent 26 days in isolation in an all-male, maximum-security prison to avoid a place like Holloway. She had prevented Gareth from having her moved from Woodhill for that very reason. Now she was mixing with criminals who openly bragged about stabbing people. She had reached her lowest point yet.

Elaine and the other women were led to a prison wing where cells appeared to be randomly assigned to them. She recognised two of her cellmates as the women from the waiting room who had remained silent as the others boasted about their unsavoury activities. There were five beds in the cell, two of which were already occupied, along with lockers and a tiny bathroom. To Elaine, it resembled a maternity ward. A bubbly Australian woman introduced herself to Elaine and suggested that she take the bed next to her. She seemed excited by the arrival of fresh company. Camille, or Cam, as Elaine later came to know her, helped break the ice in the cell by keeping the conversation flowing. She announced that she was on remand for deception. Ann, one of the newcomers, revealed that she had been remanded into the custody of Holloway for arson. For some reason, Cam completely by-passed another new prisoner, a tall, heavyset woman in her mid-20s, in the discussion. When it came to Elaine's turn to explain the reason for her imprisonment, she replied with a polite but blunt: "You don't want to know."

The subject was dropped – but not for long. About one hour later, as the other prisoners slept, Cam quietly offered Elaine some stark advice on how to survive Holloway. She explained that if a prisoner refuses to say why they're in jail, it's automatically assumed by other inmates to be a charge relating to child abuse, neglect of an infant or a heinous attack on an elderly person. "That sort of thing will get you killed in here," Cam warned.

"If I were you I'd make up a crime; then they'll leave you alone." Elaine was deeply disturbed by her cellmate's comments but appreciated the tip-off. She confided in Cam that she had been wrongly linked with an IRA splinter group and charged with conspiracy to cause explosion and possession of explosives. Cam was spellbound. "For

God's sake girl, you don't do things by halves!" she exclaimed. Emphatically declaring her innocence, Elaine joked that most of the girls in Holloway were probably saying the same thing. Cam and Elaine formed an immediate bond that night and talked into the early hours about everything from their arrests to their family backgrounds and love lives. Before going to bed, Elaine washed her suit and underwear in the sink and hung them up to dry. She had been informed that it would be up to her solicitor to send in fresh clothes. She climbed into bed still wearing the towel she had borrowed from Cam.

"Ah, the deprivation Cam," Elaine laughed in a bewildered tone.

"You ain't seen nothing yet," Cam replied.

She was right.

Chapter Fourteen

HOLLOWAY NIGHTMARE

Elaine found it comforting to wake up the following morning and see a familiar, friendly face in the cell, even if she had only known Cam for a few hours. She got out of bed and put on her damp clothes as an obnoxious bell announced the serving of breakfast. Flanked by Cam and another cellmate, Ann, Elaine proceeded cautiously to the kitchen area. It was a far cry from the isolation of Woodhill; the sheer volume of prisoners moving through the wing amazed her. As a newcomer, Elaine inevitably found herself the unwelcome centre of attention. Cam had already fielded numerous inquiries about the mysterious young woman sharing her cell. Some had her down as a solicitor or social worker due to the fact that she was smartly dressed in a business suit. Immediately after breakfast, Elaine was anxious to return to the comparative privacy of her cell. Cam had suggested that they spend some time together in the prison gym or exercise yard but there was no way Elaine was going to draw further unnecessary attention to herself.

Like Elaine, the majority of women incarcerated in this section of the prison were also on remand. Even in the short space of time she had spent in Holloway, Elaine was cognisant of the hierarchical system that existed among inmates. In an unnatural, dehumanising environment such as prison, she learned that an individual's status was determined by the nature of their crime; it decided your circle of friends and how others perceived you.

Accordingly, gang rivalry within the prison was rife; stories of physical abuse and bullying abounded. Then, of course, there were the friendships between inmates that took on a more intimate, sexual nature. Lesbian behaviour was seemingly not just confined to the prisoners. Elaine became uneasy when a female officer, the one she had mistaken for a man at Belmarsh, winked at her suggestively. Elaine glared contemptuously back at her, dashing any hopes the officer might have had of getting familiar with her.

From her cell window, Elaine could see the entrance to the prison and its prominent red-brick walls – a well-known landmark in this part of London. She was bored senseless as she waited for Cam to return from her morning workout in the gym. There wasn't even a book or magazine to read. But boredom was the lesser of two evils – there was no way she was going to participate in any prison activity. Not knowing how long she would be staying at Holloway compounded her sense of desperation. Elaine tried to remain positive. She was convinced that every effort was being made to secure her release. The fact that she could be shipped out of Holloway at any moment was another reason for her to remain in her cell. Wishful thinking, perhaps, but it was better than being miserable.

When Cam returned from the gym, they visited the prison shop together. To Elaine's utter frustration, she had neglected to bring any money with her to Holloway and was allocated a miserly two pounds by the prison. Still, it allowed her to purchase a 10 pack of cigarettes, which wouldn't go too far at the rate Elaine was smoking. She kicked herself afterwards when she learned that she could have bought a telephone card with the money instead. Unlike the controlled regime at Woodhill, this prison had a more flexible policy when it came to making phone calls. Cam gave Elaine one of her cards to allow her to contact her solicitor. The Australian seemed intrigued by her Irish cellmate's case and was as eager to find out what was happening in court that day as Elaine was. Unable to recall Gareth's phone number, Elaine was directed to an office where she was assisted by a kind, elderly nun. Number in hand, she joined the queue for the telephone.

Elaine knew that Gareth would still be away but got through to her secretary, Tracy. The news was not good. Tracy informed Elaine that the magistrate was still being unbelievably difficult; her family and legal team were being put through the mill. Gareth had been kept updated of the situation by telephone but so far all efforts by solicitor Tim Greene to satisfy Magistrate Cooper had failed. It was becoming increasingly unlikely that Elaine would be released that day. To make matters worse, it was a Bank Holiday weekend in the UK. Elaine realised that this could result in her remaining in Holloway until at least Tuesday, or even for the duration of the remand period, if the magistrate reserved judgement on her bail application. It would be the second time in a month that a Bank Holiday weekend had impeded her freedom.

* * *

Fresh efforts to satisfy the magistrate's surety demands were being made by Elaine's legal team throughout that day, Friday, 28 August. He approved a surety of £10,000 provided by a lifelong friend of Tom Beirne's, who ran a pub in south London. However, Mr Cooper continued to find fault with other alternative guarantors proposed. A member of Fine Gael, Eric Lynch, who owned a number of properties in London, had offered himself as a replacement surety. When he turned up in court to sign for Elaine, the magistrate insisted that the man's wife also appear. The woman was contacted and later presented herself in court, but Mr Cooper refused to accept the surety on the basis that they had a young child and would be signing over the family home. The couple also owned an apartment in north London, which they were prepared to offer as an additional surety. After Mr Cooper insisted on an auctioneer's valuation report, Eric Lynch left the court and made the lengthy journey to Muswell Hill to find a local estate agent. When he eventually returned with the required documents, the magistrate was not satisfied that there was a £20,000 difference between the valuation and the mortgage due on the property. Late that afternoon, he also ordered that police checks be carried out overnight on the tenancy agreement for the apartment. The magistrate indicated that police could notify him of the situation on Saturday morning. For the second day in a row, time had run out for Elaine. In the meantime, she would have to remain at Holloway prison. Gareth Peirce later noted: "There is no question in the eyes of all who were present in court, whether they be defence lawyers, family, press or observers, that the actions of Mr Cooper were arbitrary, capricious, illogical and unreasonable."

* * *

That evening in Holloway, Elaine's thoughts were with her mother. She was afraid of the possible impact the stress would have on Kathy's health; she had suffered three heart attacks in recent years. Even during her period at Woodhill, Elaine had always played down the hardship of prison life when it came to her mother. In one letter home she wrote: 'I know that it's impossible for you not to worry but things could be a lot worse, Mum. Imagine, if you will, if I were desperately ill in hospital. I would still be confined to a room in which I would be unable to leave. I would still be miles away from family and friends. At least I'm safe and well. I have my health, which is the main thing, and I have been in no way physically harmed. Most of the officers have been quite compassionate here.' While she was being somewhat economical with the truth, Elaine knew her mother would take great comfort from her words.

After dinner, Elaine stuck closely to her Australian friend as lock-up time approached. Walking back to their cell, Cam was summoned by another inmate and brought into a cell where at least another six prisoners were idly chatting. Sitting on the bed was a middle-aged woman, who seemed to be the central figure within the group. After speaking with Cam, the haggard-looking woman turned to Elaine. "Wotcha in for, darlin'?" she asked in a gruff Cockney accent. "Pretty little thing like yourself; you look more like one of them solicitors." Mindful of Cam's earlier advice, Elaine decided to simply outline the charges against her. The very mention of IRA seemed to trigger off a hysterical reaction from her inquisitor, who began ranting about the babies and children that had been murdered by bombs. The atmosphere turned sinister as the other women stared coldly at Elaine. This time, however, she refused to be intimidated. "You'd want to keep your mouth shut about something you know nothing about," Elaine forcefully responded. "Unlike yourself, I'm guilty of nothing. Don't you dare tarnish me with the same brush as other people in this kip who have caused pain and suffering. I've done nothing and I'll be out of this place in no time – you mark my words!" At this point, Cam intervened and assured the others that Elaine was "fine". The London woman appeared to have been caught off-guard by Elaine's outburst and conceded that she might have prematurely jumped to the wrong conclusion.

Back in her cell, Elaine was shaken by the incident, although proud of her handling of it. The adrenaline was still pumping through her veins as Cam congratulated her on her performance. There had been no other option but to challenge that woman's remarks. Had they been allowed to go unchecked, rumours would have been in full flow in no time. She would have been branded as a woman who hurt children by planting bombs, placing her in immediate danger. Elaine had played the prison game – and won. She noticed that a woman had vacated one of the beds in their cell: the one who had been excluded from their conversation the previous night. According to Cam, she had been moved into isolation for her own protection. A fellow inmate had recognised her from an earlier prison stint, where she had served time for child neglect. As news of the woman's past spread throughout the wing, she had been targeted by the other inmates and viciously attacked. That's simply the way it was at Holloway. Elaine stayed well clear of the notorious shower blocks in the prison, which were the scene of regular physical and sexual assaults. It was a particularly terrifying place for an attractive young woman to be. She never once showered while at Holloway and would simply wash herself in the cell's small bathroom.

Elaine felt deeply troubled the next morning. The fact that it was now the Saturday of a Bank Holiday weekend indicated that she would not be leaving Holloway any time soon. She began to regret confiding so openly and honestly with Cam about her prison experience. On reflection, it was the worst possible thing she could have done. Up to that point, Elaine had coped in silence, particularly when she had been placed in solitary confinement at Woodhill. Now, speaking about it only seemed to reinforce the severity and reality of her situation. As she exited her cell for breakfast, she felt more conspicuous than ever at Holloway; her height, Dublin accent and the argument she had had with the other prisoner certainly didn't help. Eyes seemed to follow her every move. It was vital that she maintained the hard, tough exterior she had displayed in front of the other women the previous night. In a strange sense, the fact that the words 'Irish' and 'IRA' were associated with her probably helped protect Elaine from the other prisoners; it certainly made them more wary of her.

* * *

Hopes for Elaine's release faded early on Saturday, 29 August. Despite the fact that police checks on the apartment's tenancy arrangements had proved satisfactory, they were unable to get in touch with the magistrate. When Mr Cooper was eventually contacted in the early afternoon, he still refused to find the proffered surety acceptable. It now looked increasingly likely that Elaine would have to remain at Holloway indefinitely until the matter was dealt with in court. Frustratingly, the magistrate had not refused bail; he had merely objected to the surety offers. As far as their dealings with Magistrate Cooper were concerned, Elaine's legal team had reached the end of the road. At the insistence of Kathy, an urgent approach was made to the clerk of the High Court and the duty judge was contacted. After verifying details of the bail application with the police officer involved, the judge. was satisfied that bail could be granted by accepting the

additional £20,000 originally offered. The only proviso
was that the original surety, who was away on holidays,
would have to re-sign within seven days of the hearing. A
simple, straightforward decision by a High Court judge
had reversed Elaine's fortunes. Although bail was granted
at 3 p.m., it would be more than three hours before she
walked free from prison. A courier dispatched to Holloway
with the relevant paperwork was delayed by traffic, the
Notting Hill carnival brought the streets to a standstill,
so the documents authorising her release eventually had
to be faxed to the prison. Nothing, it appeared, ran
smoothly when it came to Elaine's case.

A tired and emotional Kathy praised the valiant efforts
that had been made on behalf of Elaine by her legal team,
friends and supporters. In some cases, people had allowed
their personal financial affairs to be opened up to public
scrutiny by the magistrate; others had missed two days'
work to appear for Elaine in court. Through the media,
Kathy also acknowledged the professionalism of the police,
who had carried out the required checks on Eric Lynch's
apartment in the most expedient manner. Even the Crown
Prosecution Service was praised for not objecting to the
proposed alterations to Elaine's bail conditions in the first
place. Kathy's contempt was solely reserved for the
magistrate. An equally weary Tim Greene told *The Irish
Times* that the whole episode had been 'completely
unnecessary'.

* * *

Elaine had spent most of Saturday afternoon staring out
through the window of her cell. At approximately 5.30
p.m. she heard the cell door open. "Moore, you've been
released – gather your possessions and come with me," a

prison officer announced. Elaine couldn't believe what she had just heard and looked to Cam for confirmation. After excitedly exchanging their contact details, the two friends vowed to stay in touch and possibly see each other again "on the outside". Elaine felt a tinge of sadness leaving Cam behind in that bleak and desolate place. They had become so close in such a short space of time. Cam's advice had almost certainly saved Elaine from being attacked by other inmates. The Australian cheerfully assured her that she would be fine and made Elaine promise to keep her updated on her case, which she did.

Unlike the exit procedure at Woodhill, no strip-search was necessary as Elaine was brought out to the reception area. She was simply frisked and asked to sign her release form. The entire process took less than 30 minutes – she was free to go. But given all that had gone wrong that week, Elaine remained sceptical. What if Cooper changed his mind? Had the police been informed of her release? What if she was picked up again? Elaine was taking no chances. Before leaving, she demanded some form of documentation that would verify her release from Holloway. A senior officer complied with her request and stamped a piece of paper that read: 'Bail Conditions: Prisoner CF7885 – Moore, Elaine. Report to Belmarsh Magistrate Court on 17 September 1998 at 10 a.m. To live and sleep each night at 28 Reddington Road, London, NW3.' It was dated 29 August 1998. To this day, Elaine still carries that piece of paper in her wallet.

Elaine inquired if there was anyone waiting to greet her. After all, she had no money for a taxi or even to make a phone call. The prison officers could only confirm the presence of members of the media outside. She was taken across a courtyard to a large iron gate, which incorporated a small door to facilitate pedestrian access.

The door creaked as a prison officer, who wished Elaine the best of luck, opened it for her. She felt she would need it. She glanced back towards where she believed her cell had been, wondering if Cam could see her leave. When she turned around, a beaming Kathy was standing there, bouquet of lilies in hand. Her mother's feelings of relief and delight were clearly palpable. The mother and daughter reunion was captured by a RTÉ television crew. The station's reporter, Sean Whelan, sensitively requested that the camera stop rolling to allow them a few moments of privacy. Even he seemed touched by the emotion of Elaine's release. She agreed to appear in an interview with RTÉ, which went out live on the Six-One News. Elaine remained silent throughout, however, and simply let Kathy, a consummate media performer by that stage, do all the talking. Viewers back in Ireland witnessed a young woman standing by her mum looking dazed and confused. Following the interview, Kathy and Elaine chatted briefly with the television reporter, who had been incredibly supportive throughout the bail drama. They then hailed a cab and left HMP Holloway.

The image of Elaine emerging from prison alone, still dressed in the suit she had worn to court three days earlier, remains as poignant as ever for her today. "I was a different person as I walked through the gates of Holloway," she says. "I felt lost, hopeless even. From that moment onwards, bail was just a temporary privilege for me, one that could be taken away at the discretion of a bitter man. Before 27 August, I felt confident that I had achieved freedom, limited as it was. We planned to work tirelessly in preparation for a committal hearing. With the grace of God, I would be returning home to Ireland soon after. But now my belief in the course of justice had diminished. I no longer considered that a committal hearing would enable me to put the record straight. Because of Cooper's actions, I felt that even if the prosecution decided not to pursue a case against me, the magistrate would still insist that I be committed for trial. It may not have been possible for him to do so but it still terrified me."

Chapter Fifteen

CAMPAIGN FOR FREEDOM

A night out on the town was hastily organised to celebrate Elaine's release from Holloway. But the events of the previous few days had clearly taken their toll on the Moore camp and the atmosphere was noticeably subdued. Elaine, as usual, laughed and joked along with friends and family despite feeling deeply troubled inside. There was one small consolation prize to be salvaged from the wreck of her disastrous court appearance. The magistrate had agreed to a change of address from the Irish Chaplaincy in Tollington Park to a religious retreat house on Reddington Road. The day after her release, Elaine packed her belongings and said her goodbyes to the priests and staff at the chaplaincy. While glad to be moving out, she deeply valued the friendships she had made during her short time living there.

Elaine had not expressed a preference for any particular area of London when requesting a change of address. The sleepless nights at the Irish Chaplaincy had seriously depleted her energy levels. She simply needed to live somewhere she could feel safe and secure. Run by the Columban Missionary Society, her new home at St Columban's, on Reddington Road, was an exceptional property located in a leafy suburb of north-west London. Fr Mick Duffy and his housekeeper greeted Elaine on her arrival. She felt awkward as she was introduced to the Brothers and staff but sensed she would soon settle in. She was shown to a magnificent bedroom at the front of the house, which had a large en suite bathroom with a dressing table and wall-to-wall mirrors. Elaine marvelled at the level of privacy the bathroom afforded her; it reminded her of a movie star's dressing room. She was notified by staff about meal times but had no intention of eating at the house if she could help it. Not wishing to impose further on the hospitality of the religious order, Elaine decided to make herself as scarce as possible. Reddington Road would be somewhere to simply lay her head at night.

The location of Elaine's new accommodation was perfect. It was within walking distance of the lively Hampstead area and, more importantly, just 20 minutes away from Rory's house. She knew the area pretty well. It was hugely comforting to be back on familiar territory, which gave her a renewed sense of freedom. Best of all was being able to venture beyond the hall door on her own without feeling intimidated by her surroundings. It was exciting to be living close to such a cosmopolitan part of the city as Hampstead, where she had socialised many times in the past with Rory. The area was an oasis of high street and designer stores; the streets were lined with trendy cafes, restaurants and bars. Also nearby was Hampstead Heath, a popular picnic spot. It was a world away from Tollington Park, where Elaine had become increasingly fearful for her safety. Shortly after the Omagh atrocity, she had noticed the words 'IRA Scum' sprayed across a wall near the Irish Chaplaincy. There was every possibility that the graffiti had been there for some time. Nevertheless, Elaine was concerned that it may have been specifically aimed at her.

Just as she was settling in to her new life at Reddington

Road, Elaine was told that a slight problem had arisen with her accommodation. The religious order had not been informed as to how long she would be staying and sought clarification from Gareth Peirce's office. It emerged that Elaine's room would only be available up until her next remand hearing, which was set for 17 September, as the Brothers were expecting guests from China. The situation would have to be resolved as quickly as possible. Elaine didn't want to have to apply for another change of address and run the risk of displeasing the magistrate – the last thing she needed was to give him an excuse to send her back to jail. It was imperative that he would not be able to accuse her of breaching any of her bail conditions or even suggest that she was taking liberties. Thankfully, a compromise was reached whereby Elaine would simply move to another bedroom in the house, albeit a far less luxurious one. Her new accommodation was located to the rear of the building on the ground floor. Although considerably less comfortable and secure than her original bedroom, it backed on to a beautiful woodland garden. The downside, however, was that she had to run a gauntlet of fear each night to gain access to her room, which was separated from the main house by a poorly lit walkway. After dark, it was a journey that required a considerable amount of Dutch courage. Elaine always returned alone, as she didn't want to abuse the hospitality of the Brothers at Reddington Road. Because there was no key to lock the bedroom door, Elaine would place a large wooden chest up against it to deter a possible intruder. She remained as security conscious as ever.

There was a possibility that Elaine would be remanded on bail indefinitely if her case was committed to trial. This would effectively force her to remain in London for at least a year. Since losing her job at Netlink, her lifestyle had been funded by her mother and, indeed, Rory. While she appreciated their generosity, Elaine yearned for her independence, having always paid her own way from an early age. She had discussed the possibility of seeking new employment with Gareth and Rory. Both agreed that she would benefit, both emotionally and financially, from working again. Having an established routine was exactly what she needed to take her mind off her troubles. There were some obvious obstacles: how would she even get past the interview stage with a prospective employer when she explained her reason for leaving her last job? Then, of course, there was the instability of life on bail. Elaine was afraid that Magistrate Cooper might decide to send her back to jail as he had the authority to do so. With the odds stacked firmly against her, Elaine temporarily shelved plans to look for a job. She decided she would revisit the matter in the event of her case proceeding to trial.

Even prior to her release from Woodhill, the campaign to clear Elaine's name was well underway. Back in Ireland, Elaine's mother had become a ubiquitous presence on the airwaves and in the newspapers, relentlessly declaring her daughter's innocence at every possible opportunity. In London, Rory was working tirelessly behind the scenes to achieve justice for his friend. Apart from organising personal character references for Elaine, he had attempted to bring a number of prominent human rights activists on board the campaign. They included Kevin McNamara, the Labour MP for Hull North, a prominent Liverpool-Irish Catholic radical and former party spokesman for Northern Ireland. British Irish Rights Watch, an independent non-governmental organisation that monitors the human rights dimension of the Northern Ireland conflict, also took an active role in highlighting Elaine's case. Among the group's sponsors were Baroness Helena Kennedy QC, a distinguished lawyer who has been involved in many leading civil liberties cases, including the Guildford Four's successful appeal against their convictions. A prominent member of the Labour Party, she was appointed to the House of Lords and is said to be close to the British Prime Minister, Tony Blair, and his wife, Cherie. She had sent a letter of support to Elaine in Woodhill. Another sponsor of British Irish Rights Watch is Michael Mansfield QC, who had represented Elaine at an earlier successful bail hearing. The barrister had been involved in the cases of the Birmingham Six and the Guildford Four.

Much to Rory's frustration, Elaine was reluctant to become involved in her own campaign. He tried to press upon her the importance of making personal representations to the various politicians and human rights groups that could possibly assist in her case. But Elaine continued to place all her stock in Gareth, in the belief that her solicitor alone would see her through. She also feared that associating with certain groups could prove counterproductive and possibly harm her defence. Gareth recognised the merit in what Rory was trying to achieve, but felt that the legal process had to take its course regardless. Pressure groups would only succeed in highlighting Elaine's case; they would not have any bearing on the outcome of a court hearing. As far as Rory was concerned, Elaine had simply resigned herself to being returned to prison, which led to numerous heated debates between them. "I was continuously pushing her to become more involved in her campaign," he admits. "I said to her: 'Right Elaine, if you go to trial and are found guilty and jailed, how bad am I going to feel? You are going to make me feel awful for not letting me do everything in my power; you won't even help yourself.' 'She was very reluctant to get involved in the campaign. She didn't want to go and meet anyone from British Irish Rights Watch (BIRW), who were 100 per cent behind her and very influential." In truth, Elaine felt that pleading for assistance would be humiliating. She wanted to enjoy what little freedom she had. She also worried about the risk of pressure groups further agitating the magistrate.

Elaine did make a couple of concessions to Rory, such as agreeing to visit Kevin McNamara MP. They wanted him to make representations on their behalf to have Magistrate David Cooper removed from any possible committal hearing. A briefing document initially prepared by the Britain and Ireland Human Rights Centre (BIHRC) and tailored by Gareth outlined Elaine's earlier experiences with Cooper during her failed bail applications at Belmarsh Magistrates' Court. Particular emphasis had been put on his most recent decision to revoke her bail and send her to Holloway. In her report, Gareth had written: 'In view of the fact that there is likely to be a very serious submission of no case to answer at the committal stage for Elaine Moore, there is real concern that should Mr Cooper preside over this hearing, not only will he come to the case with a prior view of Elaine Moore . . . he has [been] shown to consider on two occasions that she should not be granted bail; and on a third occasion that the bail granted to her should not have been granted in the terms it was granted . . . so that justice will never be seen to be done by Elaine Moore or her family. The defence will, of course, ask that Mr Cooper disqualify himself from sitting on such an occasion.' Mr McNamara appeared convinced by their submission and promised Rory and Elaine that he would do everything in his power to ensure a fair hearing. Elaine didn't feel particularly encouraged by the meeting. Politicians provided references for her in the past and Cooper had still refused her bail. What good could they do for her now? Rory took the opposite view, believing the resultant publicity from an MP's involvement would put any ruling under closer public scrutiny. While holding conflicting views on what was best for her case, Elaine did placate Rory somewhat by sending off letters to MPs, who had been sympathetic in similar cases, from the priests' office in Reddington Road.

The Britain and Ireland Human Rights Centre (BIHRC), in conjunction with the Labour Committee on Ireland, held a House of Commons meeting, 2 September 1998, to discuss the implications of new security legislation brought forward as a result of the Omagh atrocity. Among those addressing the meeting were Labour MPs Kevin McNamara and Tony Benn; Billy Power, the former Birmingham Six Prisoner; Fr Gerry McFlynn, the London director of the Irish Commission for Prisoners Overseas; and Rory Hearty, who planned to talk about the circumstances of his own arrest and Elaine's ongoing case.

Entering the House of Commons – where she would most likely be viewed as a serious security threat – was a deeply stressful experience for Elaine. She was highly agitated as she stood in a large hall with Niall and Rory awaiting the arrival of Paul May, the press officer for the BIHRC. To pass the time, they viewed the historical artefacts that adorned the room. Elaine's attention was drawn to a plaque set into the stone floor. Dated 23 August 1305, the plaque marked William Wallace's trial before a bench of noblemen in Westminster Hall. She was now standing in the actual place depicted in the jigsaw given to her by prison staff at Woodhill. The extraordinary coincidence sent a shiver down her spine. Elaine believed it was an omen but was unsure as to interpret it as a good or bad one. His trial and cruel punishment were typical of law and order in the medieval ages. Given her predicament, she wondered just how much times had changed.

When the meeting eventually got underway, Elaine was happy to take a back seat and let the more experienced people take centre stage. A representative of the Britain and Ireland Human Rights Centre warned against rushing in new anti-terrorist legislation. The meeting was told that in 1974 the climate of panic and rushed security measures allowed police to secure the wrongful convictions of 18 innocent men and women. This, in turn, meant that those guilty of the murders of 40 people in the Birmingham, Guildford, Woolwich and M62 bombings were never brought to justice. "The recent arrests in London and Dublin of Rory Hearty and other innocent Irish people – and the continuing ordeal of Elaine Moore – highlight the insanity of allowing convictions on the word of a single police officer," a spokesperson for the group warned. "Justice for the innocent victims of Omagh, Ballymoney and other atrocities will not be achieved by the imprisonment of yet more innocent people."

After Rory made an impassioned speech on Elaine's behalf, they met with various MPs and other supporters of her campaign. The proceedings made Elaine feel distinctly uncomfortable. She excused herself from the meeting and opted to wait outside for the others until it was over. It was the last time that Elaine would become actively involved in her own campaign.

An uneasy stand-off developed between Rory and Elaine because of this. But simmering tensions soon boiled to the surface when Elaine accidentally came across a copy of the controversial *Sunday Independent* article that her family and friends had kept from her for over a month.

One evening, she had been hanging out at Rory's flat and went into his bedroom to lie down for a while. Unable to sleep, she picked up a book off his bedside table and casually flicked through it. Uninterested, she put the book down on the floor where she noticed the *Sunday Independent* under the bed. Rory will never forget Elaine's reaction after she read the offending article. "She came out of the room and was completely hysterical," he shudders. "She really lost the plot. I tried to explain that her mother had asked me to keep her from seeing it, but there was no reasoning with her at all. I tried to calm her down by pointing out that nobody quoted by the journalist had been named; that anyone could go and write an article like that. She was so terribly distraught and I couldn't console her." Rory recalls that Elaine became very distant towards him for a few days after the incident. As the closest person to her in London, he naturally bore the brunt of her fears and frustrations. The article implied that the prosecution had damning new evidence that would prove their case against her. If convicted, she could be facing a 20-year stretch in prison. Although Elaine knew that no such evidence existed, she came to the dramatic conclusion that she was being set up by the prosecution. "That article had a devastating effect on me," she says today. "There had been so many setbacks and unusual turns of events throughout my case that nothing would have surprised me. It was a damning article. I was inconsolable after reading it and became very withdrawn. Not even Rory or Mum could offer me any comfort. I needed to speak to Gareth – she was the only one who would be able to make sense of it all. I knew she wouldn't shy away from the truth or say things just to make me feel better. Gareth always gave it to me straight."

A few days later, Elaine showed a copy of the article

to Gareth, who was completely dismissive of it. She, too, pointed out the obvious flaw in the report – not one single person quoted had been named. She stressed that if the prosecution had more solid evidence against Elaine, they would surely have presented it during the bail hearings. As they had objected to bail on the first two occasions, it would not have been in their interest to withhold any evidence. Even the magistrate had expressed annoyance at the apparent lack of evidence against her. Gareth then read through the article again and took Elaine through it line by line. As far as the solicitor was concerned, there was nothing to worry about. Having been completely reassured by Gareth, Elaine left her office in Camden on a complete high. She decided to celebrate by buying herself a new handbag. "When she came back that day it was like she had won the lottery," Rory recalls. "Gareth had given her such hope. It was as if the charges had been dropped." Although any fears that the article had generated had subsided, Elaine could not entirely forget about it and carried the burden of its implications with her for some time.

Gareth recalls that the police did, at a later stage, try to present some 'tenuous' new evidence against the other men charged in relation to the terrorism offences, but not Elaine. "There was some evidence that the prosecution tried to rely on against the young men, but in the end they didn't because it was pretty much rubbish," she recollects. "It was to do with a so-called lip-reader. The police had taken video footage under surveillance of the two young men sitting on a park bench. Then they had someone provide them with a lip-reading. But it actually turned out that this so-called expert was making it up as she went along, by and large. It was not scientific evidence."

Elaine's next hurdle was the upcoming remand hearing. She didn't savour the thought of appearing before Cooper again. Her twenty-second birthday was to fall on 22 September, just days after the remand hearing. Prison is a lonely place at the best of times; Elaine couldn't even begin to contemplate how she would feel having to celebrate her birthday behind bars. Just thinking about Cooper kept her awake at night. As 17 September approached, Elaine tried to emotionally prepare herself for yet another setback. Gareth was determined not to let that happen again. An emergency meeting had been convened with Elaine after her last disastrous court appearance. Since then, Lynn Solomon, the film producer who had been away on holidays, had returned from America and re-signed as a surety. This time, Gareth would personally be in court to deal with any unforeseen problems, should they arise. Elaine remarked that Cooper had had no right to deny her bail on the last occasion, but Gareth insisted that his actions had been lawful, regardless of how callous they seemed.

According to Gareth, the remand dates existed for several reasons: firstly, for the court to ensure that progress was being made in the prosecution of the case and to monitor that progress; secondly, where individuals were in custody, to ensure that they were produced before the court at least every 28 days. In Elaine's case, there was no real necessity for her to have to attend court as she was not in custody. However, until a committal date was given, there was simply no occasion for her to be bailed other than the remand hearings. Given her most recent experience in court, Elaine was unable to enjoy the reassurances of bail because of the obstacles that had been arbitrarily placed in her way by the magistrate.

On the morning of 17 September, Elaine entered

Belmarsh Magistrates' Court defiantly, accompanied by Gareth. When her case was called, she walked past the bench where Cooper would be sitting and took her seat in the dock as Gareth offered a warm, reassuring smile in her direction. She shivered in cold anticipation as Cooper entered the courtroom and proceedings got underway. Again, there was no request for bail for her three co-accused, who were further remanded in custody. The prosecution presented no new evidence against the four; results from the forensic laboratory were still awaited. During the 13-minute hearing, the prosecution lawyer, Carol Wiseman, told the court that there were 1,200 exhibits in total covering various aspects of the case. Gareth, in her opening address, insisted that there were no grounds for a denial of bail for her client. This time, incredibly, the magistrate seemed to agree and remanded Elaine on restricted bail until 15 October 1998. He expected to be in a position to give a date for the commencement of committal proceedings against her by then. Elaine couldn't believe it. For the first time, Cooper had allowed her to walk free from his court. Elaine couldn't thank Gareth enough; yet again, she had been mesmerised by her solicitor's remarkable performance that morning.

There were unrestrained celebrations that night as Elaine gathered with family and friends in The Shawl pub in south Harrow, Middlesex. It was run by Ambrose Gordon, an old friend of Tom Beirne's who had signed as a replacement surety for Elaine. Kathy had flown over for the hearing and to be with her daughter for her twenty-second birthday. Elaine's confidence levels had been replenished following the hearing. The fact that bail had been granted without any complications considerably boosted her morale. It would be another month before her next remand hearing, where a committal date would most likely be set. She decided not to panic for at least two weeks. Elaine simply wanted to stave off the inevitable and enjoy life to the full.

For the first time since her release on bail, Elaine was starting to spend some time alone. She would occasionally browse around the shops in Hampstead or stop to have a coffee in the late summer sunshine. Most days, she hung out at Rory's house and spent the evenings socialising with friends. On one memorable day she passed the afternoon roller-blading in Hyde Park with Niall and Rory. The trio enjoyed several happy hours there, followed by a nice meal and a trip to the cinema. They were all in high spirits; it was just like life had been prior to her arrest on 10 July. Elaine recalls it was the closest thing to normality since her ordeal began. Niall was scheduled to return to America on 15 October. Elaine was not looking forward to him leaving. Niall was extremely laid back; nothing seemed to faze him. He had an uncanny ability to talk to her for hours on end without once mentioning her situation, even though she knew he would always be there for her should she wish to discuss it.

There were good and bad days, punctuated by extreme highs and lows. One night Elaine decided to treat Rory and Niall to a meal in a fashionable Camden restaurant; it would be her way of expressing her gratitude for their ongoing support. It was a memorable night, blurred only by the copious amount of wine consumed over dinner. A flamboyant woman who – much to everyone's amusement – danced and sang with puppets and teddy bears, entertained the diners. For once, Elaine's worries were furthermost from her mind. They left the restaurant in great form, picking up a bottle of wine en route to Rory's flat. Elaine wouldn't be able to stay too long because of the curfew Gareth had imposed on her. Their drunken banter was interrupted by a phone call conveying some tragic news. A young man who was close to some of Elaine's friends back home had been stabbed to death in Canada. Although she had not known him personally, she was deeply upset about the impact it would have on 'the lads', as she affectionately referred to them. This time, the floodgates were well and truly opened. On hearing her cry, Niall entered the bedroom and protectively wrapped his arms around her. Rory watched on sadly, knowing that – despite her fragile condition – Elaine would soon have to make the lonely trip home alone to Reddington Road. It was yet another cruel and unjust twist in this ongoing saga.

* * *

Throughout her ordeal, Elaine always gave the impression that she was coping remarkably well. It was during this period that family and friends, even Gareth, worried most about Elaine's state of mind. Preparation work for a possible committal hearing had been hampered by a delay in receiving all the prosecution statements. In Gareth's view, working on the case would have been a therapeutic experience for Elaine. Unfortunately, they had reached a temporary hiatus. "It was as if she was in limbo and being in limbo wasn't good for her," recalls Gareth. "If I phoned her and asked how she was, she'd always say 'fine', and yet I was fairly sure that she wasn't fine. She didn't feel she could somehow confide in people sufficiently to explain why." The solicitor believes that Elaine may have put up a 'protective veneer' in response to having a criminal allegation made against her. "I think it disabled her," she elaborates. "She couldn't think of the future;

she couldn't think of normality; she couldn't have normal relationships with her friends or other people because it was as if she was being taken into a different place."

Gareth expected that a date for a committal hearing would be set for sometime in November. As far as Elaine's legal team was concerned, this was a crucial juncture in terms of her case. "That would have been the opportunity to say: 'Stop it here – there is not enough evidence to go to trial'," says Gareth. "It is a difficult thing to do but we could have succeeded in Elaine's case. If we didn't win that day, then she would have to stand trial." It was Gareth's contention that, ultimately, Elaine would have been acquitted. But it could have meant at least a year on bail before her case was heard. It was therefore a scenario to be avoided at all costs. "It was extremely clear that Elaine was the odd one out in that prosecution," Gareth believes. "If it progressed to trial, there would have been a serious risk of the prosecution not winning the case. The prosecution authorities are not meant to proceed if they think they have less than a 50 per cent chance of winning. For a range of reasons, anyone who looked at the case in a detached way must have seen that they didn't have sufficient evidence to obtain a conviction."

In the meantime, the campaign to have Magistrate David Cooper removed from a committal hearing continued apace; Elaine's legal team began the lengthy trawl through the prosecution statements. They contained one particularly significant revelation. Full details of the surveillance operation revealed that Nicky – who was supposed to be Elaine's new flatmate – was, in fact, an undercover policewoman. While Nicky's observations didn't go so far as to exonerate Elaine, they unquestionably verified her version of events. Now that this information was in Gareth's possession, the prosecution would be forced to disclose Nicky's evidence in court. Ironically, the police had unintentionally bolstered Elaine's defence.

Elaine was able to relax a little after realising how flimsy the prosecution's case against her was. But she still had a profound distrust of the British judiciary, along with a deep-rooted fear of returning to prison. Gareth reflects that getting the woman to masquerade as a prospective tenant was "disturbing" and an "odd and unusual" step for the police to take.

Chapter Sixteen

THE ORDEAL ENDS

The morning of 8 October 1998 was uneventful. After tidying her room and doing her laundry, Elaine spoke briefly with Fr Mick. She then left the house on Reddington Road and walked the short distance through Hampstead to Rory's place on Malden Avenue. Elaine spent most of the day there, idly watching TV and chatting with Rory and Niall. Rory had not returned to work since his arrest on 10 July. His unexpected sabbatical allowed him the time to fully immerse himself in the campaign to clear Elaine's name – whether she wanted him to or not.

That evening, Elaine decided that she would cook a nice meal for the Hearty brothers and Rory's flatmates at Rory's flat. She had just served up dinner shortly before 8 p.m. when the phone rang. Rory took the call – it was Gareth, looking for Elaine. Reluctantly, she came to the phone. It was an unusual time for her solicitor to call, she thought. Gareth was brief and to the point – she had an inherent distrust of the telephone. She simply asked if Elaine could call to her house in Camden as urgently as possible; she needed to speak to her in person about an important matter. As Elaine hung up the phone, the atmosphere in the flat became tense.

The meal she had cooked remained on the table, untouched and uneaten. She went into Rory's room and sat motionless on his bed, preparing herself for the worst. The most likely scenario was that her bail had been revoked. Rory was also deeply concerned. Gareth had sounded strange when she spoke to him on the phone. She had asked him to drive Elaine down to her house – but she was to go in on her own. "I started to get really nervous as well," Rory admits "there had obviously been a significant development, one Elaine had to hear directly from Gareth."

There was an awkward silence when she re-entered the living room. Rory had already explained the possible implications of the call to everyone. There was simply nothing more to be said. To Elaine, the silence of her friends spoke volumes. It was as if they were speculating about the possible outcome but couldn't bring themselves to articulate the conclusions they had reached. The situation reminded Elaine of sitting in the cell at Belmarsh Magistrates' Court while she awaited her fate at the hands of Cooper. There was little conversation as Rory drove Elaine the short distance to Gareth's house. "Well, this is it, pet – I'll let you know what's wrong as soon as I do," she said to him as the car came to a halt. She hesitated slightly before walking up the garden path and ringing the doorbell. Time seemed to stand still as she waited for Gareth to open the door. Her solicitor asked how she was feeling. "I've been better," a noticeably shaken Elaine responded. As she braced herself for the worst possible news, all she could think was: "Oh my God – I'm in Gareth's Peirce's gaff!" It was a truly surreal moment. Gareth explained that she had received a fax late that evening, just before she was about to leave her office. She handed it to Elaine, who frantically scanned it for anything of obvious significance. The fax, dated Thursday, 8 October 1998, was from the Crown Prosecution Service. It read:

'I write to inform you that I have today sent a notice to the Clerk of the Justices under Section 23 of the Prosecution of Offences Act 1985, discontinuing the following charges against your client, Elaine Nan Catherine Moore:

(1) Conspiracy to cause an explosion contrary to Section 3(1)(a) of the Explosive Substances Act 1883; and

(2) Unlawfully and maliciously possessing an explosive substance contrary to Section 3(1)(b) of the Explosive Substances Act 1883.

The effect of this notice is that your client no longer need attend court in respect of these charges. The decision to discontinue these charges has been taken because the available evidence is insufficient to provide a realistic prospect of conviction.

This decision has been taken on the evidence and information provided to the Crown Prosecution Service as at the date of this letter. If more significant evidence and/or information is discovered at a later date, the decision to discontinue may be reconsidered.

Your client has the right to require the discontinued proceedings to be revived. If you wish to exercise this right, you must give written notice to the Chief Clerk at the above Magistrates' Court as soon as possible (and in any event within 35 days).

Should your client wish to apply for any costs incurred in respect of these proceedings, you may make a written request to the Clerk of the Justices. It is not necessary to apply for the proceedings to be continued in order to apply for your costs.

CAUTION: this notice only applies to the charges specified in it, and does not have any effect in relation to any others that may be pending or other proceedings against your client.'

Elaine looked at Gareth searchingly. "Does this mean what I hope it means?" she asked nervously.

"Yes, Elaine – they've dropped the charges," the solicitor replied.

Elaine remained seated and re-read the fax, struggling to comprehend the enormity of what she thought it was saying. Could it be possible that her ordeal was finally behind her? Gareth watched on patiently. But the solicitor's angelic smile said it all – it was over. Elaine leapt from the sofa and threw her arms around her. "We did it, Gareth – I can't believe it!" she squealed as tears streamed down her face. She wanted to ring her mum immediately but was so overwhelmed that she couldn't remember her number. Elaine started laughing uncontrollably – she was truly overjoyed. That evening, Kathy was working late in the women's refuge centre. Elaine left a message with a colleague for her mum to contact her urgently. Kathy became concerned when she didn't recognise the number that Elaine had left. Her heart was racing as she went to make the call. Gareth answered the phone and handed it to Elaine.

"Are you all right, Elaine – what's going on?" asked Kathy in a worried tone.

"I'm coming home Mum," was her daughter's simple reply.

There was a long pause. Kathy told Elaine that she had to go and get a cigarette and asked if she could ring her back. "Gareth – I think mum just hung up on me," said Elaine, laughing. In the meantime, her mother contacted Tom and Martin. "Elaine is coming home," was all she was able to say. She was completely in shock. Kathy tried to compose herself before calling Elaine. She wanted to know everything and sought validation of this incredible news. It was only through talking to her mother that the realisation of what had just transpired finally dawned on Elaine. "When I heard myself repeating the good news to Mum, it somehow felt real," she remembers.

"I had become so sceptical about everyone and everything. It was incomprehensible that I was now free of all the restrictions and could return home to my family." Elaine phoned her brother and her father, unaware that Kathy had already been in touch with them.

Suddenly she remembered that Rory was waiting for her outside, completely oblivious to this amazing development. She approached his car, her face displaying no emotion. She told Rory that Gareth wanted to see him inside. "What's wrong – tell me," he pleaded. As he emerged from the car, Elaine couldn't keep up the cruel charade any longer. "I'm going home!" she screamed. Stunned but elated, Rory picked her up and swung her around in his arms. Needing to hear every detail, Rory went back into the house where Gareth recounted the evening's sequence of events for him. The fax had been sent at 7.44 p.m., long after business hours. It was by pure chance that Gareth and a colleague were working late and happened to come across it. Otherwise, Elaine would not have been given the news until the following day. As with every decision relating to this case, there appeared to be a deliberate attempt by the authorities to prolong her misery. Rory suddenly remembered that he had to get something from his car. Earlier, as he sat waiting for Elaine outside, the possibility of her receiving good news had crossed his mind. Always prepared for any eventuality, he drove to a nearby off-licence and bought a bottle of champagne. It was popped open in Gareth's living room where the three of them toasted Elaine's reversal of fortunes.

Although delighted at the outcome, Gareth also felt angry when she learned that the charges against Elaine had been dropped. "There was never any need to charge her," she believes. "It was very clear that even if the police suspected her, they couldn't and shouldn't have gone beyond that and charged her without considerable thought. I thought that they destroyed her whole existence here. They fought to keep her inside; their evidence hadn't changed for a moment, from the beginning to the end. The fact that someone saw sense in the end doesn't make it any better that they didn't see sense in the beginning."

Gareth's most enduring memory of Elaine's case is the sight of such "an unusually attractive and beautiful young woman" standing in the dock. "When she appeared in court everyone was struck by her beauty," she recalls.

"She was the focus of everyone's attention for a range of reasons. If she had been sitting in the public gallery, people in court would have been looking at her. But she wasn't sitting in the public gallery – she was in the dock. So it wasn't normal; it was unusual for a young woman to be on a charge of conspiracy to cause explosions in all the years that people in this country have been on those charges. In any event it was a rarity."

Gareth urged Elaine to get a flight out of the UK immediately; that very evening, if possible. It wasn't that she feared Elaine would be re-arrested or had anything to be frightened of; she just believed that leaving London was the only way to begin to put such an awful experience behind her. "I felt it had all been a bad dream for her," Gareth explains. "Although she had been on bail, she was very affected by being, in lots of ways, still a prisoner here. I am sure I did say to her [that night]: 'Look – just go. Get out of here; leave it all behind.' I thought the quicker she could get all this behind her, the better." For the first time, Elaine felt unable to accept this advice, even though she knew her solicitor had her best interests at heart. Gareth's word had always been Gospel. But Elaine was adamant that she should stay in London for a couple of days – this time as a free woman – before embarking on the journey home to rebuild her life. She also wanted an opportunity to say goodbye properly to her friends and the many people who had supported her. Elaine may have been free to go – but she was equally free to stay if she so chose to. She planned to relish that freedom in all its forms.

Elaine was bursting with anticipation as they drove back to Rory's house to announce the good news. They resisted the urge to phone the others in advance and instead hatched plans for a devious prank. Pulling up outside, the pair struggled to keep a lid on their exuberance as they danced along the street, bottle of champagne in hand. Elaine stayed in the background as Rory entered the flat with his head lowered, signalling to Niall and his flatmates that all was not well. "They're sending her back to prison," he deadpanned. Rory was notorious for winding people up but, given the seriousness of the situation, this was a particularly impressive performance. They averted their eyes and stared at the television when Elaine entered the room. The tension was unbearable. "Well lads, what can I say?" she said, pausing, then screaming: "I'm going home!" She was immediately engulfed in a rugby type scum as all three jumped on her. The celebrations were officially underway.

The flat was soon awash with well-wishers from the other flats in the house. Champagne continued to flow as preparations were made for a major night out on the town. Finally, there was something truly worth celebrating. Elaine was met by smiling faces everywhere. After topping up her glass and lighting a cigarette, she sat in the corner of the sitting room and soaked up the atmosphere. She felt a solitary tear of joy trickle down her face. Niall approached her and said: "You did it, pet. Now get moving – it's time to celebrate." A fleet of taxis had been summoned to the house, each one bound for Scruffy Murphy's. On her arrival, Elaine met her good friend, Paddy Cohen, who managed the bar. Rory asked if he would open the bar upstairs, but neglected to mention what the celebrations were all about – he wanted Elaine to tell Paddy personally. When she did, it took some time for it to hit home for him. Throughout the night, as the party went into overdrive, Elaine remained in close contact with her loved ones back home. A party of similar magnitude had erupted in the Moore household in Dublin. Kathy informed her that she would be flying over to London first thing the next morning – this time, to bring her daughter home.

Chapter Seventeen

THE HOMECOMING

The ending of Elaine's London nightmare was front-page news in Ireland the next day, Friday, 9 October. 'This is the moment we've been waiting for,' Kathy told the *Irish Independent*. Speaking to *The Irish Times*, the Taoiseach, Bertie Ahern, said he was pleased for Ms Moore and her family that the charges had been dropped and her ordeal was over. In the same article, Mary Banotti declared she was 'absolutely delighted' at the news. 'It was what I expected all along but it has come about a little quicker than I thought it would,' the Fine Gael MEP said. 'I was always completely convinced of her innocence and I'm sure it must be a great relief to herself and her family and everyone who supported her campaign.'

Meanwhile, in London, the partying had continued into the early hours of Friday morning. After leaving Scruffy Murphy's pub, everyone descended on Rory's flat where the revelry began all over again. It was one of the most incredible nights of Elaine's life, although it saddened her to think that she would be leaving behind some of the most amazing people she had ever met. This tight-knit, ex-pat Irish community had been the very backbone of her existence in London. Having vowed to never return to England again, Elaine realised that her relationship with each individual would be changed forever. The celebrations were temporarily marred when a fracas occurred between two party-goers at around 5.30 a.m. In a sense, it was inevitable that underlying tensions would come to the surface that night due to the heady concoction of alcohol and pent-up emotions. Elaine decided that she wasn't going to allow the incident to dampen her spirits. Discreetly, she left the flat alone and took a taxi back to the house on Reddington Road.

Elaine tiptoed through the house, conscious of disturbing the other residents. Catching a glimpse of her drunken demeanour in a mirror, she had to cover her mouth to suppress a giddy laugh. For once, she felt no fear as she entered her room with new-found confidence. No sooner was she in bed than there was a knock on her door – it was Fr Mick. Elaine cringed – perhaps she had overstepped the mark by returning to the house at such an ungodly hour. She needn't have worried – the priest was simply letting her know that two men had called to the house looking for her; he had asked them to wait in the sitting room. Apologising profusely for the inconvenience, Elaine explained that the charges against her had been dropped. Fr Mick was delighted for her. He graciously dismissed her apology, explaining that he awoke at dawn each morning and had been preparing breakfast when the knock came to the door. She got dressed hurriedly and made her way back out to the main house where she was greeted by Niall and Tony, a flatmate of Rory's. "We were worried," said Tony, by way of explanation. "No one saw you leave the house – are you all right?" Elaine appreciated their concern but couldn't understand why they simply hadn't phoned her. She laughed at the state of her two friends, who were showing all the signs of a night of excess. Elaine was relieved to learn that the row back in Rory's flat had been quickly diffused soon after she left.

Elaine and her friends were invited by Fr Mick to stay for breakfast at the retreat house. Niall wasn't able to join them, unfortunately, having finally succumbed to a drink-fuelled slumber there and then in the sitting room. Elaine and Tony gladly tucked into the generous helpings of food put before them as they regaled the priest with an epic account of the night before. She asked Fr Mick to convey her heartfelt thanks to the Brothers and staff at Reddington Road and inform them of her good news. After breakfast, they opted to walk back to Rory's flat – the fresh air would clear their heads. There was no time for sleep – this was to be Elaine's last day in London and she intended to enjoy every moment of it. Top of the agenda was meeting up with her friends in a local café. Before joining them there, she received a phone call from Kathy – who sounded as fragile and hungover as her daughter. Elaine was aghast to learn that she was expected to give an interview that morning with Pat Kenny for his radio show. "Mum, I haven't slept since yesterday and am still slightly tipsy as we speak," she pleaded. Reluctantly, Elaine agreed to take a call from Kenny. In a desperate attempt to regain her composure, she decided to do the interview while sitting on the pavement outside the cafe. After all, she couldn't be heard to be slurring her words on national radio.

Pat Kenny seemed genuinely delighted that Elaine was finally coming home, which helped put her at ease. She thanked the broadcaster and his listeners for all their support over the previous three months. The response to her mother's initial interview with the RTÉ host had been phenomenal. In Elaine's view, it had helped shape the public – and the media – perception of her and resulted in her receiving hundreds of cards and letters from well-wishers while in prison. She told the show she was disappointed that the fax sent by the Crown Prosecution Service announcing her release did not include an apology.

"It was pure business format," she said. "There was no apology – no nothing." Elaine also expressed reservations about ever going abroad in future. "I swear, I don't think I'll ever leave Ireland again. Even going on a two-week holiday will be a fierce hard thing to do. I don't think I'll be leaving for a long time."

Elaine had a busy day ahead of her. There were so many people she needed to say goodbye to and, naturally, a major farewell party to attend. Her mother was also due in London in the next few hours. As she packed, Elaine learned that the media had tracked her down. Rory had already taken a call from RTÉ's London editor, Brian O'Connell, who had previously covered Elaine's case in a fair and impartial manner. She agreed to meet him later for an interview but was keen to leave Reddington Road as quickly as possible due to the presence of journalists outside. This, she felt, was an unwelcome intrusion on the sanctuary of the retreat house. Elaine refused to comment to awaiting reporters as she jumped into the car with Rory and sped off. As arranged, they met up with the RTÉ reporter a safe distance away from the house. Elaine desperately hoped that her initial TV interview – which was first aired on the lunchtime news – would help quell the media interest in her story.

Back at Rory's flat, Elaine chatted incessantly on the phone with friends and relatives – it was a story she would never tire of telling. Her best friend, Tracy, told how her father had interrupted his work and burst into the house to announce Elaine's homecoming. Elaine was delighted to speak to Rory's mother, Doreen, who had been kept fully briefed on developments by her son. Finally, she called Gareth to see if there was a possibility of meeting up before she went back to Ireland – unfortunately, there wasn't. The solicitor reiterated her view that Elaine should leave the UK as soon as possible and put the experience behind her. "Don't look back, Elaine," she told her.

That evening, Kathy and Tom flew to London and took a taxi directly to Rory's flat where they received an ecstatic welcome from Elaine. It had been a long time since she had seen her mother look so happy. After their reunion, they travelled together to the Irish Chaplaincy in Tollington Park. During their last visit, the Brothers had told Kathy and Tom that they were welcome to stay any time they were in London; they had even been given their own key to allow them to come and go as they pleased. Their usual room was unavailable; members of the Irish band, The Saw Doctors, had occupied it that night. Their old friend, Carmel, who worked in the chaplaincy office, came to the rescue and found Tom and Kathy accommodation nearby. Fr Joe Brown, a young priest who had always been hospitable towards the Moore family, let them into the house.

There wasn't much time to settle in – the mother of all farewell parties was just about to get started in Scruffy Murphy's. Elaine was delighted at the huge turnout, which gave her the opportunity to say goodbye properly to the people that had played such an important part in her life in London – from her former colleagues at Netlink to her friends and campaign supporters. The unavoidable absence of Gareth was the only thing missing in an otherwise perfect night as the champagne, and Guinness, flowed.

* * *

By Saturday, 10 October, media focus had shifted to the handling of Elaine's case by the authorities. Scotland Yard's tactics were severely criticised as full details of the surveillance operation carried out on Elaine emerged. The duplicity of 'Nicky' – who had surreptitiously recorded her conversations with Elaine while posing as a prospective tenant – drew howls of protest from commentators. The late Labour TD, Pat Upton, called on the Irish Embassy in London to make urgent representations to the British authorities regarding the conduct of the police. Deputy Upton felt that such behaviour would do nothing to improve the confidence of Irish people living in the UK. 'The way the undercover policewoman is said to have behaved sounds like she was almost encouraging Elaine to unwittingly incriminate herself,' he told *The Irish Times*. In the same article, the Sinn Féin TD for Cavan-Monaghan, Caoimhghín Ó Caoláin, said Elaine's case demonstrated the grave dangers to civil liberties posed by draconian legislation. Peter Barry, the former Tánaiste, found the reported behaviour of the undercover police-woman to be 'disturbing and bizarre'. Mary Banotti MEP, on the other hand, believed that the deployment of 'Nicky' was ultimately helpful to the defence's case. 'The evidence she collected proved that Elaine was telling the truth,' she told a newspaper.

Fr Gerry McFlynn, the London officer of the Irish Commission for Prisoners Overseas, said he had been puzzled and concerned by the Metropolitan Police's investigation of Elaine. Gareth Peirce also reserved her strongest criticism for the manner of the police in-vestigation. She told *The Irish Times* she had been 'astonished' to see the case go so far through the courts. She said the police had simply decided not to believe Elaine's 'consistent explanations', which – in her opinion – was 'tantamount to reversing the burden of proof.' The solicitor felt it was too early to consider bringing a case for compensation against the British authorities. 'She

[Elaine] would have to consider that carefully. I think she would want to be shot of the courts and not spend time looking back.'

The *Irish Independent* believed that Elaine would now have to come to terms with the psychological scars of her three-month nightmare. 'All I want to do is to go on a holiday around Ireland,' she was quoted as saying. 'I don't know how much this whole thing has affected me; I still haven't really come to terms with what has happened. That will come later. All I want to do now is go home.' The article warned of the possible effects the experience would have on Elaine: 'It's probable that when the euphoria wears off; when she has said goodbye to all her friends in London; and the celebrations with her family and pals at home in Dublin are over, the enormity of what she has endured will sink in. Fruitless anger, bitterness and deep-seated resentment at her wrongful arrest may follow. Coping with these destructive and ultimately futile emotions will be her next test. She will be a remarkable young woman if her natural openness and self-confidence is not eroded for good. From now on, suspicion may be her first instinctive recourse; obsessive vigilance her watchword; and she may never be able to stroll the streets of London without the odd anxious glance over her shoulder at a passing policeman.'

* * *

Elaine couldn't bring herself to say 'goodbye' to the many friends she would be leaving behind in London. 'I'll see you soon' sounded better; there was less finality to it. Well-intentioned plans for a get-together in Ireland were made with every farewell hug, although, privately, Elaine knew she wouldn't be seeing many of these people again for a long time – if ever. Not surprisingly, leaving Niall behind proved deeply upsetting for Elaine. The one saving grace was that Rory had agreed to travel back to Dublin with her. "I doubt I would have been able to leave London without him," she admits. "I was very dependent on him."

There was a subdued atmosphere in the car as they drove to Stanstead Airport that evening. Kathy tried to prepare Elaine for the expected media circus that would await her in Dublin by firing the most probable questions journalists would ask at her. Suddenly, they heard something explode underneath them. The car, which was being driven at speed along the express motorway, swerved violently across three lanes as Rory struggled to regain control. Thanks to his competence as a driver, he managed to bring the vehicle to a stop in the hard shoulder. There were sighs of relief all round. "Something's telling me that I'm not supposed to leave this place!" Elaine joked. "The elements are conspiring against us." Fortunately, there was a less sinister explanation – a blow-out in the left rear tyre. The incident did nothing to calm everyone's already frayed nerves. "We were very nervous as it was," recalls Kathy "On the way to the airport, we were even wondering if the car had been wired – everything was going through our minds." Rory quickly put on the spare wheel and they continued on to the airport.

Prior to checking-in at the airport, Elaine became conscious of a lone photographer stalking her. Noticing her discomfort, he eventually approached and requested permission to take a single photograph. She agreed, on condition that he would then leave her alone. Sitting in the departures lounge, Elaine felt increasingly edgy. She went to the ladies' room and applied some make-up in a futile attempt to conceal the prominent dark circles around her eyes. Having been in bed for no more than four hours since learning that the charges against her had been dropped, Elaine was showing all the signs of self-inflicted sleep deprivation. Frankly, she looked a mess – there couldn't have been a worse possible time to face the media. She informed her mother that it wasn't a prospect she particularly savoured. From her own recent experiences with the media, Kathy knew that certain elements of the press would be unrelenting in their efforts to talk to Elaine. However, she decided not to push the issue, seeing that her daughter was visibly exhausted and agitated.

On boarding the Ryanair flight, Elaine was tactfully ushered to a seat towards the front of the plane. As she left London behind her, Elaine tried to contemplate her future, but was unable to see beyond the night that lay ahead of her. She felt tense and apprehensive. Kathy, too, was unable to relax until she heard the pilot utter the words: "Welcome to Dublin." Elaine glanced over excitedly at Rory as the other passengers applauded their safe landing. The Moore party were requested to remain seated until everyone else had disembarked. A stewardess informed them that a car had been arranged to transport them to the VIP lounge. Elaine kissed her fingers and touched the ground as she emerged from the plane, overwhelmed by the familiar sight of Dublin Airport. No sooner had she sat in the courtesy car than she saw her father and brother through the window of an airport lounge. She leapt from her seat and ran across the tarmac in their direction. In a rare breach of procedure, Airport Police opened a fire exit to enable Robert to join her outside. The brother and sister reunion was a particularly poignant moment – Robert had been the only member of the family Elaine had not seen since her arrest.

Having declined the use of the courtesy car, Elaine was directed to a VIP lounge. Still high from the experience of seeing her brother and father again, her heart sank when she was informed that a press conference had been arranged in anticipation of her arrival home. All she wanted to do was cherish each and every moment with her family.

"She was very upset," remembers Kathy. "The airport staff were brilliant and told her that she didn't have to face the media if she didn't want to." When she calmed down, Elaine weighed up the pros and cons of attending the press conference. It presented her with the perfect opportunity to thank the media and the public for all their support. It would also possibly deter journalists from calling to the family home that night in the hope of being granted an interview. Elaine was surprised and delighted to meet a friend of hers, Kevin, who was a member of the Airport Police. He helped to reassure her by describing the format of the press conference she was about to give. Elaine steeled herself before entering the room – it was time to meet the media.

She was immediately taken aback by the rapturous applause she received from the awaiting journalists, photographers and camera crews. The room was packed to capacity. Elaine could not believe the level of interest in her story. She was surrounded by a succession of microphones and tape recorders as she took her seat alongside her mother; Robert, Tom, Martin and Rory stood behind her protectively. Her brother gripped her hand tightly as Elaine fielded question after question from reporters. Her voice was quivering and her hands were shaking – she longed for the experience to end. Notwithstanding her obvious discomfort at being thrust so prominently into the limelight, Elaine answered each question articulately and intelligently. Under the circumstances, it was a commendable and brave performance.

Elaine revealed that her sense of relief at the charges

being dropped had already turned to "absolute fury" over her treatment at the hands of the British authorities. "I'd like an apology at least," she said. "It wasn't just my life – my family's life has been destroyed, too. I was treated like a criminal over there. Once the PTA [Prevention of Terrorism Act] is mentioned and your name is after it, you're in big trouble. I lost everything – the life I had in London is completely lost. The amount of people affected is unbelievable – they arrested 10 people."

Elaine told the press conference that being arrested was the hardest part. "It was terrifying. I've always known an awful lot about what's happened to people [in Britain] through the years and I thought: 'Am I going to be tortured here? Am I going to be abused? How am I going to be treated? Will they slam the door and lock me up?'" She admitted that she drew parallels between her case and those of the Guildford Four and Birmingham Six as soon as Gareth Peirce walked into her cell. She paid tribute to her solicitor, describing her as "an amazing woman".

Elaine refused to comment on the cases of the three Irishmen arrested with her who were still facing terrorist charges in Britain. "Their families are going through exactly what my family went through, so I'm not going to get into that," she said. She considered it unlikely that she would be pursuing a case for compensation against the police authorities. "I'll never go back," she declared.

After the press conference ended, Elaine was escorted by Airport Police to an awaiting car and brought to the nearby Forte Crest Hotel. Unaware that she had already left the airport, numerous relatives and friends had congregated in the arrivals hall to greet her. Some became anxious and impatient when she failed to appear and quizzed reporters about her whereabouts. These particular journalists, however, were not covering Elaine's story and were waiting to interview the Taoiseach, Bertie Ahern, who was also at the airport that night. When Mr Ahern finally emerged, he took the opportunity to express his delight at the outcome of Elaine's case. Speaking to TV3 News, the Taoiseach said: "I'm pleased to see that this is all past her and it is all over. There are no charges and there are not likely to be. I've been in touch with the family during the summer . . . and I'm glad to see that it's all worked out well for them."

Elaine's friends and relatives finally tracked her down to the hotel. The number of people that had turned up to welcome her home was staggering. One by one, she embraced her aunts, uncles, cousins, friends . . . anyone she had ever cared about seemed to be around her. Elaine somehow managed to remain composed until she came face-to-face with her best friend for 10 years, Tracy Mulvaney. They almost crushed each other with the strength of their embrace as Tracy's parents, Brian and Audrey, looked on tearfully. During those long, lonely days in prison, Elaine had worried endlessly that people's opinions of her would have changed as a result of her arrest. With a deep sense of relief, she now realised that these fears had been unfounded. She was particularly struck by how deeply affected other people's lives had been by her experience. Friends spoke of how they had defended Elaine's honour in the initial stages of her ordeal; for the first time, some of these stories could now be told with comical undertones.

Just when it seemed that the evening couldn't get any more exciting, news filtered through that members of the Republic of Ireland soccer squad were staying at the hotel that night. Earlier, the team had flown into Dublin in preparation for an upcoming Euro 2000 qualifier against Malta in Lansdowne Road. Being in such close proximity to the likes of Roy Keane and Jason McAteer sent waves of hysteria through the Moore camp, particularly among Elaine's female cousins; her mother and aunts had their eyes fixed on Packie Bonner and Niall Quinn. Spurred on by her new-found fame, Elaine was persuaded to approach various members of the squad. Against the backdrop of girlish giggles, she was practically frog-marched by her companions in the direction of the team. Niall Quinn, who was Elaine's favourite player, approached and extended his hand to welcome her home. She was completely star-stuck when the player hugged her. He then introduced Elaine to the entire squad, who were extremely receptive and willingly posed for photographs. To top it all off, Niall Quinn arranged tickets for Elaine, Robert and Rory for the match on Wednesday and promised to meet up with them for a drink afterwards. In more ways than one, it had turned out to be a night to remember. "Niall Quinn was an absolute gentleman who went out of his way for us that evening," says Elaine. "He truly helped mark the occasion of my home-coming."

The Moore party later left the hotel and made the short journey home to Coolock Village. Elaine was deeply touched to notice a welcoming committee, comprising of some neighbours and their children, who had been waiting patiently outside her house for a number of hours. They cheered and applauded as she emerged from the car. "It was incredible to think that people, some of whom I didn't even know that well, would actually take the time to wait for me on a cold October evening, just to welcome me home," Elaine states. "It meant the world to me."

Inside her home Elaine was greeted by further cheers and bouquets of flowers. Even though some of the party had already gone to a local pub, the house was thronged with friends and well-wishers. Elaine immediately asked for Lana, her beloved dog that she had feared she would never see again. Cradling the little dog in her arms, she made a beeline for her bedroom, which had been preserved, shrine like, by her mother. Elaine sat down on her bed to fully relish the moment. Not a thing in the room had changed, from the duvet cover right down to the multitude of Michael Collins posters and memorabilia. "Jesus, Elaine – no wonder you were arrested," joked Rory on entering the room.

Every head seemed to turn in her direction when Elaine joined the others in the Sheaf O'Wheat pub. Due to the publicity surrounding her case, she had become one of the most recognisable women in Ireland. She realised life would never be the same again.

After a momentous night catching up with loved ones, Elaine returned home with her family and Rory. His prominent role in her safe return had been widely acknowledged that night. Rory had been a true friend to Elaine in every respect. They all sat up chatting for some time until Elaine could stay awake no longer. Taking Lana under her arm, she bid everyone goodnight and retreated to her bed for the most deserved sleep of her life – it was the sleep of the just.

Chapter Eighteen

A NEW LIFE

It took Elaine some time before any sense of normality was restored to her life. Although she was delighted that Rory had agreed to stay for a week to help her resettle, having him beside her lulled her into a false sense of security. Unwilling to contemplate not having him around, she tried to keep thoughts of their separation out of her mind. As much as she wanted him with her, Elaine accepted that Rory was still firmly rooted in London. She was given a preview of life without him when he went to Cullyhanna to visit his family for a couple of days.

On the Monday following her triumphant homecoming, Elaine received a visit from a close friend, Colin, who had made a career move to Manchester six months before she went to London. When they were both living in Britain, Elaine had travelled to see him and stayed in his home. She had been unaware of a disturbing encounter her friend had had with Scotland Yard detectives after her arrest. Colin was questioned about the time he and Elaine had spent together, as well as letters they had written to each other. She listened in horror as he related his intimidating experience to her. The police bluntly informed him that Elaine was facing 20 years behind bars. Colin was astute enough not to be intimidated by their scare tactics and never once harboured doubts about his friend's innocence. When asked to read and sign his statement, he was amazed how his answers had been misconstrued and distorted. Only after the police clarified his remarks did he agree to sign it.

Colin urged Elaine to get in touch with the group of friends she referred to as 'the lads', assuring her that they had been 100 per cent behind her from the beginning. Regrettably, she had cut herself off from this social circle in the months preceding her move to London due to the break-up of a four-year relationship with a member of the group. She agreed to meet them later that night in one of her old haunts, Harry Byrne's pub in Clontarf. She was nervous as she walked into the pub, conscious that everybody seemed to recognise her. It was also her first time to venture out alone without Rory or her family since arriving home. She felt a pang of excitement as she spotted the 11 young men, all huddled together around a table. Suddenly catching sight of her, the group jumped up and Elaine was smothered in hugs and kisses. After a few minutes, it was if she had never been away from them.

As planned, Elaine, Robert and Rory attended Ireland's showdown with Malta at Lansdowne Road. Elaine was seated next to a man in his sixties who gave her a running commentary of the match. Niall Quinn's form seemed to be the main focus of his attention. When he suggested that the player should be using his height to connect his head with the ball more, Elaine responded that, in her opinion, Quinn was playing a gem of a match. It was a good job she had defended the footballer – the man beside her was Niall Quinn's father.

Spirits were high in the VIP lounge afterwards due to Ireland's 5-0 victory over Malta. As she mingled with Ireland's elite players, Elaine noticed Pat Kenny, the man who had jumpstarted the campaign to highlight her plight. The television and radio star warmly embraced her and welcomed her home. He spoke in glowing terms about his admiration for her mother, who had first raised Elaine's plight on his morning radio show. Elaine was thrilled to finally meet Pat Kenny in person, particularly as she was due to appear, along with Kathy, on his television show that coming Saturday.

The next morning, Elaine set off for County Armagh to meet Rory's family, even though her mother had expressed concern about her re-entering a British jurisdiction. Although determined to never return to England, Elaine felt that Northern Ireland, "being only up the road", posed no real danger. She remained vigilant, however, and discussed the matter with a Garda before taking the trip across the border. She received an enthusiastic welcome from Rory's parents on her arrival. Although their sons' lives had been dramatically affected by their association with Elaine, they bore no resentment against her. She spent the next two days enjoying the beautiful countryside in the company of some of the most hilarious people she had ever encountered. Finally, she understood the origins of Rory's laid-back attitude.

As Saturday evening approached, Elaine and Kathy frantically prepared for their appearance on the Kenny Live TV show. A limousine arrived to bring them to RTÉ's studios in Donnybrook – it was a far cry from sitting in the back of a police van. Waiting nervously in the wings, Elaine quipped to a stagehand that she had changed her mind about appearing on the show. She remembers the unfortunate man turning very pale; she was the next guest to go on and had to reassure him that she was only joking. Walking out into the glare of the studio lights was a nerve-wracking experience, but the host's casual interviewing style put Elaine at ease. The fact that she had previously met Pat Kenny helped, as did the fact that most of her family and friends, including Rory and Tracy, were in the studio audience. After the interview – which was watched by thousands of people nationwide – Elaine was approached backstage by Nell McAndrew, who was also a guest on Kenny's show that night. She congratulated Elaine on her performance – which had deeply moved her – and said that she would be a hard act to follow.

After the show, Elaine and her friends hit the town with a vengeance, ending up in a city-centre nightclub. She felt like a minor celebrity as she was mobbed on the street by complete strangers, all wanting to shake her hand. Elaine, however, initially found the experience threatening and unnerving. "Every time a person approached me, I wondered if he or she would be the one to vent some kind of anger at me," she recalls. "I always remained uptight until I could figure out where they were coming from or what their agenda was. Thankfully, there were no negative incidents, which I was grateful for; it enabled me to relax in public. Back in those days, even one bad experience would have been enough to see me withdrawing completely from public view."

Finally, the day came for Rory to return to London. It was an emotional time for the two friends, who had been brought even closer, if that was possible, by their three-month-long ordeal. Ever since her release from prison on bail, Elaine and Rory had been virtually inseparable. Without him, she felt lost and alone, despite the wonderful support network of family and friends around her. After Rory's departure, Elaine became distant and withdrawn and didn't leave the house for two weeks.

True to his word, Rory phoned her every day and sent regular cards and letters. Although hearing from him would always lift her spirits, it wasn't the same as having him by her side. The loss of his company was incalculable.

To the casual observer, Elaine seemed to have emerged relatively unscathed, psychologically, from her traumatic arrest and incarceration in London. Her mother knew differently, and became increasingly concerned about her daughter's reluctance to talk about the experience. Elaine's tendency to internalise her deepest fears would manifest itself in the form of vivid nightmares, which continue to plague her.

Kathy remembers one particular night, shortly after Elaine came home. "There was this unmerciful bang – I thought somebody was breaking-in to the house. Then I heard another bang and I knew where it was coming from. I ran into the room and there she was on the floor, screaming." Elaine had dreamt that thousands of spiders and earwigs were in her bed, crawling all over her body. She leapt out of bed, landing sharply on Robert's stereo system, which left a prominent dent in her back. As she lay on the floor, she hallucinated that even more insects were devouring her. Her panicked reaction caused further injuries to her wrist and ankle. As Kathy attempted to soothe her, Elaine lay motionless on the floor, paralysed by fear and pain. "I think I've broken my back, Mum," she said quietly. She dragged herself along the floor into her mother's bedroom where she finally calmed down. Realising she had imagined the whole thing, Elaine began to laugh hysterically at the spectacle she had made of herself.

On other occasions, Elaine was found wandering around the house in the middle of the night in a trance-like state. These potentially dangerous episodes – which became more frequent as time went on – cause her acute embarrassment. She is reluctant to discuss the issue when such incidents are relayed to her. For this reason, Elaine will not stay overnight in unfamiliar surroundings. "It's debilitating in many respects," she says. "When I'm unduly stressed – or if I've had one drink too many – I often choose to stay awake for fear of what might happen while I sleep."

The nightmares continued with disturbing frequency, particularly after the death of her Aunt Mary, or May, as Elaine fondly refers to her, in December 2001. Kathy recalls a recent occasion when she shared a bed with her daughter. "There was work being carried out on the house and only one bedroom was habitable at the time. I told Elaine to sleep with me in my bed rather than take the couch. I was fast asleep and next thing I felt her leap from the bed. She was standing by the window, terrified, scanning the room as though someone had been attacking her. It made me realise that at the time, I probably didn't truly know what she had been through."

* * *

Once settled back into life in Ireland, Elaine had her career to consider. She was heartened to receive several job offers from prominent business people, many of whom had been either touched by her story or approached by her supporters. In early November 1998 she was offered a position by a south Dublin based company. The job, and salary, would be similar to the one she had enjoyed at Netlink. It came with the added incentive of a company car and a training programme to help with her transition back into the workforce. Elaine was definitely interested and met with a director of the company to discuss the position further. While more than willing to accept the job, Elaine felt compelled to tell him that she did not feel up to returning to work so soon. An agreement was reached whereby she would take up her position with the company in the new year at the end of January 1999.

In the meantime, other opportunities presented themselves to Elaine. She had been offered unlimited access to facilities provided by the NuTron Diet clinics to help her 'de-stress' after her ordeal. The company's latest venture was a concept called 'The Stressless Room', which provided health, relaxation and beauty treatments to busy Dubliners. Elaine, along with former Irish rugby star, Tony Ward, was recruited to officially open the facility in early December 1998. The media turned up in their droves; it was their first real opportunity to report on Elaine's progress since she returned home. After the Dublin launch, she was asked to travel to the company's Galway clinic for further promotional duties. During the drive, she noticed a sign for Athenry, which made her think of the well-known ballad. As she sang the words in her head, the car in which she was a passenger was involved in a collision. A car in front of them had failed to indicate and their driver was unable to brake in time due to wet road conditions. Elaine's knee went crashing through the dashboard, although, fortunately, all four passengers only sustained superficial injuries. By that stage somewhat used to performing under difficult circumstances, she had recovered sufficiently to give a radio interview in Galway 40 minutes later.

It was through her public relations stint with the stress management clinic that Elaine came to attend the 1998 Fianna Fáil Ard Fhéis. Paul Allen, the PR guru, mentioned to her that he had been invited to the event in Dublin's RDS. Elaine asked if he would pass on her sincere gratitude to the Taoiseach, Bertie Ahern, whom she credited with playing an important role in her case. There was strong evidence to suggest that the Irish Government had been involved in high-level talks with the British authorities. "The Government and the Taoiseach assisted my family during that trying time without ever seeking public credit for their efforts," Elaine believes. When Paul Allen offered to arrange tickets to the Ard Fhéis for her, she jumped at the opportunity to be able to thank Mr Ahern in person.

Elaine's attendance at the annual gathering attracted the media's attention. "I remember the delegates were looking at me strangely," she says. "I wasn't used to being in political circles. I was simply there in a personal capacity to express my appreciation to Bertie." At a reception afterwards in the RDS library, the Taoiseach approached Elaine and greeted her warmly. "I simply thanked him for everything and that was that. I was delighted to have met him; he's a man I greatly admired, particularly because of his contribution to the peace process and Irish society in general."

No journalist approached Elaine on the night but her appearance at the Ard Fhéis was pointedly reported in the newspapers – mainly, at the expense of Fine Gael. *The Irish Times* noted that Elaine Moore was one of the 'more glamorous guests' who had been 'stolen, it seemed, from under Fine Gael's nose'. The *Irish Independent* said Elaine had 'a long chat with the Taoiseach while the rest of the guests fought for a drink at the bar.'

The tone of these articles was mainly tongue-in-cheek but it was clear that Elaine's decision to attend the event had offended elements within Fine Gael. Today, Mary Banotti makes no secret of her feelings about the "extraordinary" episode. "I was both amazed and upset," she admits. Shortly after attending the Ard Fhéis, Elaine discovered that Mary had complained about the incident to Gareth Peirce. The MEP was also unhappy that she hadn't heard personally from Elaine since she came home. When interviewed in connection with this book Mary said that she had simply contacted Gareth to confirm that the bail money she had put up for Elaine had finally been returned to her. She accepts that she did mention Elaine's attendance at the Ard Fhéis with the solicitor during the conversation.

Kathy also recalls having a blazing row on the telephone with the MEP's sister, the former Fine Gael TD, Nora Owen, who sought an explanation for Elaine's attendance at the Ard Fhéis. The conversation became heated as Kathy attempted to assure the former Minister for Justice that her daughter had not intended to embarrass or offend anyone, Mary included, by her actions. Feeling that Elaine's behaviour was being scrutinised and monitored, Kathy became extremely agitated and eventually ended the call by hanging up on Mrs Owen.

Elaine couldn't understand what all the fuss was about. Earlier that summer she had met Mary for lunch in London while out on bail and thanked her personally for her support. She was furious that the MEP had aired her grievances with Gareth instead of contacting her directly and sent Mary a strongly worded letter. 'I had every intention of contacting you over the Christmas period,' she wrote. 'Surely you must understand that since my return to Ireland I have been working effortlessly to restore my life. The humiliation and stress of the ordeal I suffered in London will obviously take a lot of time and effort to heal. There are several family members whom I did not see prior to a week ago. They, like Mr Peter Barry, who was contacted by my mum, fully understood my initial lack of communication but I am sorry that you did not share that same understanding. Please understand that this is a very difficult time for me.'

Elaine also made reference to her attendance at the Ard Fhéis. 'I have never in my life had any political agenda and do not appreciate being entangled in a political debate. Our Taoiseach played a vital role in my safe return to Ireland and he, like many others, will receive my gratitude. I do, however, apologise for not having contacted you personally as of yet, but as I stated previously, I expressed my gratitude at every opportunity and then commenced the hard battle of rebuilding my life. I apologise if you misinterpreted my actions as being insensitive as I can assure you that was never my intention.'

In a letter to Elaine dated 26 November 1998, Mrs Banotti responded:

'My Dear Elaine,

Thank you for your letter received today. The tone and contents startle me as they reveal a depth of misunderstanding which I did not believe existed.

My contact with Gareth Peirce was made simply to inform her of the repayment on Monday of the bail money I had lodged on your behalf. Inevitably the question of your progress since you returned to Ireland came up and I admitted to some dismay at what seemed to be your adoption by Fianna Fáil.

You will understand Elaine that of course I accept that the last few months have been a time of confusion, distress and strain for yourself and your family. At no time did my belief in you waiver, despite the rumours provoked by the bombing in Omagh. Your several small accusations against my discretion can only be dismissed as arising from your own difficulties. I must make it clear that far from gaining any political advantage from assisting you as I did, it was in fact an act of considerable political risk.

However, the life of a politician is one of risk and in this case, as I was convinced it would be, the risk deserved to be taken. I do not regret it for a second but I am sure that on reflection you will accept that my surprise at the lack of any personal message from you is only human and is to be expected after all that has happened between us. Whatever about the knocks which are part of political life, ordinary courtesy is always appreciated.

Yours sincerely,
Mary Banotti MEP.'

Elaine has not had any contact with Mary Banotti since receiving this letter, but did send her flowers that Christmas, as had been her original intention.

When interviewed for this book, Mary Banotti insisted she was not bitter about the rift between herself and the Moores. "I wouldn't say bitter – I am indifferent."

Elaine, for her part, believes the falling out was an unnecessary situation that got out of hand because it was approached in "an emotionally charged" manner. "I was extremely annoyed that Mary Banotti had discussed the matter with my solicitor and Nora Owen contacted my mother, yet their grievances should have been aired directly with me."

* * *

Much to Elaine's surprise media interest in her lingered for some time after her return from Britain. Of particular interest to reporters were her future career plans. Kathy continued to deal with most of the media's queries, patiently explaining that her daughter needed time and space to assess her options. Most newspapers reported on Elaine's case fairly and accurately – even sympathetically. There were, however, some notable exceptions. Shortly after her return from London, Kathy reluctantly showed Elaine a copy of an article that had appeared in the September 1998 edition of *Magill*, the monthly current affairs magazine. The article, which was headlined 'Inside the Real IRA', was published in a special edition to mark the Omagh atrocity. The article named Elaine as a member of the Real IRA. The offending paragraph appeared alongside a chart illustrating the number of deaths relating to the conflict in Northern Ireland.

Elaine felt numb after reading the article. She was appalled at the notion of the Omagh victims' families in any way associating her with the car bomb attack. Elaine sought immediate redress in the form of an apology and recruited the services of Michael E. Hanahoe solicitors. Failure to secure an apology and retraction from *Magill* resulted in Elaine taking proceedings against the magazine for libel. Although terrified at the prospect of having to appear in court, her fears were outweighed by the need to preserve her good name and character. She had never been charged with membership of an illegal organisation and had fought hard to have the bomb charges against her dropped. Her freedom may no longer have been at stake – but her reputation was.

Another company had purchased *Magill* before the case came to court. In the March 1999 issue of the magazine, the new publishers printed an apology to Elaine distancing themselves from the contentious article. It stated that the former publishers, Coliemore Publications Ltd, now recognised that the allegation was 'utterly untrue' and a 'gross libel upon Ms Moore'. It added that the magazine's former editor, Vincent Browne, joined in the apology.

The case against *Magill*'s former publishers and former editor was listed for hearing in the High Court on 12 July 2000. However, when the case was called, Elaine's senior counsel, Garrett Cooney, announced that it had been settled. As part of the settlement, an apology was read out in court and subsequently printed in the next edition of the magazine. It read:

'In a special edition of *Magill* published in September 1998, a reference was made to Ms Elaine Moore which asserted that she was a member of the 'Real IRA'. At that time, Ms Moore had been wrongfully arrested in England; she had always protested her innocence of the offences charged against her and her protests were fully vindicated when the English authorities shortly afterwards dropped these charges and her liberty was fully restored to her. *Magill*, then published by Coliemore Publications Ltd and its then editor, Mr Vincent Browne, are now happy to acknowledge that the allegation which was published about Ms Moore was wholly false and that she had no connection whatsoever with the 'Real IRA', or indeed, any terrorist organisation. They further acknowledge that the ethos and activities of such organisations are wholly abhorrent to her. They now formally

retract the allegation made against her and
apologise for the damage it did to her good
name and reputation. They regret very much
the deep personal distress caused to her and
her family, which was greatly exacerbated by
the fact that the accusation was made in the
aftermath of the atrocity at Omagh, Co.
Tyrone. As an acknowledgement of their
mistake and as a measure of the sincerity of
this retraction, both *Magill* and Mr Browne
wish it to be known that they have paid
substantial compensation to Ms Moore together
with her legal costs.'

The *Sunday Independent* was also served with a writ by
Elaine's solicitors over the article published about her
case on 9 August 1998. Elaine could never forget how
upset she had been when she found the newspaper hidden
under Rory's bed while she was out on bail. The main
thrust of the article was that the prosecution had withheld
vital evidence that would help prove their case against
her. The newspaper lodged a defence to the claim but the
case was eventually settled out of court. An agreed apology
was published in the *Sunday Independent* on 25 November
2001. It read:

'In our edition of 9 August 1998, we published
an article written by Liz Allen under the
headline 'Vital evidence held back in terror
case'. This article asserted that British anti-
terrorist police then had in their possession
evidence, as yet undisclosed, which could lead
to the conviction of Miss Moore of serious
terrorist offences. We now acknowledge that

Miss Moore was completely innocent of all charges and allegations which had been made against her. We are happy to state that she was never involved in any terrorist activity and that the withdrawal by the British authorities of charges against her to that effect was an entirely proper vindication of her innocence. We regret very much the publication of the story in question and we offer our sincere apologies to Miss Moore for all harm caused by it to her and for the distress suffered by her and her family.'

* * *

Elaine's promotional work for the stress clinic had led to speculation in tabloid newspapers that she was about to 'return' to her modelling career. There was some substance to the reports. She had recently been in touch with her former modelling agency, Assets, with a view to having her portfolio sent back to her. The agency had received numerous inquires about Elaine's availability for assignments.

They informed her that there would be plenty of modelling work for her if she went back on their books. Elaine promised to think about it but never pursued it any further. "Modelling was never really a career I could consider for the simple reason that I am the most un-photogenic person I know."

Due to her impressive performance on Kenny Live, Elaine was approached by a filmmaker who felt she had a future as a TV presenter. There was also a lucrative offer to participate in a proposed television documentary about her ordeal in Britain. However, because she wanted put the entire episode behind her at the time, she politely declined. Although flattered by these exciting opportunities, Elaine really needed to return to familiar territory and didn't yet feel confident enough to venture into the unknown.

It was late December 1998 before Scotland Yard returned any of Elaine's items to her. Thankfully, Rory had been able to put pressure on the police to speed up the process. Just before Christmas, he pulled up outside Elaine's house in Coolock, with his new car packed to capacity with her belongings – much of which had been destroyed by fingerprinting dust. This reinforced just how intrusive the police had been in their investigation of Elaine.

Memories of her ordeal still preyed on Elaine's mind. On Christmas morning, Elaine and Robert Moore sat frozen with fear in their living room. Outside, they could hear the distinctive sound of a helicopter getting increasingly louder. Nervously, they peered out the window to see it land on the green space directly opposite their house in the presence of numerous gardaí. As the door of the craft opened, they half expected to see armed police jump out and converge on their doorstep – stranger things had happened. Suddenly, the helicopter's sole passenger emerged – it was Santa Claus, his sack full with presents for a local children's party. Elaine and Robert looked at each other and laughed with relief.

Having Rory back with her made for a particularly memorable Christmas. Elaine was also delighted to receive a visit over the holidays from Nick, a former Netlink colleague, who celebrated the arrival of the New Year with her. She felt hugely optimistic as they toasted the arrival of 1999. There was much to look forward to – she was particularly excited about starting her new job.

In early January, she made arrangements to visit her new workplace to familiarise herself with its operations. She was greeted with a handshake from the managing director but was somewhat taken aback when he queried her attendance at the Fianna Fáil Ard Fhéis. Elaine replied that she had simply wanted to thank the Taoiseach in person for his support. As the time approached for Elaine to officially take up her new position, she experienced difficulty in contacting her prospective boss, who failed to return any of her calls. She became increasingly anxious when her scheduled work commencement date passed without any contract being signed. When she finally made contact with a senior executive, she discovered that the job offer no longer stood. He said that somebody purporting to be Elaine had contacted the company to say they would not be taking up the position. She had made no such call. Furthermore, the company's excuse failed to explain why her numerous phone calls had not been returned.

Elaine was incensed. She had passed up several other job offers in the belief that she had already secured employment. Deciding to put the incident behind her, she recommenced her search for work. In August 1999, she took up a position with a project management consultancy firm but never fully realised her potential there.

On a personal level, things were looking up. On 16 August 1999, Robert became the father of a beautiful baby daughter, whom he named Saoire. The choice of name was a compromise between Sarah and Saoirse (Irish for 'freedom'), which seemed particularly apt given the family's experience the previous year. For Elaine, Saoire's arrival signalled the beginning of a fresh chapter in her life. She dotes on her niece and spends many enjoyable hours telling her stories. "She is a bright and inquisitive little girl," says Elaine. "There's no better form of therapy than entering the carefree world of a child. Robert had just over a year to recover from his traumatic arrest before Saoire came along. We are all so proud of him – he's a wonderful parent. Seeing how protective he is of his daughter makes me draw comparisons with how he took care of me, his little sister, when we were growing up."

In February 2000, Elaine realised a long-held ambition when she bought herself a brand new Ford Puma. Originally, she had planned to purchase a car with the proceeds of her earnings in London – but fate took her on a different course. Finally owning her own car represented a landmark in Elaine's life; it was the realisation of an ambition and a considerable achievement for a twenty-four-year-old who had been unemployed for the best part of a year. Finally, her career curve and finances were on an upward trajectory.

Elaine's first real career break came in October 2001 when she was invited to assist with the establishment of the newly-founded Programme Management Association (PMA). Being involved with the organisation from its inception provided her with the exciting new challenge she needed. Following the PMA's reconstitution from a profit to non-profit organisation, she was put in charge of a range of duties, such as events and general office management. "Working in a non-profit context makes my job all the more worthwhile," she says. "Managing our events has given me the opportunity to meet a wide number of personalities, from Government representatives to banking officials. Admittedly, I am reluctant to join in on the many lively debates that occur but the PMA is certainly helping me to come out of my shell. It has given me a platform to acquire many new skills and offers daily challenges. I couldn't have hoped for a more challenging or supportive working environment. It's a great feeling being paid to do a job I enjoy so much."

Mr Paul Dowling, chief executive of the PMA, says Elaine has played a vital role within the organisation.

"She has made many personal sacrifices along the way," he feels. "Her enthusiasm and commitment have always impressed me – she always goes that extra mile."

In October 2001, Elaine also returned to college on a part-time basis to study a diploma in public relations.

* * *

Elaine has enjoyed the stability of a loving relationship since meeting Paul Donegan through mutual friends in a Dublin city-centre pub. On that particular night, Paul – who was more than slightly inebriated – obnoxiously infiltrated Elaine's group of friends and blatantly refused to leave until she spoke to him. "I remember feeling somewhat put out when I realised that all the lads I was with knew this remarkably beautiful woman; yet, she had somehow escaped my attention down through the years," Paul laughs. "Once I set eyes on her, I was not taking no for an answer. Admittedly, I kind of imposed myself on her – in the nicest possible way, of course! I didn't see her for quite some time after that, but I was determined to get her in the end."

Elaine was soon equally smitten with Paulie, as she affectionately calls him. She describes him as "extremely handsome, charismatic and funny". Their future together was sealed when they finally met again and they have been inseparable ever since. "Paulie is one of the kindest, most patient and loving people I have ever met – I feel privileged to have him in my life," says Elaine. "His calming nature and endearing manner have been a ve positive and steady influence on me."

After a three-month whirlwind romance, the couple purchased their dream home together in Co. Carlow. It has breathtaking views of three counties. It was the stunning scenery that convinced them to buy the property, which is set on a third of an acre of manicured gardens. Paul admits that they purchased the house on a whim – but it was undoubtedly the right decision. "It's our own little paradise in many respects," he says. "Elaine has made my life complete. She is a beautiful person who leaves a positive imprint on the lives of everyone she meets. I couldn't imagine my life without her and certainly don't intend to find out."

Elaine adopted two tiny Maltese terrier sisters, whom she christened Abbey and Ellie, and Paul's dog, Sootie, moved in with them. "The girls", as she calls them, are her pride and joy and she is rarely seen without them. "I treat them like children," she admits. "They are a very calming presence and have a therapeutic effect on me. With them around, I never feel alone."

Elaine continues to spend most of her time with her mum in Dublin, mainly using her Carlow home as a weekend retreat for herself and Paul. It's an arrangement that gives her the best of both worlds – the convenience of Dublin city and the peace and tranquillity of the Carlow countryside.

"Life, by its very nature, will always throw challenges in our way but, together, I believe we can overcome just about anything," she says philosophically. "My world now revolves around my life with Paul, our families, friends and dogs."

It's a world away, she agrees, from the bleak isolation ⸢ a British prison cell.

EPILOGUE

On Friday, 21 May 1999, the three young men accused of planning a firebomb campaign in London were jailed by the Old Bailey for a total of 69 years between them. Anthony Hyland (26), of no given address, was described in court as 'the ringleader' and sentenced to 25 years for conspiracy to cause explosions. His co-accused – Darren Mulholland (20), from Dundalk, Co. Louth, and Liam Grogan (22), from Naas, Co. Kildare – each received 22 years in prison. A jury found them guilty after 13 hours of deliberation. Passing sentence, Mr Justice Klevan told the men that although he did not believe they had intended to murder, there had been 'a substantial risk of death and injury'.

Elaine shivered as she heard the news. The stiff sentences handed down reinforced the severity of the situation she had been exposed to. She realised that if the charges against her had succeeded, there was every chance she would have received the maximum permitted sentence. After all, police had even once suggested that Elaine was 'the brains' behind the operation and she had been facing two serious charges: conspiracy to cause explosions and possession of explosives. On a human level, she felt sad for the men. It was, in her opinion, a total waste of three young lives. Out of respect for their families, Elaine had refused to comment when reporters arrived at her doorstep looking for a reaction.

Elaine has never held Anthony Hyland nor Scotla

Yard in contempt for putting her through her nightmare ordeal. "Life is simply too short for that," she explains.

"In the beginning, I must admit that I played out numerous 'what if?' scenarios in my head. But pointing the finger of blame wouldn't have made me feel any better. It's important to remember that Hyland exonerated me in his statement to police. What point would there have been in publicly criticising him? He was in prison; I would have just added to the anguish of his family. As for Liam Grogan and Darren Mulholland, I have never met either of them and do not associate them with my experience. They all have their own demons to face. I was, of course, horrified and disturbed by the danger I had been placed in and the subsequent disruption to my life and the lives of all those I love. But I've moved on from all that now and have my sights set firmly on the future."

Similarly, Elaine bears no grudge against the British authorities. "I have never doubted the validity of the reasons for my arrest," she insists. "I am, however, still infuriated that four other innocent people were placed under suspicion and arrested simply because of their association with me. Scotland Yard had every right to arrest, detain and question me – but I should never have been charged. The manner in which I was detained in solitary confinement in an all-male, maximum-security prison was harsh and cruel, to say the least; it infringed on my human rights."

Elaine has good reason to feel hard done by. Two statements issued to a Sunday newspaper by both the Real IRA and the Provisional IRA insisted that she had never been a member of either organisation. Even before she had been charged, Anthony Hyland had asserted Elaine's total innocence to police. But most significant of all was the covert role played by the undercover policewoman, 'Nicky', whose surveillance report on Elaine was withheld from the defence right up to the last minute. Most observers feel there is little doubt that this evidence would have completely vindicated Elaine had it been presented in court. This implies that anti-terrorist officers knew from the outset that she was innocent – yet they still chose to arrest, charge and detain her. Designating a palpably innocent young woman as a 'Category A' prisoner had the effect of demonising Elaine in the eyes of the media and – more worryingly – the judiciary. Similarly, the high-security police escorts to and from court deliberately created the impression that she posed an implicit threat to British security.

The Britain and Ireland Human Rights Centre (BIHRC) succinctly summed it up when they said: '. . . Elaine Moore's case reinforces the dangers of allowing police officers' opinions to be admitted as evidence in court proceedings.'

On 26 July 2000, Kevin McNamara, the British Labour MP, asked the then Home Secretary, Jack Straw, what progress had been made in settling a figure to compensate Elaine Moore following her wrongful arrest and imprisonment. Mr Straw replied that he was not aware of any application for compensation having been received by the Home Office in respect of her case. "If an application is received, it will be dealt with by me in the usual way," he said.

However, Elaine, to date, has not pursued a compensation claim against the British authorities – nor is she likely to in the future. "All I ever wanted was an apology for the unnecessarily harsh treatment that I was subjected to," she says. "Initially, I had been advised to take a case purely to compensate me for the loss of employment and the expenses incurred by my family as a result of my incarceration. But in the absence of an apology, I felt that a monetary settlement would have been a brush-off and a further slap in the face. Besides, my fear of having to ever set foot inside a British court again was reason enough not to entertain the notion of compensation."

Her deepest regret, perhaps, is the life and the friends she was forced to leave behind in London. "It's the community of people and the lifestyle we shared that I miss the most," she reflects. "Leaving all that behind hurt a great deal. Had I left London of my own volition under normal circumstances, I'm sure I would have visited as often as possible. Knowing that I have no control over when or how I see Rory and the others continues to upset me."

Elaine never felt the need to undergo counselling, although people thought that she might benefit from it. If she hit a low point, there was always someone who she could turn to. Those close to her concede that she has coped extremely well given what she went through. "She is unbelievably strong and has a good outlook on life," believes Robert Moore. "In a way, she is now a lot stronger and more determined." Her brother, on the other hand, is still consumed by guilt for putting Anthony Hyland in touch with Elaine in the first place. "It's something I'll always have to live with."

Rory Hearty's arrest on 10 July 1998 was not to be his only brush with the British police. He was later prevented from boarding a Dublin-bound plane at London City Airport during a visit home to see Elaine. Refusing to answer any questions until his solicitor was contacted, he was held for a number of hours. By the time he was told he was free to go, Rory had missed his flight. There is little doubt he was stopped because of his association with Elaine. In fact, one of the police officers even sarcastically asked him how she was keeping. Rory is still devastated by what happened to Elaine. "I really miss her," he says. "It's still hard to go home to Ireland. Anytime I meet her she tells me that I am the only person she can really speak to about what happened. In a way, I remind her of all that."

Gareth Peirce believes the British authorities were extremely embarrassed by their handling of Elaine's case.

"It was a very public allegation, accusing a woman of conspiracy to cause explosions – and then they had to drop it. Yet they don't say: 'We are terribly sorry – we got it wrong.' We don't get apologies."